Psychotherapy as a Human Science

Psychotherapy
as a
Human Science

Daniel Burston
Roger Frie

 Duquesne University Press
Pittsburgh, Pa.

Published in the United States of America by
DUQUESNE UNIVERSITY PRESS
600 Forbes Avenue
Pittsburgh, Pennsylvania 15282

Library of Congress Cataloging-in-Publication Data

Burston, Daniel, 1954–
    Psychotherapy as a human science / Daniel Burston and Roger Frie.
        p. ; cm.
    Includes bibliographical references and index.
    Summary: "Provides a critical and historical introduction to the core themes
and influential thinkers that helped to shape contemporary human science
approaches to psychotherapy" – Provided by publisher.
    ISBN-13: 978-0-8207-0378-7 (pbk. : alk. paper)
    ISBN-10: 0-8207-0378-8 (pbk. : alk. paper)
    1. Psychotherapy. 2. Psychotherapy—Philosophy. 3. Psychotherapy—Miscellanea.
I. Frie, Roger, 1965– II. Title.
    [DNLM: 1. Psychotherapy—history. 2. History, 19th Century. 3. History, 20th
Century. 4. Philosophy, Medical—history. 5. Psychoanalysis—history. 6. Psychoanalytic Theory. WM 11.1 B972p 2006]
    RC480.B87 2006
    616.89'14—dc22

                                                            2006016020

Contents

This book is the culmination of many years of research, reflection, and spirited, scholarly communication about psychotherapy as a human science. We began this process with the aim of filling a gap in the current literature on psychotherapy. Much is written today about advances in neuroscience, empirically validated treatments, and quantitative methods for the practice of psychotherapy. Yet scant attention is paid to the role that history, philosophy, and our implicit theoretical assumptions play in the assessment and treatment of human behavior. Our emphasis on psychotherapy as a human science does not mean we have overlooked the significance of neuroscientific studies, or deny the fact that empirically validated treatments have improved the reduction of specific symptoms in some disorders. Rather, our view is that unless psychotherapy as a whole is understood from the perspective of history and philosophy, the contemporary focus on manualized treatments and quantitative research results in a one-sided view of human psychology. Our chief objective, therefore, is to challenge the implicit theoretical assumptions we hold by demonstrating the extensive links that exist between psychotherapeutic and philosophic approaches to human experience, with special emphasis on the enduring importance of the existential-phenomenological tradition.

The scale of issues we attempt to incorporate is broad. At the same time, there are important trends in the contemporary literature on psychotherapy to which we have not been able to give our full attention. These include, for example, the discussion of gender, race, and postcolonialism; attachment studies; and neuroscientific research. All are relevant to understanding clinical theory and practice, but are not covered extensively here. The limited discussion of a particular theme or approach should not be interpreted as evidence that we view one perspective as more or less relevant than another. Our choice of what to include — and what to exclude — has been shaped by our desire to provide readers with an in-depth historical analysis of the issues at hand, as well as by restrictions of space and length. Wherever possible we have sought to provide specific references to important contemporary themes and texts that we have been unable sufficiently to expand and elaborate ourselves.

A coauthored book like this one is only possible when the authors take on equal tasks and are in broad agreement about most of the pertinent facts and principles involved. This, in turn, is rendered possible by the fact that we came to the study of psychotherapy as a human science from similar backgrounds. We share academic training in the history and philosophy of psychology as well as in clinical psychology. Added to this is a combined knowledge of continental philosophy and the history, theory, and practice of psychoanalysis. These interests are reflected in our writings. Daniel Burston's previous books (1991, 1996b, 2000) examine key figures in the history of psychoanalysis and phenomenological psychology, while Roger Frie's previous books (1997, 2003) examine the intersection of phenomenology, psychology, and psychoanalysis.

We also bring our own individual perspectives to bear on this subject. The chapters on philosophy draw on Daniel Burston's interest in religion and its social and political ramifications. The thematic chapters draw on Roger Frie's approach to understanding the relation between contemporary philosophy, social theory, and clinical practice. In addition, we teach and practice in different settings, and as a result, our work has had a different focus. Daniel Burston chairs the Department of Psychology at Duquesne University, perhaps the only program in clinical psychology in North America that has strong historic roots in phenomenological philosophy. Prior to his training in psychology, Burston studied political theory and philosophy, and the philosophy and psychology of religion. Roger Frie is assistant clinical professor in the Department of Psychiatry at Columbia University and on the faculty of the William Alanson White Institute of Psychiatry, Psycho-analysis, and Psychology. Prior to his training as a psychologist, Frie studied social theory, continental philosophy, and the history and theory of psychoanalysis. In addition, he brings to his writing a clinical expertise in the practice and teaching of psychotherapy and psycho-analysis.

In the process of writing this book we owe debts of gratitude first and foremost to our families for their support of this endeavor. We also wish to thank Susan Wadsworth-Booth, director of Duquesne University Press, for taking on this project at a time when many academic publishers overlook the relevance of the human sciences for the theory and practice of psychotherapy. Finally, we wish to thank our students, who over the years have provided invaluable feedback as we taught and discussed many of the ideas we present in this book.

Psychotherapy and Philosophy

Training in the mental health professions is increasingly driven by political and economic forces and has become very technical in focus. Insurance companies demand that psychotherapy be objectifiable, and as a result, manualized treatment protocols are now widespread. Because of this growing reliance on a natural science approach, the fact that psychotherapy rests on a set of implicit, philosophical assumptions about human experience is largely overlooked. Yet these philosophical assumptions often determine not only the objectives of psychotherapy, but also the actual framework in which it is practiced.

We have written this book in an attempt to move beyond the narrow technical concerns of much current psychotherapy. Our aim is to elaborate psychotherapy from a human science perspective in order to help professionals, students, and interested readers appreciate the importance of theory for clinical endeavors and thus to enlarge the scope of psychotherapy training and practice. Psychotherapy cannot be studied in a strictly empirical manner without also considering the history of philosophy, the challenges of ethics, and the vagaries of politics.

Our journey will take us on an exploration of an intellectual tradition that freely combines insights from philosophers, psychiatrists, and psychologists. The interplay between philosophy and psychotherapy, and its long history in Western thought, is especially relevant to our undertaking. The juxtaposition of philosophy and psychotherapy may seem unusual to those who are unaccustomed to making this connection. In fact, we will demonstrate that philosophers have much to teach therapists. In our view, philosophy is inherent to the very practice of psychotherapy.

For many psychotherapists, the greatest impediment to the introduction of philosophy into clinical discourse is the issue of how data are accumulated, interpreted, and assessed. Many clinicians have a stereotyped conception of the philosopher as an isolated scholar who reflects only on his or her own experience in a process of introspection. This view overlooks precisely what postmodernism has taught us: the generation of ideas is always dependent upon difference and otherness. Only by engaging with what is other than ourselves is it possible to open up new ways of thinking. And, as we shall see, many of the philosophers considered in this book are directly concerned with the practical application of their ideas, whether through teaching and research or the actual practice of psychology.

What is a Human Science?

A dialogue with philosophy is not merely useful, but also vitally necessary for the grounding of theory, practice, and research in psychotherapy from a human science perspective. But what is a "human science perspective"? Prior to 1874, when Wilhelm Wundt founded the first psychological laboratory in Leipzig, psychology was traditionally linked with philosophy and focused not only on human behavior, but also on the nature of the mind or soul. Psychologists who broke with that tradition and embraced experimentalism and the natural science approach were often German or German-speaking and sought to distinguish their orientation from that of their predecessors and counterparts in philosophy and the humanities. So in the German language a distinction is often made between the natural sciences (*Naturwissenschaften*) and the human sciences (*Geisteswissenschaften*).

In the broadest sense, "natural" science seeks to study and elucidate the behavior of entities and processes that exist in nature. These are generally void of intention; that is to say, they are not endowed with experience or intentionality. Conversely, human behavior is almost always a function of an individual's experience of and intentions toward the world — a world that is constituted by and for the individual in terms of culturally and historically embedded meanings and symbols, as well as his or her own idiosyncratic choices and decisions. Unfortunately, since the rise of experimental psychology more than a century ago, many branches of psychology and psychiatry methodically seek to bracket or nullify any careful consideration of human subjectivity and intentions — the very things that render human behavior intelligible in ordinary circumstances. Under the pretext that human behavior can be explained or interpreted without reference to the subject's experience and intentions, psychology, and psychiatry tend to reify or "objectify" the individual (Laing 1960).

For most of the twentieth century, academic psychology sought to elucidate the structures, processes, and functional interrelationships that suffused the mind and mental faculties or functions like intelligence, perception, memory, language acquisition, and the like. In order to achieve this objective, it generated empirical generalizations regarding the behavior of the organism under rigorously controlled laboratory conditions or in carefully designed longitudinal studies, in surveys, questionnaires, and so on. Moreover, it prided itself on being able to express or translate its findings into measurable mathematical formulas. The problem is that, on reflection, the "laws" arrived at in this way are merely empirical generalizations that apply to everyone at once, and to no one in particular. They are quite useful for understanding overarching trends in human behavior, but in the end they refer to a disembodied, ahistorical entity — a "generalized other."

The objectification of human behavior in academic psychology poses a number of challenges for psychotherapy. From a clinical point of view, one can be thoroughly versed in these laws of behavior, yet remain utterly incapable of developing a rapport with another human being or of understanding the nuances of clinical interaction when problems arise. For clinical purposes, these data just will not do. We require an approach that addresses what is distinctive about *human* behavior, applied judiciously to real flesh-and-blood human beings.

Thus far we have dwelt on methodological issues. But for someone approaching psychotherapy from a purely naturalistic perspective, the human science perspective also raises some serious questions about the goals of treatment. Is "normality," defined as the absence of troubling symptoms, our ultimate objective? And is normality, thus defined, the same thing as "mental health"? If not, what *is* the goal of psychotherapy: symptom reduction or increased self-understanding and awareness? improved interpersonal relationships? or all of these, in some measure?

To those who embrace a human science orientation, the absence of inner or interpersonal conflict, or of manifest symptoms of mental disturbance does not always betoken "mental health." On the contrary, the absence of conflict can express a frictionless adaptation to a social role that robs persons of their full humanity. From a human science perspective, a client's confusion or emotional pain is seldom simply a "symptom" of some underlying metabolic or brain disorder, to be eliminated as quickly as possible. The contemporary culture of medication often overlooks the person's need to understand and articulate the social and interpersonal roots of deviance and distress. The theorists we discuss here would surely recommend that individuals whose suffering exceeds a tolerable threshold, or whose symptoms are not affected by therapy, avail themselves of pharmacological remedies. But they would also insist that anxiety, guilt feelings, and depression are not necessarily the expression of a disordered brain. On the contrary, these commonplace clinical phenomena are universal and ever-present possibilities of human experience and, therefore, opportunities for the development of deeper self-understanding and self-mastery.

In order to present a human science perspective, however, we need to adopt an appropriate method, one that is rigorous yet avoids the potential pitfalls of natural scientism. To that end, we borrow from a number of intellectual traditions — phenomenology, existentialism, humanism, postmodernism — that, together with psychoanalysis, provide the basis for an understanding and appreciation of human experience.

PHENOMENOLOGY

Phenomenology is an approach to philosophy that stresses the existence of a world of immediate or "lived" experience that precedes the objectified and abstract world of natural scientific inquiry. Fidelity to the texture of human experience requires a patient and painstaking description of the phenomenon in question, which must precede any attempt at explanation in theoretical, abstract, or quantitative terms. Indeed, a strict application of phenomenological method eschews causal explanations altogether. To regain the freshness of primordial experience, we have to "bracket" (or suspend belief in) many widespread preconceptions about subject and object, mind and body, organism and environment, facts and values, affect and cognition, and so on, and attend closely to the phenomenon itself.

Phenomenology comes in several forms, but one thing that remains consistent throughout is its *antidualistic* emphasis. Edmund Husserl (1859–1937), who founded *transcendental phenomenology,* was critical of the *subject/object* dualism that informs natural scientific thought. Husserl insisted that the scientific tendency to divorce subjectivity, or our experience of the object, from the object of experience, as if they were two entirely different things, does violence to the facts of experience and prejudices our way of apprehending our own experience, that is, our relations to ourselves. The subject/object bifurcation that Cartesian culture takes for granted is inscribed in our minds by prevailing cultural practices, including language. Far from being a primordial datum of experience, says Husserl, it is actually an acquired habit, a "second nature." When we sever subjectivity and objectivity in this way, subjectivity almost always gets devalued and depreciated, while a specious or superficial kind of objectivity gets turned into an idol that resists critical scrutiny (Husserl 1962, 1964).

Unlike Husserl, however, Martin Heidegger (1889–1976), who founded *existential phenomenology,* placed more emphasis on the pernicious effects of the *mind/body dualism,* which Husserl never abandoned completely. Like René Descartes (1596–1650), Husserl argued that consciousness is (actually or potentially) completely independent of the body. Husserl dwelt at some length on the logical possibility of a disincarnate or disembodied subjectivity, and thus failed to overcome Descartes's solipsistic perspective (Husserl 1970). Heidegger dismissed Husserl's claim as too "otherworldly," and always took the embodied and fundamentally social nature of *Dasein* for granted (Heidegger

1962). Heidegger's emphasis on embodied subjectivity was shared by Jean-Paul Sartre (1905–1980) and Maurice Merleau-Ponty (1908–1961), who blended elements of Husserlian and Heideggerian phenomenology in novel syntheses of their own. In addition to drawing on Husserl and Heidegger, Sartre and Merleau-Ponty drew from an older tradition of Hegelian phenomenology, taking continental philosophy in new directions. Sartre, for example, claimed that existentialism is a kind of humanism, prompting Heidegger to angrily repudiate the existentialist label.

EXISTENTIALISM

Existentialism is an approach to philosophy that states that, despite our disparate social and historical situations, we all partake of the same basic structure of existence and all need to confer value and impart meaning to our lives through action and decision. The way in which existence is structured into different modes varies from one theorist to another — such as the authentic and inauthentic modes in Søren Kierkegaard (1813–1855) and Heidegger, the "being" and "having" modes in Gabriel Marcel (1889–1973) and Erich Fromm (1900–1980), being "in itself," "for itself" and "for others," in G. W. F. Hegel (1770–1832) and Sartre, or the various *modes of relatedness* described by Martin Buber (1878–1965), Ludwig Binswanger (1881–1966), or Erich Fromm. But despite a plurality of theories on this score, it is usually possible to discern a *meta-theoretical consensus* about certain fundamentals that place existentialists in the same universe of discourse (Burston 1996b).

When did existentialism begin? That is more difficult to answer. Though Karl Jaspers, Heidegger and Max Scheler were talking about the philosophy of *existenz* during World War I, the term "existentialism" was actually coined later by a French journalist who was interviewing Sartre in 1941. Sartre liked the label, and it was soon being applied to a wide range of contemporaneous thinkers, not all of whom welcomed this avant garde designation. Nevertheless, the term "existentialism" grew quite popular during the fifties and sixties, as Sartre and Simone de Beauvoir's novels and plays enthralled audiences on both sides of the Atlantic. Because of their prodigious literary efforts, others, including Dostoyevsky, Baudelaire, Kafka, Gide, and Rilke were soon embraced by members of the movement as forerunners or fellow travelers.

There never was a stable or binding consensus regarding the actual leadership or terms of membership in the existentialist movement. Moreover, in contrast to the Anglo-American world, where existentialism has remained a commonly used term in the parlance of philosophy in France, Germany, and most of Europe, existentialism is a term used specifically with reference to Sartre and his followers. We are writing primarily for an English language audience, but to avert any possible misunderstandings, we seldom speak of existentialism, but prefer the term "existential-phenomenological," as it is broader and more inclusive, describing the intertwining of these two intellectual traditions.

When did existential phenomenology take root? To trace the lineage as far back as possible, we could follow theologically oriented thinkers like Hans Jonas and Paul Tillich, who traced the beginning of existential thought to Blais Pascal, whom we term a *proto-existentialist*. But for the sake of clarity and convenience, we defer to prevailing wisdom and date the origins of existentialism back to Søren Kierkegaard and Friedrich Nietzsche (1844–1900).

To get this matter into historical perspective, consider the historical relationships among philosophy, theology, and science. In medieval times, philosophy was considered the handmaiden of theology and only became emancipated from a subservient role to theology gradually, through long and strenuous effort. Initially, the growth of the natural sciences (from Galileo onward) contributed to this process of individuation. Indeed, by the mid-nineteenth century, the explosive growth of the natural sciences shattered what was left of the old scholastic synthesis and promised to confer many moral and material blessings on believers in the new cult of "progress."

Unfortunately, however, in this brave new world, philosophy's erstwhile ally threatened to become a new oppressor, as positivist thinkers proposed that philosophy was freed from fealty to theology only to assume her true historic mission, namely, as handmaiden to the natural sciences. Kierkegaard and Nietzsche shunned the stifling embrace of bourgeois philosophy, whether in the form of positivism or the unbridled speculation of idealist philosophy. They argued that the real goals of philosophy — self-knowledge and freedom — were not to be found on either of these paths, and that the apparent gains afforded by modern science and "progress," which was celebrated by materialists and idealists alike, masked alarming trends toward conformity, banality, and other deformations of the human spirit.

The first clinician to use phenomenological methods in the study of mental disorder was Karl Jaspers (1883–1969), who praised Kierkegaard and Nietzsche for their great insights (Jaspers 1913). But strangely enough, in doing so, he overlooked the fact that unlike himself — or Freud, for that matter — Kierkegaard and Nietzsche were not clinicians. As we see in the following chapters, Kierkegaard and Nietzsche were actually social psychologists. Admittedly, they were not plodding empiricists, accumulating facts and testing hypotheses regarding the "laws" of social behavior. Rather, they were critics and partisans who hoped to rescue their readers from complacency, spiritual slavery, and the galloping malaise of modern European civilization. Thus, in contrast to their admirers among twentieth century clinicians, Kierkegaard and Nietzsche wrote mostly about diffuse social pathologies, or what Fromm later termed "socially patterned defects" (Burston 1991).

Thus, unlike psychoanalysis, which began as a clinical technique and was only applied to social psychology afterward, the existential-phenomenological approach to treatment derived from a body of thought that had initially addressed the manifold deformations of the "collective psyche," and only then was it applied to individuals' personal situations. In the process, of course, Kierkegaard and Nietzsche wrote some probing reflections on phenomena that clinicians encounter routinely, like boredom, anxiety, guilt, depression, despair, madness, and so on. But when they dwelt on them, as they often did, it was not for the sake of describing or explaining discrete forms of psychopathology. On the contrary, they were exploring and explaining perennial possibilities of human experience that are rooted in the human condition.

PSYCHOANALYSIS AND THE EXISTENTIAL-PHENOMENOLOGICAL TRADITION

This was not the case with Sigmund Freud (1856–1939), the founder of psychoanalysis. Freud's training as a neurologist and specialist in "nervous diseases" prompted him to view guilt, anxiety, and depression through psychopathological lenses. Moreover, unlike Jaspers, and most of the theorists we examine, Freud's unwavering determination to align psychoanalysis with the natural sciences led him to disparage the idea of a separate methodology for the human sciences, and to distance psychoanalysis from philosophy at every opportunity. Fortunately, many of Freud's heirs were less intransigent on this score, and welcomed dialogue with philosophers. This allowed for the gradual inclusion of continental European philosophy in the conceptualization of theory and technique after Freud's death. As we will demonstrate, existential-phenomenological and Lacanian psychoanalysts in Europe, and interpersonal, relational, and intersubjective psychoanalysts in North America have either reformulated or altogether rejected key aspects of Freud's instinct-oriented metapsychology, including the tripartite theory of mind, the notion of instinctual energy and drives, the unconscious, childhood and gender development, and classical analytic technique — particularly the notions of neutrality and the "blank screen." In order to fashion new conceptions of the mind, body, and interaction, these revisionist psychoanalysts have drawn on the work of continental philosophers, particularly phenomenological, existential, hermeneutic, and postmodern thinkers.

The interest shown by revisionist psychoanalysts in continental philosophy has not extended to Anglo-American analytical philosophy. In fact, until recently, much analytical philosophy has been cool, if not hostile, toward psychoanalysis, demonstrating the same kind of antipathy toward Freud that it has for modern continental philosophers. Conversely, continental philosophers have embraced psychoanalysis and applied its methods to the realms of social theory, politics, history, feminism, textual analysis, and many other fields.

The deep and evolving convergence between psychoanalysis and continental philosophy is not fortuitous. Both developed out of European intellectual traditions that address questions relevant to clinical practice. How can we achieve insight into the way we live our lives? How can we understand the nature of human love and intimacy? What is the role of the body in my experience and perception of the world around me? How can we account for the multifaceted, often opposing tendencies of human interaction? And how is the human being, or subject, situated in a world of shared understandings?

As we shall see, existential-phenomenological philosophers reject the traditional Cartesian conception of the subject as isolated and closed in upon itself. They argue that Descartes's famous dictum "I think, therefore I am" makes it difficult to account for the reality of other minds. In its place, continental philosophers seek to formulate a concept of subjectivity that is true to our lived experience. They elucidate the implicit connections between the self and other within the context of *intersubjectivity*. They pay particular attention to embodied experience and consider the ways in which we are always and inevitably enmeshed in social contexts. Many revisionist psychoanalysts embrace these same changes, including themes and experiences that were similarly excluded from the purview of classical Freudian clinicians.

In their effort to move beyond Freud, many psychoanalysts have recently adopted the label of "postmodernism" to describe their work. The bifurcation between modernism and postmodernism in contemporary psychoanalysis is essentially a product of the tension between classical and contemporary psychoanalytic traditions and represents the efforts of some interpersonal, relational, and intersubjective psychoanalysts to differentiate themselves and their work from their Freudian colleagues. It is also the result of integrating into psychoanalysis the postmodern philosophical critique of such modernist ideas as subjectivity and individuality.

The distinction between modernism and postmodernism in psychoanalysis and psychotherapy takes many forms, affecting the way clinicians formulate theory and view technique. The reliance on the analytic neutrality and objectivity that defined classical psychoanalysis has given way to an analytic relationship based on mutuality, in which traditional assumptions about authority and reason yield to ambiguity and uncertainty. In place of foundational concepts such as objectivity and truth, postmodernists emphasize constructivism or perspectivism. In contrast to the materialistic, isolated entity that characterizes the so-called modernist self, the postmodernist tends to see the self as generated and maintained by the relational, linguistic, and cultural contexts in which it is embedded.

Yet the attempt to differentiate neatly between modernism and post-modernism begs many important questions. Do all modernists really adhere to the notion of an immutable core self, and do all postmodernists truly see the self as illusory? Is there a place for modernist concepts such as agency and individuality in postmodernism? On close reflection, the boundaries between modernism and postmodernism in psychoanalysis and psychotherapy are often quite porous. Moreover, long before the advent of postmodernism, the pursuit of analytic neutrality and objectivity that defined classical psychoanalysis had frequently given way to an analytic relationship based on mutuality in which traditional assumptions about authority and reason yielded to an emphasis on ambiguity and uncertainty (Frie 1999a, 2002).

Like existentialism and phenomenology, "postmodernism" eludes precise definition. Some people use the term in a global, encompassing fashion to denote several intellectual trends, including poststructuralism, deconstructionism, and social constructivism. Others define it more narrowly, taking care to differentiate among these different points of view. Either way, the prevailing tendency to distinguish between modern and postmodern psychoanalysis overlooks the efforts of earlier revisionist psychoanalysts who differentiated themselves and their work from their Freudian colleagues.

Many ideas embraced or embedded in the postmodernist turn in psychoanalysis were anticipated by European psychoanalysts and psychiatrists who identified with the existential-phenomenological tradition. This neglected but nonetheless influential intellectual tradition includes clinicians such as Karl Jaspers, Ludwig Binswanger, Medard Boss, Erich Fromm, R. D. Laing, and the early Jacques Lacan. To a large extent, the existential-phenomenological tradition developed in reaction to modernism and, in the process, set the groundwork for postmodernism. These clinicians introduced the concept of a socially and historically constituted person; they emphasized the interpersonal and embodied basis of human experience, questioned the myth of analytic neutrality, and introduced the notion of a "two-person psychology." Yet in contrast to many versions of postmodernism, they sought to develop a theory of human agency that was true to our lived, embodied experience and could account for progressive change and understanding. In effect, if not by design or deliberate intention, their aim was to reconcile such key modernist themes as agency and subjectivity with an emerging postmodern framework.

Curiously, contemporary interpersonal, relational, and intersubjective psychoanalysts in North America seldom cite existential-phenomenological clinicians or recognize them as forerunners of their work. This is, in part, a result of a widespread Anglo-American antipathy toward philosophical ideas. Clinical education in North America has become rather narrow, and input from other disciplines, particularly the humanities, is often given scant attention. As psychotherapy and psychoanalysis move beyond the medical model, however, there is the possibility for greater inclusion of the human sciences in our conceptualization of therapeutic theory and technique.

Humanism and Postmodernism

By the late 1920s and 1930s, European psychiatrists had created a new and distinctive approach to the study and treatment of mental disorder, inspired by the intellectual current of existential phenomenology. However, since the literature was mostly in French, German, Dutch, and other European languages, most of it was completely unknown in England and North America. However, in 1958, an anthology edited by Rollo May, Ernst Angel, and Henri Ellenberger, *Existence: A New Dimension in Psychiatry and Psychology,* introduced the existential-phenomenological perspective in the United States and became a runaway best seller. This was around the same time that an indigenous American movement, humanistic psychology, emerged on the scene.

Humanistic psychology arose as a spirited response to the rival orthodoxies of Freudian theory, which dominated American psychiatry, and behaviorism, which dominated psychology, during the 1950s and beyond. Humanistic psychologists reproached classical psychoanalysis and behaviorism with (1) excessively mechanistic and deterministic accounts of the origins and meaning of human behavior, and (2) with doctrinal rigidity and narrowness and tendencies toward depersonalization, intellectualization, and excessive ritualism in the therapeutic encounter between clinician and patient. Their hope was to create a "third force" — an alternative to psychoanalysis and behaviorism, and in this they resembled their existential-phenomenological counterparts in psychiatry and psychoanalysis.

As a result, a good deal of confusion exists about what humanism, humanistic psychology, and existential phenomenology actually mean. In philosophy, "humanism" refers to a European philosophical tradition with a rich and varied history. Consequently, philosophers often regard humanistic psychology as a very recent American innovation, while critics see it as an embattled intellectual movement from the counterculture of the 1960s and 1970s (Milton 2002). Although it has changed and developed considerably since its inception, the relationship of humanistic psychology to the (much older) tradition of philosophical humanism is sometimes problematic, and often quite tenuous (Burston 2003a).

As a distinct philosophical outlook, humanism first emerged in the Renaissance, where it was often associated retroactively with the Roman playwright Terence, whose quote was "Homo sum; nihil humani me alienum puto," or "I am a man; nothing human is alien to me." The broad implication of this remark is that Terence refused to identify with one particular ethnic group. On the contrary, he regarded himself as what the Stoics called a *cosmopolites* — a citizen of the universe, and not the representative of a particular race, nation, or religious orientation. In short, Terence embraced a pan-human identity that transcended the vagaries of ethnicity and religious belief.

During the Renaissance, the term "humanism" was associated with the revival of pagan learning in figures like Marsilio Ficino and Pico della Mirandola, who stressed (1) the need for well-rounded people to study the humanities, and (2) the essential compatibility between neo-Stoic and neo-Platonic philosophy and the Christian faith. Later, the term "humanism" was used to describe the sensibilities of non-dogmatic Christians such as Petrarch, Erasmus, and Thomas More, who insisted that Christianity is as relevant to the problems of living in *this* world as it is to seeking salvation in the next.

Later still, the term "humanism" was attached to the work of historians like Giambatista Vico and Jacob Burkhardt, who resisted the positivist program for the human sciences, and looked back at the Renaissance as a period worthy of emulation. In the mid-nineteenth century, however, the term "humanism" was also adopted by Left Hegelians such as Ludwig Feuerbach and Karl Marx, who used it to characterize an explicitly atheistic outlook that explains belief in the supernatural and longings for transcendence as the result of the (unconscious) projection of the "human essence" into an otherworldly realm, which is conjured up as a consolation for (and the legitimation of) an unjust social order that constrains and/or deforms the unfolding of our latent sociability and capacity to reason. Unlike Burkhardt and others, whose humanism was centered on the study and emulation of the past, Feuerbach and Marx made the realization of humanism a task for the future. Marx summed this up nicely when he said that, unbeknownst to us, perhaps, we are still caught up in the era of human prehistory. By this reckoning, real human history has yet to begin and will not commence until exploitation, oppression, and the ideologies that serve to justify or disguise them all cease to exist.

In view of its long and complex history, it is evident that no one can claim ownership of the term "humanism." It means different things to different people, but what unites the disparate threads of philosophical humanism — religious and irreligious — is a consistent emphasis on the *unity* of the human species and our duty to defend and promote human dignity and welfare. Implicit in the call to promote human dignity is the emphasis placed on the role of self-authorship or self-determination in the formation of our character and conduct. According to this view, we are never entirely determined by our past experiences. Personal choice plays a significant role in who we are and what we become (Burston 2003a). By this account, will and volition are the defining attributes of human nature, even if they only operate in a sphere bounded by finite alternatives. Accordingly, for most of the thinkers and clinicians we examine, heredity and environment, instinct and adaptation, play important roles in shaping character and conduct, but they do not necessarily determine what we are or who we become. Our own choices, our agency or will, are potent factors as well. Put another way, although we exist in multiple contexts and forces that are beyond our control, our ability to make choices continues to be an important part of the human condition. In this sense, for the thinkers and clinicians we consider, agency is never simply an isolated act of choice, but a complex process of reflection informed by personal history and fundamentally embedded in biological, cultural, and social contexts (Frie 2003).

This issue of self-authorship sets humanism and existential phenomenology apart from postmodernism, which is deeply suspicious of such notions as identity, objectivity, truth, and reason because it sees the world as ungrounded, fragmented, diverse, and contingent. In the postmodern universe, there is a deep suspicion of all forms of essentialism, including the venerable notion that we have the freedom to determine our own paths through agency and choice. To understand the appeal of postmodernity, it is important to recognize that postmodern skepticism is actually grounded in the social, cultural, and economic shifts of contemporary Western society. Postmodernity refers to a decentralized world of culture, technology, industry, and politics. A persuasive feature of contemporary social life is its ever-increasing capacity to enmesh human subjects in destructive relations of power, in situations of conflict and in processes of domination. In the midst of these changes, the human subject has undergone a radical transformation in which personal identity and subjectivity have been utterly refashioned to the point that they are believed to be mere fictions. The contrast to humanism could hardly be more striking.

Despite the wide spectrum of opinions they encompass, all varieties of postmodernism share a rejection of the isolated Cartesian subject and its solipsistic perspective on our relationship to the world. By this account, the Cartesian subject is aligned with such modernist notions as autonomy, agency, and authenticity. Postmodernism, in contrast, celebrates the dissolution and dispersion of the self-determining human subject.

For some observers, the postmodern notion that meaning is derived less from a single mind than from interdependent relationships implies that theory, research, and practice in psychology must all be revisited from a postmodern perspective (Gergen 2001). For others, however, the stridency with which postmodernism attacks the human subject and psychological agency is anathema to the very practice of psychotherapy (Frie 2003; Martin and Sugarman 2000). Indeed, the postmodern attack on the subject raises a vital question: can psychotherapy be conducted in a setting where notions of the subject, agency, and authenticity are held in suspension or entirely dismissed? This requires a careful analysis of what these terms actually mean, not only in theory, but also in practice. It also depends on how closely or consistently the psychotherapist adheres to postmodern philosophical dicta in practice. Taken to its logical conclusion, postmodern theory generates a series of challenges for any practicing psychotherapist.

At the same time, postmodernism has played a constructive role in calling attention to many of Cartesian rationalism's excesses and oversights, and to the many invidious agendas and ideologies that are cloaked in the guise of dispassionate "objectivity." The recognition that dominant forms of rationality represent hidden and not so hidden assumptions about power and patriarchy has led to a new exploration of sexuality, gender, and race in the treatment setting and beyond. In particular, the feminist analysis of culture and language has reintroduced the marginalized other into clinical concerns and provides an important critique of classical psychoanalytic theory.

As the postmodern critique of science has shown, every observation, no matter how objective, always has an implicit agenda. Scientists need to have preexisting theories and suppositions in order to ask the question that will lead to data. The scientist is always situated in a specific time and place and his or her scientific theory is itself a project of that culture. When applied to the clinical situation, this suggests that the therapist's subjectivity and clinical perspective will inevitably influence what the therapist knows about his or her patient.

In psychotherapy, the questioning of objectivity allows for a range of innovative clinical possibilities. Because clinical phenomena can only be understood in the contexts in which they take form, the interpersonal dyad has become a domain of therapeutic inquiry. There is much at issue here: a sense of agency and identity on the part of both the patient and therapist; the power relations among the patient, therapist, and society at large; the role of repressed, inhibited, or unformulated desires, wishes, and needs; and the problem of conformity and ideological values and assumptions woven into the therapeutic discourse, which reflect the wider sociopolitical contexts in which we exist.

THEMATIC OVERVIEW

In light of these reflections, it should be clear by now that the various philosophical traditions we draw on are not distinct or discrete bodies of thought. On the contrary, they are often densely intertwined. Moreover, thinkers and therapists often situate themselves (or are situated by others) in more than one school of thought at once. This fact prompts a great deal of philosophical discussion, which precedes or accompanies our reflections on the theory and practice of psychotherapy throughout this book. The practical, clinical application of the ideas that make up the human science perspective in psychotherapy will be addressed in the concluding "Clinical Postscript."

The first chapters, which span the interval from Descartes to Dilthey, say little about psychotherapy as such. Instead, they survey a wealth of reasoned reflection on issues such as reason, faith, and emotion, the nature of love and work, the sources of human conflict and aggression, conscious and unconscious mental processes, authenticity and inauthenticity, and the scope and impact of self-deception in individual and group psychology.

Those with a clinical focus may balk at this lengthy preamble, for fear of losing their way in the dense thicket of ideas, or losing sight of the common ground that unites the therapists of today with philosophers of the past. To keep these common concerns clearly in view, we employ a series of binary classifications that enables us to make instructive comparisons between theorists in these different (but closely linked) fields of endeavor.

Unfortunately, like all heuristic schemata, the labels we use to classify thinkers across disciplinary boundaries may promote an oversimplification of very complex perspectives on the human condition. We are well aware of these dangers. Nevertheless, for the sake of drawing comparisons and of making instructive contrasts, we found it very helpful to discriminate between religious and irreligious thinkers, between rationalist and irrationalist thinkers, utopian and anti-utopian thinkers, and between moderns and postmoderns.

Because religion plays a central role in the work of many of the thinkers we examine, we begin with the contrast between religious and irreligious thinkers. Though not common in the American vernacular any longer, we deliberately chose the term "irreligious" to indicate that more than simple atheism is at issue here. Taken at face value, the word "atheism" simply betokens an absence of faith, which could easily be the expression of an indifferent or merely skeptical attitude toward the existence of God. The thinkers we deem to be "irreligious" were not merely indifferent or skeptical. On the contrary, they were atheists who rejected supernaturalism and the otherworldliness of traditional piety in principle. They thought of belief in God as an illusion, or as an ideological instrument wielded for the benefit of one group of people at the expense of another. Alternatively, they saw belief in God as a measure of our psychological immaturity, our inability to face up to the challenges of existence, and take responsibility for our own lives. Despite deep differences on other matters, there is a striking convergence on this point among the works of Feuerbach, Marx, Nietzsche, Freud, Alexandre Kojève, and Sartre.

Alternatively, among thinkers who cherish religious convictions, there is a startling diversity of perspectives, ranging from Pascal's "deus absconditus" to Hegel's "Absolute Spirit," Kierkegaard's "Single One," and Buber's "eternal Thou." Though we discuss broad trends, we cannot do justice to all the complex theological differences that exist among these thinkers. But we are aware of them and mindful of the fact that from Descartes to Dilthey, theological and philosophical perspectives on human behavior are deeply intertwined. Indeed, though often dismissed as "unscientific" by clinicians who embrace a naturalistic perspective, theological issues are still pressing concerns for thinkers like Max Scheler and Martin Buber, and several therapists in our survey, including C. G. Jung, Erich Fromm, and R. D. Laing.

The distinction between religious and irreligious thinkers, though critical, provides only one way to map, explore and interpret a person's thought. Other dimensions are equally important, and equally revealing, albeit in different ways. Let us examine the distinction between rationalism and irrationalism.

Rationalism is characterized by its emphasis on *the primacy of reason*. Though it has roots in Greek philosophy and medieval scholasticism, modern rationalism really begins with Descartes (Levi 1974). Rationalists argue that reason alone provides us with a reliable guide to the truth — or "the Truth," as the case may be. By contrast with reason, say rationalists, faith, will, instinct, imagination, and passion are apt to mislead or cloud our judgment. Therefore, reason (or "the intellect") ought to inform, constrain, or, wherever possible, *dominate* all other aspects of human existence — especially passion, which is closely bound up with the body and its appetites.

In contrast to the primacy of reason espoused by rationalist thinkers, irrationalists contend that the human intellect is an inherently limited and imperfect instrument that operates in unconscious subjection to the person's will and the imagination. Or, as David Hume says, "the intellect is the slave of the passions." Another common theme among irrationalist philosophers is that there are other, equally valid ways of apprehending the truth that rationalism habitually disqualifies, such as faith, love, will, imagination, and so on. The classic statement of this idea is Pascal's maxim that "The heart has its reasons, of which reason is ignorant." Closely related to this kind of irrationalism is a view of human subjectivity shared by Dilthey, Buber, Marcel, Binswanger, Laing, and Levinas, which is beautifully summed up in Dilthey's favorite Latin saying: *individuum est ineffabile*. In other words, the core or heart of the human personality is always an ineffable mystery that cannot be adequately captured and expressed in language, or even comprehended by the intellect alone. On the contrary, a deep under-standing of the other person requires that we address and encounter him or her with our entire being. As we shall see, this is an ethical as well as an epistemological imperative.

While rationalism and irrationalism clash incessantly in the history of philosophy, their disagreements are not purely theoretical. Leaving psychotherapy aside for the moment, they have profound ramifications for the study of politics and history. By and large, rationalists espouse a vision of the good life based on the belief that social relations are — or *should* be — regulated by contract, consent and rational delibera-tion. Indeed, for rationalists, these modes of relationship constitute the *essential* forms of social life, absent which a descent into barbarism is supposedly only a matter of time.

By contrast, irrationalists dismiss contract, consent, and rational delib-eration as relatively recent and superficial accretions in the history of culture, and they emphasize the power of specifically nonrational processes that presumably promote solidarity and social cohesion, or their opposite, fragmentation, and conflict (Avineri 1974). Irrationalists regard the rationalist emphasis on the primacy of reason as being igno-rant of the paradoxes and mysteries of the human soul. Rationalists, in turn, mistrust irrationalist politics, calling attention to their tendency to align themselves with extreme reactionary or revolutionary move-ments. And rightly so. If you survey major social movements in the nineteenth and twentieth centuries, you will find that fascism and anarchism both draw deeply on irrationalist ideologies of one sort or another.

Nevertheless, if you analyze the less virulent varieties of irrational-ism, many of the arguments adduced against the hegemony of reason are cogent and humane. Indeed, as we shall see shortly, a "moderate" irrationalism, like Pascal's, for example, looks positively balanced in com-parison with Descartes's sweeping rationalist assertions. Therefore, we maintain that not all "irrationalisms" are equivalent in terms of content, cogency, or overall merit, and that some versions of "irrationalism" are philosophically defensible. So we are not going to use the "irra-tionalist" label in a sweeping, indiscriminate fashion. And because so many thinkers in our survey have been labeled as irrationalists at one point or another, we hasten to point out that there are also strong strains of rationalism embedded in the human science perspective in the work of Hegel, Husserl, Jaspers, Sartre, and Fromm. Though convenient for polemical purposes, it is actually quite misleading to represent the human science perspective as a specifically irrationalist one. The tension between rationalism and irrationalism runs right through it, as it does through all modern, and to a lesser extent, postmodern philosophy.

Beyond what we have said to this point, it is difficult to generalize about rationalism and irrationalism because this way of describing and apprehending a particular theoretical perspective cuts across the other relevant dimensions. Thus, irrationalism cuts across the traditional distinction between left- and right-wing ideologies. But it also complicates the distinction between religious and irreligious thinkers. This comes as a surprise to many people because, in the Enlightenment and post-Enlightenment context, when faith was often justified on the basis of "feeling," rationalism was often associated or simply equated with atheism. Nevertheless, Descartes was both a rationalist and a religious thinker, while Pascal, who was more devout, viewed Descartes's professions of faith as deluded or insincere. Leap two centuries ahead and you will find a similar drama played out between Hegel and Kierkegaard. Though no Cartesian, Hegel was a rationalist of sorts, while Kierkegaard was an irrationalist like Pascal, who doubted the sincerity of his *bête noire's* religious convictions.

Contrary to popular misconception, then, rationalism and irrationalism are perspectives or styles of thought that are actively at play *within* the theologico-philosophical perspective, as well as *between* religious and irreligious thinkers. And these reflections bring us to the inimitable Friedrich Nietzsche, who was both irreligious *and* an irrationalist at the same time. In this, no doubt, he was an original, and possibly the first of his kind. Indeed, Nietzsche was the only major thinker in the late nineteenth century who forcefully combined these two attributes, becoming the progenitor for the "postmodern" turn in philosophy.

Another issue we employ here that cuts across centuries, disciplines, and the other classificatory schemata is the role assigned to conflict and sociability in human existence. Beginning with Pascal, one school of thought, which we call "anti-utopian," says that human beings are constituted such that we are often at variance with one another, and indeed, with ourselves, and therefore destined to suffer from intractable inner and interpersonal conflict. From this point of view, peace and harmony, personal or interpersonal, are actually somewhat ephemeral goals because the roots of conflict and aggression are built into the human condition and no amount of inner transformation or social reform can alter this basic fact of life. This emphasis on the ubiquity of conflict characterizes theorists as diverse as Pascal, Nietzsche, Freud, Sartre, and Lacan. At the other extreme are theorists who stress human solidarity and sociability and our potential to mitigate or transcend inner and interpersonal conflict.

These divergent ways of framing the role of conflict and sociability in human affairs play an important role in how we manage and interpret (inner and interpersonal) conflict, and what we hope to achieve through clinical interventions. In psychoanalysis, for example, Freud's pessimism about human nature affected his austere approach to therapeutic interaction, while Binswanger's optimism led to a dialogical perspective on theory and practice. In fact, Freud told patients that the only thing the analytic process held in store for them was the prospect of exchanging their "neurotic misery" for "everyday unhappiness." Conversely, many post-Freudian analysts suggest that analytic therapy, if properly conducted, should yield robust improvements in the patient's interpersonal relationships.

Moreover, attitudes on this point — the presence and persistence of conflict — are often closely correlated with a theorist's views on love. Freud, Sartre, and Lacan subscribe to the view that love is blind, and they see love as an involuntary passion, or even an affliction. Others, like Scheler, Buber, Binswanger, and Fromm, claim that love bestows deeper insight into the beloved than is possible in any other way. Similarly, Freud, Sartre, and Lacan see love as a mode of relatedness to others that springs from a need for gratification, and they interpret attachment and desire as a response to that need. In other words, they see love as a creature of scarcity, driven to compensate for an experienced absence in the individual's existence. By contrast, Scheler, Buber, Binswanger, and Fromm see love as a mode of relatedness rooted in abundant strength, and in the presence, the particularity, and the immediacy of the other apprehended in a fully human way.

Finally, we return to the distinction between modernism and post-modernism. In some ways, this should be the least troublesome classification. After all, with the well-known exception of Nietzsche, a distant progenitor, it is often assumed that postmodernism only becomes truly relevant after its inception in the political and social upheavals of 1968. In truth, however, many of the ideas implicit in postmodernism — the emphasis on perspectivity, the deconstruction of the isolated Cartesian subject, and recognition of our fundamental embeddedness in contexts beyond our awareness and control — were already introduced much earlier by the thinkers we will examine. The tension between modern and postmodern perspectives, which was supposed to have begun in the late twentieth century, already had shown up in the twenties, thirties and forties, demonstrating that modernism is a far more complex and ambiguous entity than its postmodern critics would have us believe. The tension between modernism and post-modernism will provide a means to understand the excesses of rationalism and irrationalism and will be a focus of the chapters ahead.

Truth, Method, and the Limits of Reason
Descartes and Pascal

René Descartes

René Descartes is commonly regarded as the founder of modern philosophy. He was born in La Haye, France, in the province of Tours in 1596, the youngest son of an eminent lawyer. He was a promising student and was sent to the Jesuit academy at La Fleche, where he studied literature, languages, philosophy, science, and mathematics. When he graduated at age 16, Descartes was baffled and dismayed by the startling diversity of opinions held by philosophers and doctors of the church on a wide range of subjects. But Descartes was less interested in discerning the real meaning of Scripture than in reconciling Scripture (and by implication, faith) with the findings of the newly emerging natural sciences championed by Galileo and others —a far more difficult task. Stranded at the intersection between faith and science, between medievalism and modernity, Descartes was obsessed with discovering the truth. But what is "truth"?

For the sake of simplicity, let us define truth as parsimoniously as possible, as what actually is the case. But how do we discover what is (or is not) the case? Are there rules or procedures to follow? The oldest method for ascertaining the truth is Pythagorean in origin. Pythagoras said that rational introspection and the contemplation of mathematical formulas hold the key to the mysteries of the universe.

He predicated the practice of rational introspection on the control and repression of the body's senses and appetites, which he said led the soul astray. Pythagoras did not trust naturalistic observation to establish anything reliable or incontrovertibly true. The senses deceive, the passions confuse and mislead us. Reason — equated with mathematical reasoning — must somehow rise *above* the body, a task for which few are suited (Russell 1946).

Plato agreed with Pythagoras, and by use of introspection claimed to discover *innate ideas,* which are accessible to rational introspection, which he likened to mathematical formulas, for example, proportion, justice, beauty, and truth. These forms, or ideas, are unchangeable and imperishable, and supposedly superior to the transient and corruptible evidence of the senses. Observable nature is thus, in a very important sense, less real than these quasi-mathematical forms he was talking about.

Another way to ascertain the truth, said Plato, is the Socratic method, which attempts to elicit the truth in *dialogue* with others through a process of patient and prolonged questioning, in which the fundamental assumptions underlying various discussants' ideas and assertions are gradually clarified, and their cogency or credibility examined critically, in light of other evidence and beliefs. In other words, the truth can sometimes be elicited or established *intersubjectively,* through rational discourse, provided we know how to ask the right questions and attest honestly to what we actually experience (Russell 1946).

After the scathing dismissals of Pythagoras and Plato, naturalistic observation rebounded in the hands of Aristotle, who did not think that reason and sense perception were inalterably opposed. Unlike Plato, Aristotle credited patient and careful observation with supplying the intellect with the raw material it needs to infer the causal connections between various entities and processes in nature, leading us gradually to a rational intuition of the underlying structure of the cosmos (Clagget 1963).

Thus, there are three ways of ascertaining the truth left to us by Greeks: (1) rational introspection, an *intrasubjective* process, (2) Socratic dialogue, an *intersubjective* process, and (3) naturalistic observation of the nonhuman world. To this venerable list the Hebrews added

(4) the discovery of "revealed" truth through the careful and methodical exegesis of an authoritative text, an approach that spawned the modern discipline of hermeneutics (Ricoeur 1980). Another method for discovering truth was popularized by Francis Bacon, but only codified clearly and effectively by Descartes's older contemporary, Galileo Galilei (1564–1642): (5) the *experimental method*. For Galileo and his followers, truth cannot be found in a book, or in the interiority of faith, or even in dialogue with friends or adversaries. These methods are quite fallible and as likely to mislead us as they are to inform. Truth is *out there,* so to speak, and its discovery depends on the proper coordination of patient, naturalistic observation, rigorous experimentation, and methodical theory building. Experiments enable us to *quantify* natural processes in controlled, artificial contexts that are designed for the purpose of manipulating dependent and independent variables and minimizing or excluding extraneous ones. If properly executed, experiments, in turn, yield data that furnish the basis for new theories, which prompt new observations, fresh experiments, and so on.

Where does Descartes fit in? Descartes had a strong Pythagorean and Platonic streak that favored rational introspection and mathematical intuition. While he did not disparage interpersonal dialogue, textual exegesis, or scientific experiments as avenues to truth (at least in so many words), he pursued them much less diligently than many of his contemporaries.

In the winter of 1619–1620, Descartes was traveling through Bavaria (en route to a military posting) when he interrupted his journey to seclude himself in a rented apartment. During that three-day interval, he spent most of his time meditating inside a large cast-iron oven that was relatively common in those times, and which eliminated all unwanted light and sound.

Without realizing it, Descartes had embarked on an experiment in what is nowadays called "sensory deprivation," which gave him unparalleled concentration and freedom for reflection. Unless you have practiced meditation for prolonged periods of time, it is very difficult to imagine Descartes's thought processes, holed up as he was alone in his dark, silent cell. To begin with, said Descartes, he resolved to reject as false all opinions in regard to which I could suppose the least ground for doubt, in order to ascertain whether after that there remained aught in my belief that was wholly indubitable. Accordingly, seeing that our senses sometimes deceive, I was willing to suppose that there existed nothing really such as they presented to us; and because some men err in reasoning . . . I, convinced that I was as open to error as anyone else, rejected as false all the reasonings I had hitherto taken for demonstrations; and finally, when I considered that the very same thoughts which we experience when awake may also be experienced when we are asleep, while there is at the same time none of them true, I supposed that all the objects that had entered into my mind when awake, had in them no more truth than the illusions of my dreams. But immediately upon this I observed that, whilst I thus wished to take all as false, it was absolutely necessary that I, who thus thought, should be somewhat; and as I observed this truth, I think, hence I am, was so certain and of such evidence that no ground of doubt, however extravagant, could be alleged by the skeptics capable of shaking it, I concluded that I might, without scruple, accept it as the first principle of the philosophy of which I was in search. (Descartes 1949, 26–27)

In other words, Descartes resolved to dispense with half measures, that is, to stop doubting this or that particular claim, and to doubt the truth of *absolutely everything.* But try as he might, he could not dispel the impression that he, the doubter, doubted, and therefore thought, and therefore, by implication, existed in some fashion. Hence the famous formula known as the "cogito": "I think, therefore I am." After all, if he did not exist, what was the source of the persistent doubt that plagued him?

However, Descartes adds that it was only his existence as a rational, thinking subject that was absolutely certain. His corporeal or bodily existence remained on a more precarious epistemological footing:

In the next place, I attentively examined what I was, and as I observed that I could suppose I had no body, and that there was no world or any place in which I might be; but that I could not therefore suppose that I was not; and that, on the contrary, from the very circumstance that I had thought to doubt the truth of other things it most clearly and certainly followed that I was; while, on the other hand, if I had only ceased to think, although all the other objects which I had ever imagined had been in reality existent, I would have had no reason to think that I existed; I thence concluded that I was a thinking substance whose whole essence

> consists in thinking, and which, that it may exist, has need of no place, nor is dependent on any material thing; so that "I," that is to say, the mind by which I am what I am is wholly distinct from the body, and is even more easily known than the latter, and is such, that although the latter were not, it would still continue to be all that it is. (1949, 27)

In other words, Descartes's reveries compelled him to conclude that he, that is, his real, rational self, is utterly independent of his body, and that he would, therefore, survive its eventual extinction. This conclusion allowed him to satisfy two desires, namely, (1) to affirm the immortality of the soul and, at the same time, (2) to preserve the idea of free will. However, to achieve these objectives, Descartes also needed to distinguish between *res extensa,* or the world of material objects, which are characterized by the attributes of extension and motion in space and time, and the timeless, bodiless *res cogitans,* or mental universe. The body, being an object in *res extensa,* is subject, presumably, to natural law. It is basically a mechanical device, although a complex and sophisticated one. It is also the seat of the passions, which prompts the body into action. The mind, by contrast, is governed by reason and free will — up to a point, anyway. Unfortunately, the passions often interfere with our clarity of mind and the exercise of rational choice.

So in Descartes's model of the mind, reason and passion are adversaries, antagonistic forces that influence behavior by different means, and with vastly different results. This was also the case for Pythagoras and Plato, who invoked reincarnation to explain how mind and body become intertwined (Russell 1946). For Descartes, a devout if unconventional Christian, reincarnation was not an option, so he hit upon the pineal gland as the locus of the soul in the body. Why? Because, anatomically, the pineal gland is a small, quasi-spherical organ near the center of the brain that extends into the largest ventricle, or brain cavity. According to Christian theology, the soul is one and indivisible, and the pineal gland was the only part of the brain known to Descartes and his contemporaries did not appear to be double or divided.

Another reason Descartes seized on the pineal gland was that it seemed ideally situated to interact with the cerebrospinal fluid that flows through the ventricles of brain — a fluid that Descartes endowed with "animal spirits," or small, fine particles that supposedly flow in a fluid medium through the nerves to activate specific muscle groups and thereby set the body in motion. These same animal spirits, in varying proportions, precipitate the states of physiological arousal that accompany our strongest feelings and desires — hunger, lust, fear, rage, wonder, mirth, and so on. According to Descartes's hydraulic theory of the emotions, outlined in *Discourse on Method* (1637) and in *Treatise on the Passions of the Soul* (1649), the intensity of emotional arousal is grossly proportionate to the number of animal spirits and the volume of the fluid flowing through the nerves, and an individual can act rationally only as long as the animal spirits are not in a state of internal commotion. Then the rational soul, acting through the motions of the pineal gland, can influence the speed and course of the animal spirits flowing through the ventricles and either initiate voluntary action or inhibit inappropriate responses to external events. However, when the internal commotion is too great, the rational soul, operating through the pineal gland, is powerless to change or modify the person's behavior, and they act instinctively or reflexively.

Although original and intriguing in their day, Descartes's ideas about the brain and human behavior were also quite fanciful. The pineal gland is important, of course, but it is not the source or center of the so-called "executive functions" of rationality, will, and so on. To the extent that they even recognize these problems at all, contemporary neurologists locate Descartes's "animal spirits" and "rational soul" in the limbic system and the frontal lobes, respectively. Nevertheless, while it still enjoyed some currency, Descartes's physiological psychology played a significant role in perpetuating an idea that dates back to Plato and before and was later embraced by Hegel and Freud, namely, that reason is an active, ordering principle and is closely associated with human agency and choice. By contrast, the passions have a driven, involuntary character that effectively places them outside our control and usually puts them at variance with the promptings of reason. Fin-ally, and above all, perhaps, Descartes's hydraulic theory of the emotions and his theory of the "rational soul," which initiates voluntary action and inhibits inappropriate ones, vividly anticipated Freud's theory of the id and the ego.

Descartes did not publish *Discourse on Method* until 1637, more than a decade and a half after his actual epiphany. In the meantime, he left Paris for Holland, which, being Protestant, was more tolerant and supportive of independent inquiry. But even there Descartes ran into difficulty with local clergymen when he published *Meditations on First Philosophy* (1641) and *Principles of Philosophy* (1644), and he published very little after that. Fed up with Holland, he left for the court of Queen Christina of Sweden in 1649. However, the harsh climate and the crushing frivolity of a courtier's life soon finished him off. He died of pneumonia in 1650 (Levi 1974; Russell 1946).

What is Descartes's legacy to psychology? Descartes is described as the father of modern rationalism because he assumed that if people examine their thought processes carefully, they invariably discover the existence of certain innate ideas, like "perfection" and "infinity," or the axioms of geometry. In due course, said Descartes, serious reflection on these innate ideas leads to a rational comprehension of the necessity of God and the immortality of the soul. But though labeled a rationalist, how rational was Descartes? Someone who doubts the existence of his own body and the world at large — someone whose doubt is not a mere thought experiment, a playful conjuring with hypotheticals, but *real* doubt, fraught with urgency and conviction — is not just your average skeptic. Survey some of Descartes's celebrated contemporaries — Galileo, Hobbes, and Pascal — for the sake of comparison. It never occurred to them to doubt the existence of the world or their own bodies. So why did Descartes?

Moreover, despite his professed fondness for "clear and distinct ideas," on closer inspection, many of Descartes's ideas were actually quite wooly. Even if the pineal gland did play the pivotal role that Descartes scripted for it, this would not address (much less eliminate) the larger issue of how two radically disparate realms, "mind" and "body," coexist and interact in the first place. If mental and physical phenomena represent two distinct "worlds," or levels of existence, locating their ostensible intersection spatially in a semispherical gland in the brain's center is not a genuine solution. At best, it is a way of dancing around the problem, a clever expedient that defers dealing with the *real* problem that, fundamentally, the co-inherence of "mind" and "body" are an unfathomable mystery. And if we do not bifurcate human existence, or frame things in this dualistic fashion, the mystery in question is promptly transformed into a pseudoproblem, and not worthy of serious attention in the first place.

With his famous dictum, "I think, therefore I am," Descartes championed the human ability to reason and ushered in the age of the Enlightenment. Following Descartes, as we shall see, many philosophers and psychologists celebrated the individual mind as the locus of reason and knowledge. However, Descartes's belief that the knowledge we have of our own minds is not connected in any essential way to the world around us raises intractable problems. Indeed, much of modern philosophy and psychology can be read as a reaction to the dilemmas implicit in Descartes's thinking. If our minds are really the only thing we can be certain of, then the external world, other minds, even the existence of our own bodies are eventually in doubt. For this reason, many of the thinkers we survey in this book stress the constitutive role of "intersubjectivity" and "embodiment," or the communal and corporeal dimensions of personal awareness, arguing that human existence is never truly separated between body and mind. For psychotherapists who embrace a human science perspective, the self is never an isolated, sovereign entity, but a product of history, culture, and language as well as personal agency or choice. And in direct contrast to Descartes, postmodernism also rejects any concept of the self or subjectivity that is not understood as culturally, linguistically, or socially constructed.

BLAISE PASCAL

Cartesian rationalism had several key features that can be summarized as follows. With respect to epistemology, there was

(1) the (alleged) separation between "mental" and "physical" reality, with reason assigned to consciousness and the mind, and passion assigned to the body;

(2) the insistence on the existence of innate ideas in the mental domain;

(3) the idea that physical or "external" reality (which includes one's own body) is intimately and exhaustively knowable by the rational mind, provided a correct methodology guides the process of inquiry; and, finally, on a normative or prescriptive plane,

(4) an assertion that, ideally, reason ought to inform, curtail, or indeed *dominate* all other aspects of (bodily) human existence.

In contrast to Descartes's emphasis on the primacy of reason, Pascal argued that the human intellect is (1) an inherently limited and imperfect instrument that operates in unconscious subjection to the will and imagination, and (2) that there are other, equally valid ways of apprehending the truth of human existence, such as faith.

Moreover, said Pascal, reason is not sovereign in its own domain, and the rationalist insistence on the primacy of reason has a quasi-delusional quality.

Blaise Pascal was born in 1623, at Clermont, where his father, Étienne, held a judicial post. He was educated at home by his father in accordance with the principles of Montaigne, a philosopher whom he alternately revered and reviled in later life. Like Descartes, Pascal excelled in mathematics, and in 1640, at the age of 17, published his first book on conical sections. In 1646, after a prolonged illness, Étienne Pascal converted to an austere branch of Catholicism known as Jansenism. Like Calvinism, Jansenism was based on a close adherence to the doctrines of Saint Augustine, which antagonized the Jesuit order, whom Pascal attacked for intellectual complacence and moral laxity in his "Provincial Letters" (1656–1657). Still, Pascal was somewhat less ardent in his embrace of Jansenism than his father and sisters, remaining a sympathetic but slightly skeptical outsider. Besides, he was busy with "worldly" matters. After his father's recovery, the family moved to Rouen, where Blaise performed some ingenious experiments on atmospheric pressure — the first in a long series of experiments that won Pascal lasting fame as a natural scientist (Pascal 1995).

In 1648, Pascal published new works on conic sections and atmospheric pressure, which kindled controversies that pursued him all through 1651. In 1652, his sister Jacqueline entered a Jansenist convent in Port Royal, and in 1654, Pascal, who had wavered somewhat in his attitude toward Jansenism, experienced an ecstatic illumination that led to his definitive conversion. In 1655, following Jacqueline, he retreated to the Jansenist enclave at Port Royal, where he passed away in 1662, eight years before his *Pensées* was published.

Pensées is an intriguing book. Mathematics and experiments are seldom mentioned in it, except tangentially, and fully half of the book is devoted to searching reflections on the Hebrew Bible and the relationship between the Jewish and Christian faiths. The first section of *Pensées* consists of 27 fragments, including one entitled "Rabbinism," while section 2 devoted 13 (out of 31) fragments to discussing the Jews and their faith and the similarities and differences between Christians and Jews. The titles of these fragments are quite suggestive: "Advantages of the Jewish People," "Sincerity of the Jewish People," "True Jews and True Christians Have the Same Religion," and so on. So it is probably no coincidence that in his hour of ecstatic illumination, Pascal inscribed the following entry in his diary: "God of Abraham, Isaac and Jacob — not of the philosophers and scholars." This entry was then copied and sewn into the lining of his coat, which he wore until his death.

If you bracket off the theological material, *Pensées* consists chiefly of reflections on the paradoxes of human nature, the role of power, coercion, and human suggestibility as the basis of worldly authority, the elusive and ambiguous character of "earthly" justice, and so on. Though Pascal never systematized his legal and political thought, these fragments contain ideas that anticipate existentialism and psychoanalysis. As Hans Jonas points out, there are passages in *Pensées* where Pascal describes our basic "worldly" condition in ways that clearly prefigure Heidegger's account of "thrownness," or *Geworfenheit*. Moreover, like Kierkegaard and Heidegger, Pascal stressed the role of boredom, anxiety, and the incessant search for distraction in human affairs, and the way they divert attention from the inevitability of our death (Jonas 1963).

That being so, it is instructive to note that while Descartes defined our humanness in narrow, rationalistic terms, Pascal insisted that "We know the truth not only through our reason but also through our heart" (1995, 28). Moreover, Pascal emphasized repeatedly that will and imagination play a large role in shaping or deforming our conscious judgment, emphasizing that consciousness is often blinkered or opaque to itself and oblivious to the real source of its ideas and beliefs:

> The will is one of the principal organs of belief, not because it creates belief, but because things are true or false depending on the aspect by which we judge them. When the will likes one aspect more than another, it deflects the mind from considering the qualities of the one it does not care to see. Thus the mind, keeping in step with the will, remains looking at the aspect preferred by the will, and so judges by what it sees there. (190)

The modern term for what Pascal was describing here is "selective inattention" — a state of *motivated inattention* to those features of phenomena that do not please us, for one reason or another. Freud's theory of unconscious motivation hinges on the idea of unconscious wish-fulfillment, or "primary process thought," so it is instructive to note that when Pascal talks about imagination, he sounds remarkably Freudian. For example, in section 1, series 2 of *Pensées,* he says:

> It is the dominant faculty in man, master of error and falsehood, all the more deceptive for not being invariably so; for it would be an infallible criterion of truth if it were infallibly that of lies. Since, however, it is usually false, it gives no indication of its quality, setting the same mark on truth and false alike.
>
> I am not speaking of fools, but of the wisest men, amongst whom imagination is best entitled to persuade. Reason may object in vain. It cannot fix the price of things.
>
> This arrogant force, which checks and dominates its enemy, reason, for the pleasure of showing off the power it has in every sphere, has established a second nature in man. Imagination has its happy and unhappy men, its sick and well, its rich and poor; it makes us believe, doubt, deny, reason; it deadens the senses, it arouses them; it has its fools and sages, and nothing annoys more than to see it satisfy its guests more fully and completely than reason ever could. . . . Imagination cannot make fools wise, but it can make them happy, as against reason, which only makes its friends wretched; one covers them with glory; the other with shame . . .

> Man has been quite right to make these two powers into allies, although in this peace imagination enjoys an extensive advantage. . . . Reason never wholly overcomes imagination, while the contrary is quite common. (9–10)

With the benefit of hindsight, one could argue that these remarks adumbrate the conflict between primary and secondary process thought sketched by Freud in *The Interpretation of Dreams* (1900) and "Two Principles of Mental Functioning" (Freud 1911), where the pleasure principle, which lacks the ability to discriminate between truth and error, gratifies us by wish-fulfillment, while reason, or the reality principle, desperately tries to hold its own, unaware that its purposes and perspectives are frequently subverted by wishful thinking and infantile grandiosity. Did Pascal influence Freud? Probably not. But the parallels are quite impressive, and they don't stop here. Like Freud much later, Pascal emphasizes the presence of inner and interpersonal conflict as an inexorable feature of human existence: "All men naturally hate each other. We have used concupiscence as best we can to make it serve the common good, but this is mere sham and a false of charity, for essentially it is just hate" (Pascal 1995, 68–69).

In short, like Hobbes, Nietzsche, Freud, and Sartre much later, Pascal felt that civic morality, prevailing notions of justice, the common good, and so on, were merely expedient disguises contrived to mask our underlying antipathy to others, and the fact that beneath the veneer of civilization the basic relation of one human being to another is essentially predatory or adversarial, lacking in genuine love, or even mere consideration for the welfare of others. From this perspective, all social and interpersonal harmony is merely temporary, a deliberate (if often disavowed) deferral of conflict, a truce maintained by a social contract. There will be no kingdom of God upon earth. Conflict is ubiquitous, and so, indeed, is acute *inner* conflict. At any given moment of time, said Pascal, we are at variance with ourselves, with reason contending against the passions, and vice versa, and with the various passions vying incessantly for supremacy within us (189–90). No one is immune to this sort of suffering, and the only road to redemption is through faith. This view of the human condition stands in marked contrast to the utopian vision in Marx, Buber, Binswanger, and Fromm, who suggested that it is possible to create or perhaps merely restore a substantial harmony or convergence of interests among people living in genuine fellowship — a new dispensation that can overcome our seemingly innate antipathy toward one another, a secular equivalent to the messianic time.

Though he seldom mentioned Descartes by name (for example, pt. 1, sec. 5, no. 84), Pascal's derisive allusions to people who doubt the possibility of a vacuum, and skeptics who doubt the existence of the world or their own bodies (for example, pt. 1, sec. 7, no. 130), leave no doubt that René Descartes was frequently in his thoughts. Though not spelled out as clearly as we would wish, given our objectives, Pascal's critique of Descartes prefigures Kierkegaard's critique of Hegel two centuries later — that speculative reason, no matter how clever or elaborately justified, abstracts so far from the thinker's real existence that it ultimately dooms him to irrelevance or inadvertent farce.

Despite differences with Descartes, however, Pascal did not disparage reason or scorn science, as Kierkegaard and Nietzsche did later. He even said that human dignity consists essentially in our ability to reason. But Pascal never imagined that reason would yield absolute or universal truths. On the contrary, Pascal dwelt on the tentative, provisional character of human knowledge and saw the human mind as capable of indefinite advancement, but never of completely fathoming the mysteries of the universe. This epistemic humility stands in stark contrast with the hubristic designs of both Cartesian and Hegelian rationalism, which literally sought to encompass the entire world in their respective "systems."

How does Pascal compare with the late nineteenth and twentieth century thinkers in our survey? Pascal acknowledged the limited, provisional truth and the inherent dignity of natural scientific inquiry, expressing a measure of trust in reason and scientific method. By contrast, Nietzsche accused science of conjuring with appearances, while for Heidegger, Galilean science was a perfect vehicle for *Seinsvergessenheit* — "forgetfulness of Being." Why? Perhaps because in the nineteenth and twentieth century, science ceased to be the domain of learned gentlemen like Descartes and Pascal, inviting the involvement of the "common man." And as scientific discoveries came to dominate the European intellectual landscape, the fear of collectivism, conformity and bourgeois complacency assumed greater urgency than before.

But a fear of the masses and the mistrust of science need not take on such a sweeping or dismissive form. In the twentieth century, there are more "moderate" strains of irrationalism present in the work Martin Buber, Max Scheler, Gabriel Marcel, and R. D. Laing that remain closer to the spirit of Pascal. Thinkers of this persuasion acknowledge that rationalism and the scientific way of grasping the world is valid when taken on its own terms. But it is also one-sided, fragmented, and potentially disfiguring if left unchecked. By their account, faith, imagination, and intuition, which rationalism routinely disparages or disqualifies, are all legitimate ways of "knowing" in certain circumstances. Indeed, they disclose a great deal about reality that is inaccessible to us through the intellect alone. Moreover, they insist, with respect to the human sciences, the absence of love and a sense of awe and mystery severely restrict what a researcher can really know about his or her subject. The idea that love and reverence is a vital prerequisite to a deeper understanding of reality has a decidedly romantic coloration and stands in the starkest possible contrast to the argument — found in Freud, among others — that love is "blind," an illusion that compromises our judgment.

Reason, the Unconscious, and History
Kant, Hegel, and Marx

IMMANUEL KANT

If Descartes ushered in the Age of Enlightenment, with its character-istic emphasis on reason, then Pascal, who dwelt on the mystery and power of the unconscious, prefigured the Romantic reaction against it. Wedged between the Enlightenment and Romantic movements was Immanuel Kant, who was born in 1724 in Königsberg, East Prussia, in what is now Kaliningrad, Russia. His parents were poor, uneducated followers of Pietism, a branch of Lutheranism. Fortunately, at the age of eight, Immanuel's pastor gave him a free but thorough education in the classics, and in 1740 he enrolled at the University of Königsberg as a theology student, but quickly gravitated toward physics, mathe-matics, and the work of Isaac Newton.

In 1755, Kant finished his formal education and assumed the posi-tion of lecturer at the University of Königsberg. During the early 1760s, his work was somewhat derivative, following faithfully in the footsteps of Christian Wolff, Leibniz's leading expositor. However, in the 1760s, the ideas that made him famous erupted in startling pro-fusion. In 1770, Kant was appointed professor to the chair of logic and metaphysics at Königsberg, where he stayed until shortly before his death in 1804. It was during this period that he published his three critiques — the *Critique of Pure Reason* (1787), *The Critique of Practical Reason* (1788), and *Critique of Judgment* (1790).

We cannot possibly do justice to Kant's critical philosophy here. Suffice it to say that he admired the audacity of Diderot and the Enlightenment and adopted their motto: "Dare to know." However, unlike Diderot and his contemporaries, Kant did not imagine that reason can fathom all the mysteries of the universe, and insisted that reason is not transparent, as Descartes imagined, but utterly opaque to itself. Indeed, Kant factored unconscious mental processes into the inner structure of the rational mind, saying that a significant part of our minds are unconscious — that consciousness itself is a product of unconscious mental operations that cannot be directly experienced, but only inferred or reconstructed ex post facto. This marked a radical departure from Cartesian rationalism, on the one hand, and from the naive empiricism of John Locke (1632–1704) and his followers, on the other.

The Lockean account of learning stipulated that perception is a passive process in which external stimuli impinge directly on our sensory apparatus. Consciously experienced sensations then give rise to conscious processes of reflection, which then create simple ideas such as shape, color, number, solidity, which in due course give rise to complex ideas such as space, time, causality, and so on. In short, said Locke, the mind is a tabula rasa, or a blank slate, that passively accumulates sense impressions and then gradually renders them intelligible through the construction of an internal "picture" of the world. Ideas like space, time, and causality — the building blocks of natural scientific discourse — are not innate, intuitive, or simply present to consciousness, as rationalists insisted, but constructed through the *association of ideas,* which are acquired, in turn, from experience (Fancher 1996).

At first glance, these epistemological debates have little bearing on theories of psychotherapy, until we remember that most systems of psychology are based on theories of "internal representations" of objects. The same is true for many theories of psychopathology and psychotherapy, though they emphasize internal representations of other people rather than the ways that we constitute our nonhuman environment. Depending on the particular school or orientation, these internal representations may be called imagos, archetypes, constructs, schemas, or "mental maps." Regardless of what we call them, every psychotherapist must grapple with the patient's "inner" world, eventually. So, the question of where these representations come from is not an idle one, either from a theoretical or a therapeutic standpoint.

In any case, Locke assumed that the process of constructing internal representations through the association of ideas is a conscious one, for the most part. He also assumed that the ideas of space, time, and causality are valid. David Hume (1711–1776), whom Kant also admired, radicalized Locke's epistemology by proposing that the concept of causality need not refer to a real relationship between objects in the world. Nor is it an "innate idea," as Descartes insisted. On the contrary, the concept of causality is a kind of mental reflex, a product of learning and habituation.

To support this contention, Hume noted that when we observe one billiard ball *(A)* strike another *(B)*, and then watch *B* suddenly move across the table (while *A* slows to a stop), we tend to infer that one object or event — namely, the impact of *A* on *B* — *causes* the other one. This impression may be dim or tentative at first, but it is *reinforced* every time the experience is repeated until, eventually, we assume as a matter of course that what we experience is a straightforward *perception* of a real causal relationship — *A* causes *B* to move.

So, unlike Locke, who took causality for granted, Hume distinguished himself by stressing that when we witness *A* hitting *B*, we infer, rather than *perceive*, the existence of a causal nexus. Our inference is based on probabilities, which in turn derive from past experience rather than air-tight ontological certainties. We infer causality in such cases because one event precedes the other with such striking regularity that experience promotes the *habit* of thinking in causal terms. Nevertheless, Hume said, it is always possible that the causal sequence we *think* that we see is the product of other, intervening processes (Fancher 1996).

Kant accepted Hume's critique of Locke, up to a point, but countered that the idea of causality is not merely derived from experience or habit. Following Locke, said Kant, Hume had mistakenly tried to derive complex ideas like space, time, and causality from sensory experience. But he did so in vain, said Kant, because in truth, *there is no such thing as passive or unmediated sensation.* The mind is not a tabula rasa, or blank slate, nor does it accumulate sensory stimuli in a purely passive manner. On the contrary, the mind actively sorts out and organizes sensory data prior to its entry or registration in consciousness. Indeed, said Kant, in order to be intelligible at all, all sensory stimuli must be "processed" through the a priori categories deemed essential to judgment, including (1) *quantity* (unity, plurality, totality), (2) *quality* (reality, negation, limitation), (3) *relation* (substance and accident, cause and effect, reciprocity between patient and agent), and (4) *modality* (possibility/impossibility, existence/nonexistence, necessity/contingency).

Leaving specific categories aside, the real point is that Kant attributed the mind's ability to sort out and synthesize sensory data *prior to* its entry into consciousness to an entity he called the "transcendental ego." By his reckoning, the "transcendental ego" is never experienced directly because its operations transform our sensory worlds *prior to* any given conscious experience (Jaspers 1962). The only access we have is by reflecting on the logical preconditions for experience — in other words, by asking, "What makes (rational) human experience *possible?*" Having posed this question carefully, Kant concludes that the operations of our own minds are never completely transparent or accessible to us; that some of our most crucial mental operations remain inaccessible to normal efforts at introspection at all times.

As most psychotherapists in training know that Sigmund Freud made some similar claims, so we hasten to add that the kind of unconscious mental processes Kant was addressing here are not the instinct and affect-laden type that preoccupied Schopenhauer, Nietzsche, and Freud — irrational, instinctual desires that engender inner conflicts and that impair our capacity to reason. If anything, the opposite is true. Kant's categories and the operations of the "transcendental ego" were posited as a vital precondition to intact cognitive functioning. Nowadays, most psychologists refer to the domain of mental operations Kant subsumed under the "transcendental ego" as "the cognitive unconscious." Unlike the dynamic unconscious discussed by Freud and others, the "cognitive unconscious" consists of mental processes that are free of instinctual or emotional conflict and that enhance, rather than impair, our grasp of reality (Burston 1986).

However, even when it is functioning and intact, said Kant, reason can only take us so far. For, in addition to asking what makes human experience possible, Kant asked the other crucial question for epistemology: What are the *limits* of human knowledge? Kant's answer was that our grasp of reality is limited to what can be rendered intelligible in light of these innate categories of cognition. Beyond that, our poor intellects cannot travel. So Kant took a bold step and synthesized the rationalist and Romantic perspectives. He adhered to the rationalist idea that the mind is active and endowed with innate ideas, but he also said that the depths of nature and of our own minds are forever inaccessible to us; that, despite our magnificent scientific achievements, the world around (and "in") us is shrouded in mystery. The knowing subject can never grasp reality fully in consciousness because consciousness is shaped and constrained by the categories that make the world intelligible and therefore render experience possible. The *noumenal* world of the *ding-an-sich* exists "in itself," of course. But it does not, and cannot, exist *for us*, except in the realm of phenomena, or appearances, as an object of thoughtful, deliberate, and persuasive conjecture that is forever beyond the reach of definitive proof.

Like Pascal, then, Kant challenged rationalism by stressing the inherent limitations of human reason. But again, like Pascal, he did not disparage or dismiss reason nor seek to replace it with anything ostensibly deeper or more reliable. Unfortunately, this did not deter more ardent and uncompromising irrationalists like Arthur Schopenhauer and Friedrich Nietzsche from misconstruing Kant's philosophy as a total refutation of the natural sciences, or claiming that they were faithfully following in his footsteps.

Georg Wilhelm Friedrich Hegel

Next to Immanuel Kant, Georg Wilhelm Friedrich Hegel (1770–1831) was probably the most influential German philosopher of all time.

Hegel built on some of the novel and subversive aspects of Kant's critical philosophy, taking them far beyond anything Kant imagined. Kant introduced the concept of the unconscious in the philosophy of mind, and Hegel built this concept into his philosophy of history. But Hegel did not share Kant's view that reality is ultimately beyond the grasp of reason. Indeed, Hegel said that nature exists "in itself," but becomes "for itself" by reflecting on its own processes through the medium of human thought. And whereas Kant argued his position by refuting earlier thinkers' ideas about epistemology (for example, Locke, Leibniz, Hume), Hegel took a more conciliatory tone. Rather than refuting his predecessors, he said that earlier philosophers had attained partial or distorted premonitions of the truth that could be integrated into a new, dialectical synthesis that reconciled seemingly disparate points of view (Hegel 1967).

Born in Stuttgart in 1770, Hegel studied the classics as a young man and enrolled in the study of philosophy and theology at the University of Tübingen in 1788 with a view to becoming a minister. There he developed friendships with the poet Friedrich Hölderlin and the philosopher Friedrich Wilhelm Joseph von Schelling, with whom he roomed as a student. Graduating in 1793, Hegel decided against becoming a minister and became a tutor in Bern and then Frankfurt, where he entered into the circle of Hölderlin and his friends (Hegel 1979). In 1801, at Schelling's invitation, he moved to Jena, where he completed his habilitation for professorship, entitled "De orbitis planetarium," on Kepler and Newton. In 1805, Hegel became a professor at the University of Jena, publishing his main work, *Phenomenology of Mind,* in 1807. In 1816 he accepted a professorship in philosophy at the University of Heidelberg. Two years later, in 1818, Hegel was invited to teach at the University of Berlin, where he concentrated almost exclusively on his lectures, which quickly made him famous. He remained in Berlin until his death in 1831, during a cholera epidemic.

Hegel's first major work, *The Phenomenology of Mind,* was followed by *The Science of Logic* (1812) and *The Philosophy of Right* (1821). He also composed a three-volume *Encyclopedia of the Philosophical Sciences,* of which volume 1 dealt with *Logic* (1830), volume 2 *The Philosophy of Nature* (1817), and volume 3 *The Philosophy of Mind* (1830). Posthumous publications (edited and issued by students) included *Lectures on the Philosophy of History* (1833), *The Philosophy of History: Introduction* (1837), *Outlines of the Phenomenology* (1840), and *Outlines of Logic* (1840).

Mention Hegel to most people, and the word that generally springs to mind is, of course, "dialectics." Definitions are hard to come by, but for the purpose of our discussion, dialectics will be defined simply as the dynamic interplay between opposing polarities, entities, or forces, leading eventually to their reconciliation, transcendence, or synthesis (German: *Aufhebung*). In ancient and medieval times, philosophy was preoccupied with the interplay between several *antinomies*, including the One and Many, the Creator and Creation, appearance and reality, essence and existence, being and becoming, subject and object, the finite and infinite, freedom and necessity, and so on. According to Hegel, the constitutive dualisms of traditional metaphysics can all be reconciled, but their eventual transcendence is not just a cognitive, but also a *historical* process, one that takes several millennia to accomplish. According the Hegel, the "truth" of any entity, whether organic or metaphysical, lies not in its pristine or initial form, but in the completed process of its unfolding. To buttress this contention, Hegel took the bold (if not reckless) step of equating the laws of logic with the laws of history and developed a whole new way of thinking about reason. Instead of positing a set of timeless, transcendent categories that govern the operation and limits of reason, as Kant had, Hegel *historicized* reason by treating it as a "work in progress," in a process of perpetual unfolding (Avineri 1974). While seldom entirely persuasive, this interpretive strategy provoked manifold responses from Marx, Kierkegaard, and Nietzsche — responses that, in may ways, furnished the basis for twentieth century existentialism.

Cartesian rationalism was based on the idea that reason and consciousness are transparent to themselves. Kant broke with Cartesian rationalism and offered a somewhat *decentered* theory of reason, one in which the rational, cogitating subject is actually unaware of many mental operations by means of which he or she constitutes his or her picture or "map" of the cosmos. Kant's contention that reality is not apprehended directly by the subject, but (unbeknownst to him or her), *constructed* in accordance with certain criteria, was the progenitor of virtually all constructivist theories of the mind, including those current in the psychotherapy field today.

Nevertheless, according to Kant, reason is still a faculty or an attribute *that resides within the individual,* even if its operations are not entirely available to conscious self-inspection. Hegel approached reason in an even more radically decentered fashion — not as a individual attribute, but as an ordering and animating principle that is diffusely present in all of nature and human history, a kind of cosmological constant that transforms the raw, insensible "in itself" of nature into a sentient "for itself," using human beings as the vehicles for its self-discovery.

According to Hegel, human history is a slow, unilinear progression in which *Geist* — which is translated variously as reason, God, or Absolute Spirit — gradually overcomes its dispersion and fragmentation in nature and attains authentic self-consciousness. Far from being ends in themselves, Hegel depicted individuals as the vehicles or instruments of *Geist,* which uses us to achieve its own ends. So whereas Kant located the unconscious mental processes that shape (and distort) our judgment and behavior squarely in the individual's transcendental ego, Hegel described reason being diffusely distributed through the culture or society as a whole, or what he called the "Zeitgeist." Indeed, said Hegel, the various empires and epochs of history, with their respective religions and philosophies, are really way stations on the road to cosmic consciousness and the ultimate transcendence of dualism. As a result, Hegel thought of individual, egoic consciousness as historically conditioned and limited by the level of development attained by members of a particular culture or civilization (Hegel 1952).

Oddly enough, Hegel seemed to think that he was personally immune to the problems of perspectivity that bedeviled previous thinkers and philosophers as a result of the historicity of *their* windows on reality — that he alone had plumbed the depths of Being in its process of historical becoming. Hegel's theodicy was dramatically at variance with mainstream Protestant theology, which stresses a personal relationship to a transcendent God. But this did not trouble him, apparently. Hegel said that philosophy does *not* disprove the God of revelation, but merely translates the latent content of religious dogma from the symbolic realm into abstract concepts that can be discursively explained and justified through reason. Indeed, much of *The Phenomenology of Mind* is devoted to this task (Hegel 1967).

As a result, many of Hegel's finest expositors have construed him as a profoundly *irreligious* thinker. To prove this thesis, Giorgi Lukacs, Alexandre Kojève, and more recently, Robert Solomon and Tom Rockmore all drew on the writings of the young Hegel, who furnished plenty of evidence of a rebellious, atheistic phase (Hegel 1979). However, those who maintain that Hegel basically *remained* an atheist as he matured are also, by implication, accusing him of cowardice and insincerity in his public pronouncements (Fackenheim 1970).

Leaving the debate on Hegel's (alleged) atheism aside, there is one lengthy section in *The Phenomenology of Mind* — the master-slave dialectic — which influenced twentieth century thought and letters in a way that is vastly disproportionate to its actual length. Indeed, with the exception of Descartes's "cogito," these passages probably elicited more learned commentary than any other in the history of philosophy. Ever since Marx first seized on it, scholars have generated an enormous amount of literature that attempts to apply Hegel's ideas about the master/slave relation to the psychology of class, race, and gender, and more recently, to clinical issues like sadomasochism and the resolution of the transference (Frie 1997; O'Neill 1996). Some of the better known writers in this genre are Alexandre Kojève, Jean-Paul Sartre, Simone de Beauvoir, Frantz Fanon, Jacques Lacan, Jessica Benjamin, Tzvetan Todorov, Judith Butler, and Paul Gilroy.

Among other things, the master-slave dialectic warrants our close attention because it addresses the origins of self-consciousness, the meaning of freedom, the formation of identity, the struggle for recognition, and the process of conflict resolution. Unfortunately, however, it does not address these issues in a very straightforward fashion. Section 178 of *The Phenomenology of Mind* opens with the statement that "Self-consciousness exists in and for itself when, and by the fact that, it so exists for another; that is, exists only in being acknowledged" (1967, 229).

Hegel goes on to discuss this proposition, and it is clear from context that, for Hegel at any rate, there is no such thing as an isolated or monadic ego, as there was for Descartes. The other person is always there implicitly, as an indispensable precondition and ineluctable mediator of my own self-consciousness, my being "for-itself." Complete solipsism — or a solitary, self-contained consciousness, à la Descartes — is never a real option. It simply does not exist. However, said Hegel, in the struggle between two competing egos, the person vigorously attempts to create conditions approximating solipsism. In an adversarial relationship, like the one that precedes the master-slave relation, the solution sought by each party it is a kind of *pseudoautonomy* that results from the disavowal of my ineluctable dependence on others, which can only be sustained through self-deception. Since I cannot negate the existence of the other person or my dependence on them completely, I attempt to minimize my awareness of it by the exercise of power, by constricting their freedom, by making my existence central or primary, and that of the other person peripheral or secondary. In short, I try to be — or become — a "being-for-myself," while rendering the other a "being-for-me" — an instrument or mirror of my own self-being. I try, in other words, to wrest recognition of my essential worth and freedom from the other person without reciprocating in kind. The other's freedom, subjectivity, and so on, is of no concern to me except as an obstacle to my own freedom and self-expression (Burston 1996a).

That said, the final result of two power-seeking persons clashing is not genuine solipsism, but what Hegel calls a "life and death struggle" in which the only the death-defying party ultimately triumphs:

> Thus the relation of the two self-conscious individuals is such that they prove themselves and each other through a life and death struggle. They must engage in this struggle, for they must raise their certainty of being *for themselves* to truth, both in the case of the other and in their own case. And it is only through staking one's life that freedom is won. . . . The individual who has not risked his life may well be recognized as a person, but he has not attained to the truth of this recognition as an independent self-consciousness. Similarly just as each stakes his own life, so each must seek the other's death, for it values the other no more than itself; its essential being is present to it in the form of the "other," it is outside itself and must rid itself of externality. (Hegel 1967, sec. 187)

It is interesting to note that the origins of egoism, as Hegel described them, reside in the creation or quest for an *illusion* of noncontingent individuality. As Hegel stated, *individual self-consciousness is inherently eccentric to itself, inherently dependent on the existence of the other for its own self-being.* Despite the inherent and insuperable eccentricity of self-consciousness, the life and death struggle that ensues in the service of its evasion (according to Hegel) ultimately creates two antithetical poles in which "being for oneself" and "being for another" become bifurcated into two disparate modes of consciousness, two distinct mentalities, an "independent" and "dependent" consciousness.

The independent consciousness, or the lord, says Hegel, exists solely *for himself* (we retain the male gender here in line with Hegel's original). By risking his life, the master demonstrates that he values freedom and self-assertion more than mere survival. Or, put another way, he affirms his honor unequivocally because he transcends or negates his animal instinct for survival. Conversely, the dependent consciousness, the "bondsman," values life more than his honor or freedom. He is governed by the fear of death, and therefore becomes a "being for the other" (Kojève 1969).

Now, before going further, note that Hegel assumes that the search for recognition emerges first and foremost in the context of *adversarial* social relations, rather than complementary social relations where reciprocity and respect prevail. Moreover, and more importantly, Hegel does not address how the battle between conflicting egos, a struggle between two selves, results eventually in a class or caste system that structures an entire social order. Instead, he assumes that in the wake of the bloody struggle, stable social relations ensue in which the one who wages war and those who work acquire different social roles and correspondingly different mentalities (Burston 1996a).

Now that the former antagonists have settled down, Hegel says, their relationship to one another is mediated through their respective relationships to nature. The way they relate to nature, in turn, provides vital clues to their ongoing interdependence. The lord continues to deny his essential dependence on the bondsman by appropriating and "negating" (consuming) the products of the bondsman's labor, and treats the bondsman's various productive activities as extensions or expressions of his own being. His dominion over nature is inscribed and affirmed through the bondsman's service to him.

Meanwhile, by virtue of his efforts to subdue and transform nature on the lord's behalf, and to negate or subdue his own inner nature, the bondsman's desires, which also clamor for gratification, must be deferred. And as a result, says Hegel, the bondsman comes to acquire a distinctive relationship *to himself* that the lord, by virtue of his laziness and his equivocal combination of dependence, independence, and denial, does not have:

> although the fear of the Lord is indeed the beginning of wisdom, consciousness is not therein aware that it is a being for self. Through work, however, the bondsman becomes conscious of what he truly is. In the moment that corresponds to desire in the Lord's consciousness, it did seem that the aspect of unessential relation to the thing fell to the lot of the Bondsman. . . . Desire has reserved for itself the pure negating of the object and thereby its unalloyed feeling of self. But that is the reason why this satisfaction is itself only a fleeting one, for it lacks the side of objectivity and permanence. Work, on the other hand, is desire held in check, fleetingness staved off; in other words, work forms and shapes the thing. . . . It is in this way, therefore, that consciousness, qua worker, comes to see in the independent being (of the object) its own independence. (Hegel 1967, sec. 195)

Had he analyzed these remarks, Kierkegaard would probably have said that the aristocratic consciousness lacks interiority because it is stuck in the esthetic phase of development. Freud, in a similar vein, might suggest that the aristocrat merely follows the pleasure principle, while the bondsman acquires the capacity to delay gratification and sublimate his instinctual drives. Erich Fromm would have said that the lord possesses an unlimited amount of *negative* freedom, or freedom from external constraint, but lacks *positive* freedom, the discipline and will to create, and in the process, to transform himself and the world (Fromm 1941). Either way, work puts the bondsman on a slow but inexorable journey toward self-discovery. As Hegel affirms, "in fashioning the thing, the bondsman's own negativity, his being-for self, becomes an object for him only through his setting at nought the existing shape confronting him" (Hegel 1967, sec. 196). And again, further below, "Through rediscovery of himself, the bondsman realizes that it is precisely in this work wherein he seemed to have only an alienated existence that he acquires a mind of his own" (Hegel 1967).

The formative activity of labor, while necessary, is not sufficient to transform the bondsman's consciousness, however. Absolute fear — the fear of death — is also indispensable to make labor a source of self-objectification and self-affirmation. Hegel says, "The fear of the Lord is the beginning of all wisdom," and implies that death is "the Lord" in this instance. Hegel's formulation remains somewhat opaque. But it is clear that like many existentialists, Hegel regarded the fear of death as a potentially *productive* force in the life of the individual. Though not commonly regarded as an existentialist, his concern with what was later termed "existential anxiety," and the need to confer meaning on life through action, are themes that suffuse his early work.

Hegel also had a strong (if indirect) impact on twentieth century developmental psychology. As Hegel noted in *The Phenomenology of Mind*, in our attempt to account for the being of the other, the ostensible unity of personal self-consciousness is reduplicated and fragmented, eliciting ongoing attempts to restore — or more accurately, perhaps, to create — the elusive unity of consciousness-with-itself. To borrow an expression from Piaget (who draws directly from Hegel), consciousness is a state of permanent internal *disequilibrium* that attempts to reverse or remedy its inherent instability through the construction of increasingly complex cognitive structures. Finally, Hegel is the real (if often unacknowledged) precursor of psychoanalytic theories of mind (Mills 2003), and of intersubjectivity (Benjamin 1988). This material will be covered in more depth in forthcoming chapters, but the basic thrust of these therapeutic approaches is that the self cannot exist without the other: there is no such thing as isolated self-experience.

KARL MARX

Born in Trier, Germany, in 1818 to assimilated Jewish parents, Karl Marx received a classical education. He studied law in Bonn and philosophy in Berlin, where he affiliated with the "Left Hegelians." Marx became editor of the radical newspaper *Neue Rheinische Zeitung* in 1841, where he met Ludwig Feuerbach. Known as a Left Hegelian, Ludwig Feuerbach (1804–1872) was an influential philosopher who espoused a new kind of humanism. Borrowing from Hegel, Feuerbach noted that self and other, the "I" and the "Thou," are always reciprocally constituted, and he devoted much thought and reflection to what Buber later called the "interhuman," or the social foundations of human existence. Like Marx, Buber, and Erich Fromm, Feuerbach was a utopian thinker who treated egoism as the product of a sick society rather than an intrinsic dynamism inherent in all social relations. According to Feuerbach, Hegel's *Geist* is actually an alienated objectification of what he termed "the human essence," which he thought of as a kind of rational sociability inextricably intertwined with perception and our sensuous, embodied being (Feuerbach 1972): "Thus the very essence of God is characterized by the fact that he is an object for no other being but man, that he is a specially human object, a mystery pertaining to man. But if God is exclusively an object to man, what does God's essence reveal to us? Nothing but the essence of man" (Friedman 1994). According to Feuerbach, disembodied reason, either in the Cartesian or Hegelian form, is not real, but a figment of the philosopher's imagination. Real human reason is always embodied and not detached from nor antagonistic to sociability or sensuous experience. Indeed, eliminating the supernatural and reconciling (or reintegrating) reason with sensuousness and sociability was the sole purpose of Feuerbach's philosophy (Feuerbach 1957).

Shortly after encountering Feuerbach, Marx "converted" to the Communist cause in 1842. As a result, his criticism of the Prussian state became so galling to King Frederick William IV that Marx was exiled in 1843 and fled to Paris and then to Brussels in 1845. After the failed 1848 revolution in Germany, Marx emigrated to London. Though his educational background was literary and philosophical, Marx's burgeoning interest in legal, political, and historical questions prompted an intensive immersion in "the dismal science" of political economy. His first, tentative critiques of Adam Smith and Ricardo were published posthumously in *The Economic and Philosophic Manuscripts* of 1844, also known as the Paris manuscripts. In these essays, Marx blended Feuerbachian humanism with "revolutionary socialism" or communism, and developed his theory of alienation, which had a profound effect on twentieth century social thought (Avineri 1976).

In 1845, Marx published his famous "Theses of Feuerbach" where he coined the memorable phrase: "The philosophers have interpreted the world. The problem is to *change* it." Then in 1846 he published *The German Ideology* with Friedrich Engels. In 1848, he and Engels published *The Communist Manifesto* with the express purpose seizing the leadership of the (rapidly emerging) International Working Men's Association, and to discredit competitors like Moses Hess, Pierre Proudhon, Wilhelm Weitling, and Mikhail Bakunin. Fierce quarrels and bitter polemics with other leaders of the working class absorbed much of his energy until his death in 1883, but these conflicts did not deter him from publishing three volumes of *Das Kapital* and authoring scores of unpublished manuscripts, some of which appeared posthumously. During that time, Marx lived in London and worked as a freelance journalist writing for English and American newspapers on politics and international affairs.

In the Paris manuscripts and, more emphatically, in *The German Ideology* and *The Communist Manifesto,* Marx differentiated his program for social change from the ideas of "utopian socialists" and "vulgar communists." Though his characterizations of Hess, Proudhon, Weitling, and Bakunin were often unkind, and occasionally quite slanderous, Marx was nevertheless quite right to stress the uniqueness of his approach, which was rooted in Hegelian dialectic. Hegel and Marx agreed that labor, which political economy treated merely as a means to an end, or a necessity to be endured, is actually an integral part of the formation of the individual and the species as a whole. Marx was more explicit and emphatic on this point, perhaps, but he drew his inspiration on this point from Hegel (Avineri 1976). In a fragment from Paris manuscripts entitled "Critique of Hegel," Marx declared that

> the greatness of Hegel's *Phenomenology* and its final product, the dialectic of negativity as the moving and creating principle, is on the one hand that Hegel conceives of the self-creation of man as a process, objectification

as loss of the object, as externalization and the transcendence of this externalization. This means, therefore, that he grasps the nature of labor and understands objective man, true, because real, man as the result of his own labor. The real, active relationship of man to himself as a species being . . . is only possible if he uses all his powers to create (which is again only possible through the cooperation of man as a result of history). (O'Neill 1996)

However, the main difference between Hegel and Marx is in terms of methodology. Hegel had undermined the seeming self-evidence of the cogito in the master-slave dialectic, but Marx (following Feuerbach) called attention to the fact that there was still an abstract and distinctly otherworldly feel to Hegel's theorizing. According to Marx, Hegel had inverted the nexus between being and consciousness, deriving the former from the latter, putting the cart before the horse. Like Descartes, Hegel deduced life from thought, whereas our engagement with nature and with others at a practical, bodily, and social level precedes and conditions consciousness, not the other way around. So in contrast to Hegel, Marx did not claim that the laws of logic and the laws of history are identical. On the contrary, he insisted that the "logic" of historical development cannot be deduced from any set of abstract principles, but must be *discovered* by studying the actual conditions of life in different societies and periods of history to discern how class relationships are played out against the backdrop of a society's (technologically mediated) relationship to nature. He called his method *historical materialism* (Avineri 1976).

One of the main tasks of historical materialism, says Marx, is to analyze the dominant ideology of any given society. The term "ideology" was used so often and so promiscuously during the twentieth century that it takes an effort to recall what it actually meant to Marx in the nineteenth. According to Marx, an ideology is a system of beliefs that misconstrues certain features of our social and historical situation as ontological givens rather than as contingent historical phenomena, which can or will be superseded in due course. As a result, ideology promotes *false consciousness,* a false ontology based on a limited and deformed conception of human nature and human potential. The prototypical example is the idea of slavery, which both Plato and Aristotle deemed "natural," and a vital precondition for the freedom and happiness of the free-born citizen. According to Plato and Aristotle, some people — "barbarians" — are naturally slaves, while others are "essentially" noble or free, and any attempt to deviate from nature through extending freedom or education to the rabble is tampering with the natural order — a recipe for disaster (Avineri 1976).

A little closer to home, Descartes provides a perfect illustration of philosophical introspection mediated through the filter of ideology. From a Marxist perspective, the formula, "I think, therefore I am," and Descartes's famous bifurcation of mind and body are not ontological givens, but artifacts of a class society, reflecting the rigid division of labor among aristocrats and commoners (or slaves), in which "mental" labor is reserved for the privileged while physical labor is the domain of servants, serfs, and peasants. Furthermore, Descartes's "systematic doubt," which puts the being of other persons (and the world at large) in question and finds certainty only in itself, reflects the imaginary self-sufficiency of an aristocrat living comfortably off a generous inheritance. If Descartes had actually *worked* for a living and collaborated with others on a daily basis for his livelihood, no such "systematic doubts" would have arisen. And if they did, he would have promptly dismissed them as idle speculation. Had Descartes been a peasant or a worker, rather than a bookish, retiring gentleman, he would have said (with Hegel's bondsman), "I work, therefore I am."

Though poised on the threshold of modernity, Descartes's philosophy of mind still reflected a predominantly feudal, agrarian ideology (Levi 1974). And capitalism, which supersedes feudalism, provides bold new methods for the production and distribution of goods and services — a whole new "mode of production" — that opens up unprecedented possibilities for human development while disguising and obscuring new forms of oppression. Thus, unlike Hegel's bondsman, who is actually a prototypical serf or peasant, the industrial wage laborer is nominally free to sell his labor to a higher bidder, or to take up another line of work if he can. But the legal freedoms he enjoys in theory are meaningless in practice if work is scarce, wages low, and mind-numbing, back-breaking work is the only way to keep himself and his family alive.

Meanwhile, the capitalist's tendency to dehumanize and "objectify" the worker is reflected (and perpetuated by) the transformation of labor into a commodity that is bought or sold by contract. Rather than being a vehicle toward self-discovery and enhancement of human dignity, labor in the new industrial order became nothing more than numbing toil. And this is tragic, says Marx, because work ought to be (1) a vehicle for self-expression and self-development, as it was for Hegel's bondsman, for example, and (2) a way of contributing to society as a whole, and not just to the fortune of this or that particular capitalist. In *The Economic and Philosophic Manuscripts,* Marx declared:

> Supposing that we had produced in a human manner; each of us would in his production have doubly affirmed himself and his fellow men. I would have: 1) objectified in my production my individuality and . . . thus . . . enjoyed realizing that my personality is objective. . . . 2) In your enjoyment . . . I would have had the direct enjoyment of realizing that I had satisfied a human need. . . . 3) I would have been for you the mediator between you and the species, and thus acknowledged . . . by you as a necessary part of yourself. . . . 4) In my expression of my life, I would have . . . realized my own essence, my human, communal essence. (O'Neill 1996)

The striking thing about this passage is that Marx did not conceive of labor merely as means to bodily survival or the accumulation of wealth, but as a way to gratify what Erich Fromm later called our "existential needs" — needs for communion with others, for recognition, and the affirmation of our worth and dignity (Fromm 1961). In Marx's mind, labor was not just a means to avert starvation or amass wealth. It was a kind of secular sacrament, or a vehicle for what Martin Buber later called "meeting" and self-discovery (Avnon 1998). By transforming work into a mere commodity, capitalism "alienates" the worker from his own powers of self-discovery and self-expression. Moreover, it constrains the worker and the capitalist alike to fill their material needs in ways that are at variance with their human or existential needs for solidarity and self-expression. The whole sordid arrangement is justified through the new science of "political economy." Rather than claiming that this sad state of affairs is a product of divine providence, the "dismal science" legitimated our cruelty and indifference to our own kind by what were (mistakenly) construed as natural laws. Contrary to the claims of economists, the "laws" enumerated by Smith, Mill, and Ricardo and others (that is, the law of wages, of rent, and so forth), did not *describe* impersonal natural processes, such as the laws of physics or chemistry, as they claimed to do. Instead, under the deceptive guise of neutral, scientific description, political economy tacitly *prescribes* ways of relating to other human beings *as if they were things* in the natural world: a process Marx termed *reification*. The reification of social relations fosters a *profoundly ahistorical mode of consciousness* that mistakes the existing state of affairs for a merely "natural" one, rather as a product of concerted human agency over historical time (Avineri 1976).

So in effect what Marx proposed — and what his harshest critics seldom catch sight of — was much more than an equitable distribution of wealth; it was nothing short of the total transformation of work from mere toil at the behest of others to free and creative self-expression *for all* (Fromm 1961). And behind his program of socializing the labor process lay the optimistic, indeed utopian conviction that the self-interest of the individual and the interests of society at large are not inherently opposed; that contingent circumstances — above all, scarcity, ignorance, and vested power interests, which can be abolished or transcended — merely make them seem so.

Although Marx was very skilled at ideological critique, he was quite reticent when it came to spelling out the normative implications of his concept of socialized labor. By 1848 Marx had distanced himself from his earlier socialist humanism and stressed the superiority of his approach to working-class emancipation by emphasizing its "scientific" character. His friend and collaborator, Friedrich Engels, called this approach "scientific socialism," or "dialectical materialism," which Lenin and his followers renamed "orthodox Marxism."

As a result of their bid to become more "scientific," Marx and his followers embarked on a descent into a natural scientism that masked an unconscious messianism in which the proletariat was conscripted to play the role of the elect. This is quite ironic, given that Marx was so opposed to religion and so adept at exposing the scientific pretensions of bourgeois political economists. Barring the efforts of a few theorists, Marxism quickly degenerated into an arid dogma — a new ideology — that was used to justify mass murder and the ruthless domination of ordinary working people by a class of bureaucratic party officials that resorted to force and deception in order to retain their hold on power.

What relevance, then, does Marx have to the theory and practice of psychotherapy today? First, the distorted development of Marx and Marxism demonstrates the power of unconscious fantasy as a force in the individual and in mass movements. Marx's flight from humanism, his lapse into natural scientism, and so on, were abetted by powerful messianic ideals and aspirations that were sublimated into a secular belief system that was largely disavowed. Of course, there is nothing wrong with secularizing normative ideals that have religious roots or ramifications, provided one acknowledges their normative character. But Marx went to such exorbitant lengths to deny that his methodology was harnessed in the service of ethical ideals that he quite possibly ended up deluding himself and his followers.

Whether Marx was motivated by vanity, fear, or a dreadful misjudgment on tactical or strategic grounds, is not relevant here. But we should note the parallel between the drift toward natural scientism and sterile dogmatism in Marxism and somewhat later, in psychoanalysis (Jaspers 1952). Indeed, the more ardently Marxism and psychoanalysis embraced natural scientism to gain prestige, respectability, or to rally the faithful during the twentieth century, the more nearly they resembled secular religions, complete with dogma, orthodoxy, schisms, and so on. Just as Marxism harbored independent theorists who kept the spirit of open inquiry alive, so psychoanalysis generated no shortage of creative theorists among existentialist and revisionist psychoanalysts who rejected the blinkers of conventional opinion.

Another important point to consider is that the role of labor in human ontology — as envisaged by Hegel and Marx — points to a gaping lacuna in most clinical approaches today. Judging from case histories and textbooks, love, pleasure, security, and optimism (or the lack of any or all of these) are explicitly addressed in the clinical literature. So, indeed, is creativity, but work and its vicissitudes is a topic that seldom intrudes on the ideas or inquiries of clinicians. As Erik Erikson declares,

> the most neglected problem in psychoanalysis is the problem of work, in theory as well as in practice: as if the dialectic of the history of ideas had ordered a system of psychological thought that would as resolutely ignore the way in which the individual and his group makes a living as Marxism ignores introspective psychology and makes a man's economic position the fulcrum of his acts and thoughts. Decades of case histories have omitted the work histories of patients or have treated their occupation as a seemingly irrelevant area of their life in which data could be disguised with the greatest impunity. (Erikson 1958, 17–18)

Has anything changed since these words were written?

Finally, Marx's suggestion that capitalism compels people to meet their basic material needs in ways that conflict with their fundamental human needs provided the inspiration for Fromm and Laing's critiques of "adaptation" in the 1950s, 1960s, and 1970s (Fromm 1955, 1970; Laing 1967). During the cold war era, the dominant school of psychoanalysis in North America was ego psychology, which defined mental health chiefly according to the person's degree of "adjustment" to prevailing cultural norms and expectations. By contrast, Fromm and Laing maintained that frictionless adaptation to one's enveloping social context often betokens a "socially patterned defect," or an acute (if unconscious) deficiency in the capacity to reason, to create, or to express and affirm oneself honestly in one's dealing with others. This calls into question the notion that the goal of therapy is "normalization," if the latter is defined as behavioral or attitudinal congruence with prevailing cultural norms. Moreover, it obligates therapists to discern when their patients' conflicts represent a "failure of adaptation" to the prevailing culture, or when the prevailing culture is really failing them, and how to address these issues in a useful and sympathetic way through what is nowadays called "empowerment."

Admittedly, Marx's contention that the process of adapting to the norms and practices of capitalist society does violence to the "human

essence" presupposes that there actually is a "human essence," o
generic human need, that is integral to our definition of "human" —
a position Marx retreated from after 1848. Some say that the notion
that society limits or frustrates human aspirations, stunts human development, and creates a pervasive malaise is more relevant to social psychology than to clinical psychology. But disturbances relating to career
choices, job satisfaction, or workplace ethics are frequently implicated
in adult disturbances, and the distinction between clinical and social
psychology is a recent social artifact, expressing a division of labor in
the academy that lacks any deep ontological foundation or compelling
rationale outside these disciplinary discourses.

ngst, Authenticity, and
Ressentiment
Kierkegaard and Nietzsche

THE COMMON GROUND

Much as they differed on important points, Hegel and Marx were both *historicists* who believed that history has an ascertainable goal and that movement toward this goal should be reckoned as "progress." For Hegel that goal was the self-recovery of Absolute Spirit, while for Marx it was the creation of a classless society, free of exploitation and oppression. Disparate as these goals seem, both Hegel and Marx construed history as a cumulative, linear process that culminates in a kind of collective epiphany, in which my deepening self-knowledge radiates outward, encompassing a deepening awareness of my interdependence with others and our collective coinherence in a process of self-authorship and self-discovery that spans several millennia. At issue, then, is a shared notion of history as a process of the self-discovery and self-creation of the human species over time.

These assumptions about history were questioned by Kierkegaard and Nietzsche, who dismissed any notion of historical progress and were wary of collective self-authorship. This tendency is evident in Kierkegaard's habit of lumping all forms of society and social action together under the derisive category of "the crowd." No other mode of sociability is even mentioned in Kierkegaard's opus. While Marx looked beyond the grim realities of class society to a time when the average

60

person embraced and embodied an idealized "life of the species," for Kierkegaard the genus or the species is nothing but a mere abstraction: "A crowd in its very concept is the untruth, by reason of the fact that it renders the individual completely impenitent and irresponsible, or at least weakens his sense of responsibility by reducing it to a fraction. . . . For 'crowd' is an abstraction and has no hands: but each individual ordinarily has two hands." A different but equally scathing appraisal of groups is found in Nietzsche. In contrast to Marx, who addresses himself to the masses, Nietzsche declares: "The masses . . . deserve notice in three respects only: first as faded copies of great men produced on paper with worn out instruments, then as a force of resistance to great men, finally as instruments in the hands of great men; for the rest, let the Devil and statistics take them!" (Nietzsche 1983, 113). Kierkegaard and Nietzsche shared a fervent antipathy to groups — a kind of *radical individualism*. And in the wake of Kant and Hegel and the tremendous pressure to *systematize* knowledge that gripped the nineteenth century, Kierkegaard and Nietzsche were both profoundly *antisystematic* thinkers. This does not mean that they were unsystematic in the sense that they lacked a system. On the contrary, they rejected the idea that the world, in all its complexity, could be encompassed in a system. Unlike Hegel, they did not aim to create a comprehensive, internally consistent and intellectually satisfying account of world history. And unlike Marx they were not invested in charting the way to collective emancipation. Their goal was to provoke and disconcert their readers, to get under their skin and compel them to confront their own existence in a stark and honest way, without pretense or subterfuge. This Socratic agenda registers indirectly in their respective styles, their quasi-confessional, quasi-confrontational modes of address, their preference for aphorisms, essays, and fragments rather than the lengthy and densely argued tomes of professional philosophers.

Finally, Kierkegaard and Nietzsche attacked Descartes, Hegel, and the whole rationalist tradition for making inflated claims to omniscience and being grotesquely divorced from the ground of existence. For Kierkegaard, the ground of existence is God; for Nietzsche, it is life, or the instincts, represented by the figure of the Greek god Dionysus.

And at this point, the parallels between Kierkegaard and Nietzsche simply cease, giving way to deep divergences in perspective. In pursuit of genuine self-knowledge, Kierkegaard stressed the profound solitude and interiority of the true Christian, in contrast to the tepid, complacent piety of "Christendom" (Kierkegaard 1968), while Nietzsche rejected Christianity altogether as a belated derivative of "the Jewish slave revolt in morals" (Nietzsche 1956). Moreover, Kierkegaard felt that genuine self-knowledge could only develop in the context of ethical resolve that deepens, in due course, into a deep (if iconoclastic) mode of piety. Nietzsche, by contrast, asserted that genuine self-knowledge could only be acquired by the total overthrow of religion and by deliberate acts of transgression that place the *Übermensch,* symbolized by Dionysus, "beyond good and evil." With these similarities and contrasts in mind, let us examine them in more detail.

Søren Kierkegaard

Søren Aabye Kierkegaard was the youngest of seven children born to Michael Pederson Kierkegaard and his second wife, Anne, in 1813. Michael Kierkegaard was a member of the Pietist "Hernhutter" fraternity and was saturated with a sense of sin and grave doubts about his own personal salvation. As Kierkegaard later recalled, his father instructed him that the world was ruled by meanness, lies, and injustice, and that, like Christ himself, the truth must suffer, be derided and scorned. Kierkegaard took this lesson to heart and applied it to his critique of Lutheran Christianity, which he said was fatally compromised by its allegiance to the state.

In 1830, at age 17, Kierkegaard entered the University of Copenhagen as a theology student and was drafted into the Royal Guard one month later. Fortunately for posterity, he was discharged because of his hunched back. During most of his university career, Kierkegaard was profoundly estranged from his father. In 1838, he experienced "the Great Earthquake," a radical reevaluation of his life, which led to the reconciliation with his father who died that same year. Around this time, Kierkegaard met Regina Olsen, to whom he became engaged in 1840.

However, after only several months and considerable anguish and soul-searching, Kierkegaard broke off the engagement and, by his own estimation, began his real spiritual vocation. Always in poor health, from the age of 25 onwards Kierkegaard had a strong premonition of an early death. This may account for his solitary ways and his astonishing literary output. In 1843, Kierkegaard published *Fear and Trembling, Either/Or, Repetition,* and several "edifying discourses." These were followed in 1844 by *Philosophical Fragments* and *The Concept of Anxiety* and in 1845 by *Stages of Life's Way.* In 1846, he considered and then dropped the idea of qualifying for ordination as a Lutheran priest and published *Concluding Unscientific Postscript* and *Two Ages.* In 1849, he published *The Sickness unto Death. The Attack on Christendom,* his critique of Danish Lutheranism, published after his death in 1855, contained several of the dozens of papers and pamphlets he had published over the preceding decade or so.

Kierkegaard did not shrink from attacking authority, nor from using humor as a weapon. When they are not simply scathing, Kierkegaard's parodies of Hegel (and Hegelians) are utterly hilarious. However, Kierkegaard also underestimated his indebtedness to Hegel on important points. For example, in the introduction to *The Philosophy of Right* (1821), Hegel outlined a three-stage sequence in what he termed the development of the will. The dialectical process that Hegel described supposedly propels the individual from (1) the level of the "immediate will," which is impulsive, insatiable, and contradictory, and which seeks novelty and excitement, to (2) the level of the "arbitrary will," which has the capacity for reflection, restraint, and commitment to a "determinate form," or identity, and then, in due course, to (3) a "universal" will that "wills itself in accordance with the Idea" and completely transcends the split between "objectivity" and "subjectivity" that bedevils the preceding two stages (Hegel 1952). This begs the question: why are "objectivity" and "subjectivity" at odds with each other initially? Because, according to Hegel, the "immediate will" vainly tries to make the objective world correspond to the contours of its subjective desires, and cherishes an illusory sense of freedom that comes from license, or mere lack of constraint, and for that very reason lacks

cohesion, direction, and resolve. The immediate will cannot uncon-
ditionally affirm one desire, or one way of being, because it cannot effectively *negate* all the other desires it harbors simultaneously. The
"arbitrary will," by contrast, possesses more capacity for reflection
and restraint, and attempts to mold its subjectivity in accordance with
the demands of reason and reality, and therefore enjoys a contingent
and limited kind of freedom, affirming some of its possibilities while
negating others. Though limited in scope, the freedom enjoyed by the
arbitrary will is genuine and self-authored, not frivolous and delusional.

In the final stage of development, says Hegel, the "universal" will
enjoys "absolute freedom" and lack of (inner or external) constraint
because it becomes fully and truly "objective" without sacrificing
either reason or subjectivity. Just *how* this happens remains somewhat
obscure, though Hegel assures us that it does, and that it entails overcoming the "false" freedom of impulsivity (which is really a form of
slavery), and the sense of finitude and self-limitation acknowledged and
embraced by the "arbitrary" will, leading to a genuine absorption in
the Infinite, which, as Hegel says, *is* freedom (Avineri 1974).

Similarly, Kierkegaard outlined a three-stage theory of consciousness in *Either/Or* (1843), *Fear and Trembling, Philosophical Framents*
(1844), *Stages on Life's Way* (1845), and *Concluding Unscientific Postscript* (1846). According to Kierkegaard, human beings can be classified
according to "types" that correspond to levels or "stages" of consciousness. The first of these is the *aesthetic* stage. The aesthete values novelty,
excitement, and variety, but deplores, indeed *fears,* boredom. He or
she loves to experiment and savors the thrill of romantic love, but flees
from commitment and avoids marriage or binding ethical commitments.
He or she lacks the decisive element of grounded subjectivity —
earnestness, inwardness, and passion. The risk entailed in becoming
stuck in this level of development — which is strikingly similar to
Hegel's "immediate will" — is the eventual awareness of the meaning-
lessness and futility of an uncommitted existence — the confrontation
with nihilism, which can lead to terminal indecision and despair. Irony,
said Kierkegaard, is a mood that arises on the threshold of the second
stage, and discloses the futility of an uncommitted existence.

Kierkegaard's second or *ethical* stage is marked by a decisive turn to action and commitment, and an attempt to live an authentic existence in the face of existential anxiety, or the awareness of the inevitability of death. Having confronted his finitude without resorting to the evasion and obfuscation of the aesthete, the ethicist experiences his existence as a task, a responsibility. He recognizes that his essential humanity is not already given. On the contrary, it is something he must make through decision, through choice. According to Kierkegaard, ethical choice confronts us at every moment of our fleeting existence and becomes the medium of our self-creation, self-authorship, or self-actualization. Accordingly, the ethicist — typified, says Kierkegaard, by Abraham, Socrates, and Kant — lives for sake of doing his duty. He possesses earnestness, inwardness, commitment, and passion — the elements necessary for a grounded subjectivity.

Thus far, the area of convergence between Hegel and Kierkegaard is impressive. Both begin with an ego dedicated to the pursuit of pleasure (and the avoidance of pain and boredom), one that defines freedom in terms of unlimited possibility and freedom from constraint, and therefore lacks coherence and the capacity for self-determination. Both graduate, in phase two, to a disillusioned but stronger and ultimately more dignified ego that acknowledges and indeed embraces finitude and attempts to bestow meaning on life through commitment and dedication to some purpose beyond or outside of itself. Though couched in nineteenth century terminology, these philosophical reflections anticipate many ideas about freedom and agency shared by existentialism and psychoanalysis. That said, however, the striking convergence that presided over phases one and two vanishes in the third stage. Why?

Kierkegaard felt that an ethical person may live a grounded, authentic existence, but that to become fully self-actualized, a third, "religious" stage is necessary. However courageous and commendable he is, said Kierkegaard, the ethicist still lacks *faith*. Indeed, in *Fear and Trembling* (1843), Kierkegaard said that clinging to the ethical perspective may even be a hindrance to making the proverbial "leap of faith," particularly if the person neglects to raise their relationship and their duty to the Absolute above their obligations to other flesh-and-blood human beings. In the course of describing the development of *homo religiosis,* or "the Knight of Faith," Kierkegaard also distinguished between two stages of religious consciousness: religiousness A and religiousness B. Although we cannot adequately describe these two substages due to lack of space, religiousness A is based on a sense of God's immanence and corresponds roughly to the Hegelian attitude toward God as a being or intelligence diffusely present in all creation. By contrast, religiousness B recognizes God as an absolute subject whose mystery and transcendence can only be apprehended in inwardness and silence.

According to Kierkegaard, Hegel's notion of *Geist* as a cosmological constant completely overlooks or ignores human temporality and subjectivity and trivializes the problems of individual anxiety and suffering. What defines individual existence is not some pseudohistorical abstraction, nor even a person's relations to others, but his awareness of temporality, of his present and future unfolding in time, moving inexorably toward death. Viewed objectively, perhaps, the individual's temporal condition — his or her being-in-time — is merely a succession of events or moments lived in serial order, one proverbial step after another. But viewed subjectively, it represents an opening to the future, an occasion for anxiety and dread, which can only be addressed by being or becoming a certain kind of person through one's ethical choices.

As a historicist more concerned with collective self-authorship than the fate of the individual, Hegel had paid scant attention to these issues. But anxiety and temporality are recurrent themes in Kierkegaard and, later, in Heidegger. To grasp what Kierkegaard was saying, contrast his approach with the standard psychoanalytic account. Freud distinguished among *realistic anxiety* (fear of an external threat), *neurotic anxiety* (fear of being overwhelmed by the strength of one's own instinctual impulses), and *superego anxiety* (fear of self-punishment, self-hatred, self-disapproval). In short, Freud distinguished between a fear of something external and an anxiety that springs from *within* as a result of a conflict among different parts of the psyche, from which comes the need for "defense mechanisms" or self-deception.

Following Kierkegaard and Heidegger, however, existential analysts like Rollo May refer to *existential anxiety,* which is not a fear of this or that specific entity, nor a product of internal conflict, but an integral feature of our being-in-the-world, a response of our whole being to the radical contingency of human existence (May 1958). To say that it originates with "external" stimuli or "internal" pressures, as a Freudian might, already bifurcates human existence in a decidedly Cartesian manner and obscures the essential feature of this anxiety. It is not the fear of a specific external threat (for example, realistic anxiety), nor the fear of internal conflicts or pressures occasioned by specific desires or experiences. These are genuine, to be sure, but existential anxiety is a total response to the emergent awareness of finitude and death. The refusal or evasion of this awareness can only lead to *inauthenticity*.

Finally, we come to another source of disagreement between Hegel and Kierkegaard, which hinges on the conflict between rationalism and irrationalism. Hegel observed that to emerge from a scattered or frivolous existence into a more dignified and coherent one, the ego's "impulses" must be "purified," must become "the rational system of the will's volitions" (sec. 19). Even if we find the logic of Hegelian dialectics baffling or unpersuasive, no clearer statement of the rationalist program of empowering reason to dominate the "impulses" is possible. The same rationalist ethos is inscribed in Freud's statement, "Where the id was, there shall ego be" (Freud 1923). Though Freud would not have relished the comparison to Hegel, their prescriptions for the good life are very similar in spirit. In contrast with Hegel and Freud, Kierkegaard did not exalt intellect or reason above all other faculties, either in the ethical or religious phase of development. He said so explicitly through his pseudonymous spokesman, Johannes Climacus, in *Concluding Unscientific Postscript:* "If thought speaks deprecatingly of the imagination, imagination, in turn, speaks deprecatingly of thought; and likewise with feeling. The task is not to exalt one above the other, but to give them equal status, to unify them in simultaneity; the medium in which they are unified is *existence*."

Had Kierkegaard merely argued for parity between reason and the other faculties, or sought to harmonize them in some way, he would not have been so radical. But Kierkegaard's irrationalism went much farther than that. Hegel sought to rationalize theology, while Kierkegaard said that Christianity is "the Absolute Paradox," and therefore repugnant to common sense, as its pagan critics rightly alleged. Hearkening back to the church fathers, Kierkegaard said that Christianity is the great *skandalon* — an obstinate object over which reason stumbles repeatedly, and therefore something no reasonable (pagan) person can bring themselves to believe. Since reason will not get you there, by this account, becoming a Christian requires the proverbial "leap of faith." So in the final analysis, Kierkegaard was not merely saying that Hegel's philosophy is muddled, abstract, or abstruse. In truth, he regarded it as un-Christian, even *anti-Christian*.

What was Kierkegaard's legacy to the twentieth century? Shorn of their theological roots and ramifications, his views on human temporality, his emphasis on existential anxiety, on authenticity and inauthenticity, his distrust of "the crowd," and so on, all had a profound effect on Ortega y Gasset, Martin Heidegger, and Jean-Paul Sartre, among others. As a result, in indirect but important ways his work informed leading clinicians like Karl Jaspers, Ludwig Binswanger, Medard Boss, Erich Fromm, Rollo May, Leslie Farber, and R. D. Laing, among others.

Friedrich Nietzsche

Friedrich Wilhelm Nietzsche was born in 1844 in the village of Röcken in Prussian Saxony. His father, Karl Ludwig Nietzsche, was a Lutheran minister who died a slow, horrific death brought on by a brain ailment when Nietzsche was four. Nietzsche's two-year-old brother died six months later. Shortly thereafter, the family moved to Naumberg, where Nietzsche lived with his mother, grandmother, two aunts, and a sister, and began to study music, which became a solace and inspiration throughout his life. Though Nietzsche might have resented the comparison, being an atheist, the quasi-religious terminology he used to describe his experiences indicates that, in a manner of speaking, music was his religion. Nietzsche studied at a prestigious boarding school in Pforta, near Naumberg, preparing for university studies. After graduating, he entered the University of Bonn in 1864. Among his teachers was Albrecht Ritschl (1806–1876), a classics scholar whom

Nietzsche followed to the University of Leipzig in 1865. In 1867, at age 23, Nietzsche entered military service, sustained a serious chest injury, and was soon discharged. After returning to the University of Leipzig in 1868, he met composer Richard Wagner (1813–1883) and struck up an intense, sometimes turbulent friendship that ended a decade later with the publication of *Human, All Too Human* (1878), in which Nietzsche sharply criticized Wagner.

Meanwhile, in 1869, Ritschl recommended Nietzsche for a professorship in philology at the University of Basel, which Nietzsche won at the astonishing age of 25. Despite these promising beginnings, however, Nietzsche was called up for service again in 1870, during the Franco-Prussian War. Never a robust specimen, Nietzsche contracted diphtheria and dysentery, and ill health plagued him until the end of his days.

In 1872, Nietzsche published *The Birth of Tragedy from the Spirit of Music,* which elicited fulsome praise from Wagner and a scathing dismissal from Ritschl and Ulrich Wilamowitz-Moellendorf, an influential classicist of that era. Bitterly estranged from his colleagues, Nietzsche spent more time in Wagner's circle in nearby Tribschen. In 1876, he proposed marriage to Mathilde Trampedach, who rejected him, and he completed *Unfashionable Observations.* In 1879, with his health failing and his increasingly turbulent friendship with Wagner over, Nietzsche quit his university post to lead a wandering existence, spending much time in the Swiss alpine village of Sils-Maria, and in 1889 he suffered a nervous collapse from which he never recovered. In the interim he completed *Daybreak* (1881), *The Gay Science* (1882), *Thus Spake Zarathustra* (1883–1885), *Beyond Good and Evil: A Book for Free Spirits* (1886), *On the Genealogy of Morals* (1887), and *The Case against Wagner, Twilight of the Idols, The Anti-Christ, Ecce Homo,* and *Nietzsche contra Wagner,* all in 1888.

The exact cause of Nietzsche's breakdown is still unknown. Though rumored to have suffered from general paresis (tertiary syphilis), this theory has never been proven. His use of chloral hydrate and other sedatives probably contributed to his decline, but physical infirmities aside, Nietzsche was a lonely, tormented soul who cherished his few faithful friends and was seldom able to replace them when they parted. To complicate matters, while visiting Rome in 1882 Nietzsche met a young Russian student named Lou Salome. Nietzsche was smitten and promptly proposed marriage. Lou declined to accept Nietzsche's hand, but six years later published *Friedrich Nietzsche in His Works* (1894), among the first serious and sympathetic studies of Nietzsche to appear in print. As an intimate of Rainer Maria Rilke and, in later life, of Freud's, Lou Salome helped to disseminate Nietzsche's ideas, though her rejection of him as a suitor probably contributed to his eventual breakdown. In any case, Salome's book was bitterly resented by Elisabeth Forster Nietzsche, Nietzsche's younger sister, who had custody of her invalid brother from 1897 until his death in 1900.

Presenting Nietzsche in a succinct and balanced way is a daunting, perhaps impossible task. For while Kierkegaard deplored systematic philosophy, the tone and content of his work was fairly consistent throughout. Unlike Kierkegaard, however, Nietzsche was not merely antisystematic. He reveled in contradictions and was so extreme or theatrical in his statements at times that it is difficult to credit his sincerity. His writings are full of wit and insight, yet frequently degenerate into political rants. There is much in his work that is disturbingly antiegalitarian and antidemocratic, and his writings on the Jews are open to differing interpretations. Yet Nietzsche's radical individualism and spirited contempt for Richard Wagner's anti-Semitism put him at odds with his sister, and with the Nazi ideologues who later heralded him as a protofascist. Perhaps a more accurate statement is that, at one time or another, Nietzsche reviled practically everyone. Jews, Christians, Muslims, Buddhists, blacks, women, and socialists — all were targets for his carefully cultivated hostility.

From the late 1870s onward, Nietzsche's proclamation that "God is dead" sought to challenge the foundational conceptions of western European culture. In the process, he unwittingly emerged as a prophet of the spiritual vacuum that produced the twentieth century's totalitarian movements. Yet he was also the thinker who best diagnosed the pathologies of fin-de-siècle European culture. Nietzsche dared to look into the underside of modernism, particularly its valorization of science and Christian morals, and his writings contain many psychological insights.

Because Nietzsche lost his intellectual faculties by 1890, his ideas, rich as they were, became a political football. His sister, Elisabeth Foerster-Nietzsche, was a vicious racist and took control of Nietzsche's estate following his death in 1900. She welcomed Hitler and Mussolini as living embodiments of Nietzsche's ideal of the *Übermensch,* encouraging fascist ideologues to quote selectively from Nietzsche. In fact, she edited his unpublished writings and correspondence in such as a way as to demonstrate his relevance to the growing fascist movement, placing particular emphasis on the notion of the "will to power." To counteract her baneful influence, Karl Jaspers, Paul Tillich, and, in due course, Walter Kaufmann sought to demonstrate the actual breadth of Nietzsche's writing following the Second World War. But because of the pervasive stench of Nazi propaganda at mid-century, misinterpretations of his work continued (Santaniello 1994).

In the 1970s, with Marxism and existentialism in serious decline, Nietzsche was hailed by Foucault, Derrida, and others as a precursor to the poststructuralist and deconstructionist sensibilities that were sweeping academia (Foucault 1977b). Nietzsche was fashionable again, albeit this time on the other end of the political spectrum. Nietzsche's metamorphosis from a fascist icon into the darling of the Left in a mere three decades is one of the strangest stories in the history of philosophy. This has much to do with his outright rejection of foundationalist philosophical ideas, which made it relatively easy for those on the right or the left to claim him as their own.

Because Nietzsche was a trained philologist, many of Nietzsche's writings addressed themes from classical Greece. Unlike many of his contemporaries, however, Nietzsche's aim was not simply to glorify the Greeks, but to use their ideas as a way of demonstrating the flaws of late nineteenth century European culture. Traditionally, philosophers tend to champion the primacy of epistemology, ethics, or ontology over other modes of discourse, but Nietzsche would have none of that. Unlike Kierkegaard's pious irrationalism, which valorized ethical and religious perspectives, Nietzsche's philosophy was unabashedly esthetic and, indeed, atheistic, though Nietzsche reveled in pagan imagery, which is apparent throughout his writings.

For example, in contrast to Kierkegaard's famous "leap of faith," Nietzsche invited his readers to join in "the dance of Dionysus" (Nietzsche 1956). *The Birth of Tragedy* (1872) was the first in a series of books to explore this theme. In it, Nietzsche explored the relationship between two gods, Apollo and Dionysus. Apollo stands for the restraint of passion and lucid, conceptual thought. Dionysus represents our tendencies toward madness, transgression, and intoxication. In Nietzsche's view, classical Greek culture had a strong Apollonian bias, demanding self-control of its people. By his reckoning, all the major figures in Greek tragedy were punished because of their secret allegiance to Dionysus. Anticipating Freud, Nietzsche used the famous myth of Oedipus Rex to develop this theme (Rudnytsky 1987). Nietzsche wrote, "It was because of his Titanic love of man that Prometheus had to be devoured by the vultures; it is because of his extravagant wisdom which succeeded in solving the riddle of the Sphinx that Oedipus had to be cast into the whirlpool of crime" (1956, 34). In this passage, the courage of Prometheus and the wisdom of Oedipus are contrasted favorably with the tepid rationality of Apollo and his followers. Oedipus ultimately commits patricide and impregnates his mother, whose children are his children, and at the same time his brothers and sisters. Most significantly, all of this takes place because he consciously attempts to avoid it, having been warned by an oracle that he *would* do so.

Nietzsche's main objective was to demonstrate the deathless vitality of Dionysian fervor beneath the brittle veneer of civilized convention. But he went even further, depicting Dionysus as a liberator:

> The chariot of Dionysus is bedecked with flowers and garlands; panthers and tigers stride beneath his yoke. . . . Now the slave emerges as a freeman; all the rigid hostile walls which either necessity or despotism has erected between men are shattered. Now that the gospel of universal harmony is sounded, each individual becomes not only reconciled to his fellow but actually at one with him — as thought the veil of Maya had been torn apart, and there remained only shreds floating before the vision of the mystical Oneness. Man now expresses himself . . . as a member of a higher community. (1956, sec. 1, 23)

In this view, Dionysus not only frees slaves and abolishes artificial distinctions and barriers, but also restores humankind to "nature," creating joy and harmony where division and discord once reigned. This is Dionysus the liberator, Dionysus the unifier, who stresses the fundamental unity of the species and the oneness of our species with nature as a whole. This vivid portrait holds us in thrall until section 9, where we encounter Oedipus Rex, a follower of Dionysus, who violates nature in pursuit of wisdom and brings destruction and disintegration in his wake. This is Oedipus as Faust, in pursuit of knowledge and power regardless of consequences.

If both characterizations are valid, then old Dionysus is a mercurial fellow. At one moment, he brings peace, harmony, and joy in human fellowship. His agenda is social and profoundly egalitarian. The next moment, in the guise of Oedipus, Dionysus could not care less about others and is engrossed in a private quest for wisdom, defying and defiling nature and bringing death and destruction to everyone in his orbit. A similar disjunction occurs at the beginning of *The Birth of Tragedy*, where Dionysus frees slaves and abolishes "rigid walls," that is, class or ethnic divisions between men. But by the end of the book, Nietzsche characterizes the "dignity of man," the "dignity of labor" derisively as "slogans," not as genuine principles. The joyous egalitarianism that Nietzsche attributed to Dionysus a few pages previously is now construed as the degenerate expression of an "optimistic" mentality that lacks realism and honesty. So from the very outset Nietzsche tended to fuse and confuse opposites and to posit tenuous symbolic equivalencies. Here we have the beginnings of the epistemic relativism that Nietzsche developed more fully in later writings, and which appealed to poststructuralist and deconstructionist thinkers.

Ultimately, Nietzsche's aim was to emphasize that the Dionysian realm cannot be completely suppressed and inevitably affects the nature of our actions and thoughts. Anticipating Freud, Nietzsche heralded the irrational in human experience and warned his late nineteenth century contemporaries against the cult of rationality. Like his philosophical mentor, Arthur Schopenhauer, Nietzsche rejected theology outright, but sought to replace it with something that played much the same role. Nietzsche rejected scientific rationality because he questioned whether any foundational conception, any ultimate explanation, can ever truly be found and relied upon.

Nietzche's last book, *On the Genealogy of Morals* (1887) is more interesting and, in truth, more subversive than *The Birth of Tragedy* because of its sustained assault on Judaism and Christianity. Although neither is mentioned specifically by name here, it is also an attack on Hegel and Marx. Nietzsche's attitude toward history was the precise opposite of Hegel and Marx, who thought of history as a gradual movement forward bringing greater self-knowledge or universal human emancipation. By contrast, Nietzsche depicted history since the advent of Christianity as a steady process of *devolution,* or of cultural and genetic degeneration. According to Nietzsche, the triumph of Christianity is merely the first installment in a process that is culminating in the triumph of democracy and socialism, which are merely updated, modern variants of old-fashioned "slave morality."

According to Nietzsche, slave morality is a product of a frustrated will to power, which results in *ressentiment* (or rancor), a trait that was common among the weak and dispossessed in the ancient world. Those afflicted with *ressentiment* habitually envied and devalued the attitudes and attributes of their masters, who were more prosperous, powerful, and favored by fortune. They rationalized their impotent hatred by attacking the old-fashioned warrior virtues of the aristocracy, that is, courage, individualism, and the unfettered expression of instinctual drives, and by making virtues out of necessities and their own apparent defects such as meekness, poverty, selflessness, reliance on others, and so on. Lacking the strength or resolve to throw off their oppressors, slaves reveled in fantasies of revenge and restitution and slowly subverted the supremacy of the ruling caste through an increasingly collectivistic ethos, since slaves sought strength in numbers, lacking the ability to challenge their oppressors "man to man." Having achieved strength in numbers, they used the powers of priestly persuasion to render the aristocracy's values and lifestyle suspect, or morally reprehensible, not just in the eyes of the underdogs, but in their own eyes as well.

Meanwhile, said Nietzsche, underneath the pious surface all the unloosed aggression of Christian civilization, which had found a "healthy" expression in individual acts of courage and self-affirmation in pagan times, became distorted and displaced into different forms of institutionalized sadism that passed for a genuine morality based on selflessness. In order to maintain appearances, the priests and administrators charged with implementing this system had to disguise the underlying motives successfully from themselves and others (Burston 2003b).

Though beyond the scope of our analysis, it is a well-known fact that Foucault's reflections on the development of penal systems in *Discipline and Punish* were directly inspired by Nietzsche's conjectures on this score (Foucault 1977a). In the wake of Foucault's efforts, Nietzsche's notion of slave morality and *ressentiment* were often compared with Marx's notion of ideology and "false-consciousness." There is a small measure of truth in this comparison because, like Marx, Nietzsche sought to unmask the real, hidden motives behind conventional morality. Moreover, albeit for different reasons, Marx and Nietzsche both invoked class interest as a potent incentive for the development of cultural belief systems based on illusions. But the resemblance ends there. The dominant ideology of any age, said Marx, is the ideology of the ruling class. It exists primarily to legitimate or enhance their power and privilege. By contrast, Nietzsche's slave morality gives rise to an ideology of the underdog, which slowly undermines the (ostensibly legitimate) pretensions and power of the ruling class. Finally, while Marx sought the origins of ideology in the clash of "objective" class interests, Nietzsche described false-consciousness chiefly as a structure of subjectivity, a product of strangulated emotions and impulses, in ways that vividly anticipate Freudian theory.

In one instance, for example, Nietzsche described a process that Freud later called sublimation. Speaking of the connection between a person's artistic energy and sexuality, in *On the Genealogy of Morals* (1887), Nietzsche states that it "may well be that the emergence of the aesthetic condition does not suspend sensuality, as Schopenhauer believed, but merely transmutes it in such a way that it is no longer experienced as a sexual incentive" (cited in May, Angel, and Ellenberger 1958, 247). Elsewhere, in *Beyond Good and Evil*, (1886), Nietzsche provides a concise formulation of the Freudian theory of repression. Freud acknowledges the philosopher's insight, stating, "But not one among all of us has succeeded in describing this phenomenon and its psychological reasons as exhaustively and at the same time as impressively as Nietzsche did in one of his aphorisms: 'I have done that,' says my memory. 'I could not have done that,' says my pride and remains inexorable. Finally, my memory yields" (Freud 1901, 158).

Despite occasional acknowledgments like these, Freud claims not to have read Nietzsche. Yet he is quoted by his biographer, Ernest Jones, as stating that Nietzsche "had a more penetrating knowledge of himself than any other man who ever lived or was ever likely to live" (Jones 1967, 385). Nietzsche was well aware of his ability as a psychologist. In his posthumously published autobiographical essay, *Ecce Homo* (1908), Nietzsche professed in a typically self-glorifying manner, "That a psychologist without equal speaks from my writings is perhaps the first insight reached by a good reader — a reader as I deserve him, who reads me the way good old philologists read their Horace" (sec. 3.5).

It is curious then, that despite Nietzsche's psychological gifts, he had little direct influence on psychoanalysis or psychology as a whole. No doubt this was due to several factors, including Freud's apparent reluctance to share the limelight with a well-known predecessor, and the fact that there were profound *stylistic* differences between the two men, which refer not to the content of their ideas, but their manner of working and addressing their readers. As Nietzsche might have said, he was a Dionysian thinker, while Freud was an Apollonian one. From our point of view, we would say, rather, that Nietzsche was an antisystematic thinker, while Freud was a thoroughly systematic one, as evidenced in his urgent desire to present his ideas in a comprehensive and systematic fashion.

Stylistic differences aside, the similarities between Nietzsche and Freud raise some serious problems from a human science perspective. Nietzsche's account of repressed aggression, sublimated sexuality, and so on, vividly prefigure Freud's intrapsychic model of the psyche, which borders on a monadology at times. In other words, it is not a fully social or intersubjective account of human nature. Nietzsche's theory of slave morality derives the process of self-deception (that he describes so vividly) from an individual's conflicted relation to his or her own impulses, rather than to himself and to other people. In the Nietzschean scheme of things, as with Freud somewhat later, other people figure chiefly as objects or obstacles to the fulfillment of the individual's will to power or instinctual desires. They never become subjects in their own right, or do so only in a derivative fashion.

Another potential problem is raised by Nietzsche's epistemological relativism, which, like his views on language and subjectivity, have a distinctively postmodern feel. They also diverge in illuminating ways from Kierkegaard's irrationalism. In *Concluding Unscientific Postscript*, for example, Kierkegaard states,

> When the question of truth is raised in an objective manner, reflection is directed objectively to the truth as an object to which the knower is related. Reflection is not focused on the relationship, however, but upon the question whether it is the truth to which the knower is related. If only the object to which he is related is the truth, the subject is accounted to be in the truth. When the question of truth is raised subjectively, reflection is directed subjectively to the nature of the individual's relationship to the thing. (Friedman 1994, 116)

Unlike their rationalist adversaries, who prized a notion of objectivity freed from all extraneous influences, irrationalists like Pascal and Kierkegaard argued that other human faculties, including faith, will, imagination, and love disclose vital truths about human existence that are hidden from those who lack them. Or, as Kierkegaard said, "Truth is subjectivity." By contrast, postmodern theorists do not dispute the primacy of reason or objectivity as a way of grasping reality any longer. They dispute the idea that "truth" or reality is graspable in the first place. This postmodern trend really begins with Nietzsche, who not only disparaged faith ("God is dead"), but admonished his readers to abandon their belief in the natural sciences as well. Freud, by contrast, believed that psychoanalysis was a natural science, though his claim was rarely accepted by mainstream academic psychology, which also claimed a scientific (that is, experimental) foundation.

In *On the Genealogy of Morals,* Nietzsche took his irrationalism even further. Citing the medieval Muslim Society of Assassins, whose motto was, "Nothing is true; everything is permitted," Nietzsche stated, in a blunt, self-assured manner, "Here we have real freedom, for the notion of truth itself has been disposed of" (1956, sec. 24). This was a radical departure in the history of Western thought. Nietzsche described truth, or more precisely, the "notion of truth" as an obstacle to freedom, rather than its vital precondition.

The question remains whether Nietzsche actually meant what he said here. He often sought to shock, provoke, or offend readers to rid them of their complacency and put them off balance so that they would be more receptive to his message. Then again, he may have been completely sincere. Many of his ideas were part of the reactionary culture of the period, and Nietzsche despised the natural sciences because he saw them as a vehicle for the masses to advance their collective will to power, much as religion had been in the past. And the idea that truth is a chimera, or utterly beyond our grasp, is completely consistent with things he said in other contexts.

What does one do if, following Nietzsche, we dismiss an absolute philosophical basis for morality? Certainly two world wars, the Holocaust, and the many instances of genocide that followed lend credence to the argument that morality is not innate in human beings. Yet Nietzsche's insistence that the moral vacuity of modern culture demonstrates the necessity of a will to power is likewise very questionable. Nietzsche is asking us to give up the need for an absolute ground from which to understand and interpret human experience, but he himself appears to rely on the notion of an absolute power. This raises more troubling questions about how individuals in a Nietzschean society would perceive morality; beyond some broad generalizations about adopting a self-affirming and life-affirming stance, Nietzsche leaves us with precious few answers.

By stressing the relationship between the knower and the known, as Kierkegaard did in the quote above, we wish to underline the fact that the rationalist effort to depict the relationship between the knower and the known as purely rational, or as void of affect, intentionality, and so on, is not a faithful account of phenomena, but a schizoid distortion of human experience. Kierkegaard and Nietzsche were quite right about this. After all, no matter what or whom we are discussing, our relationship to the person or entity in question is always conditioned by how we encounter it, and the way the phenomena initially appear *for us* furnishes diverse (and sometimes contradictory) motives that bring our cognitive faculties into play.

However, this does not mean that the concept of truth is expendable, or an obstacle to freedom. If that were actually the case, then the concepts of deception and self-deception — which ultimately hinge on the distinction between truth and falsity — become utterly vacuous, and the concept of "self-knowledge" as a goal for philosophic inquiry or therapeutic dialogue becomes irrelevant as well. We cannot imagine therapy, for example, without a concept of deception or self-deception to guide our reflections, and to assist patients in making sense of their relations to others.

Psychology as a Human Science
Dilthey and Husserl

The year 1900 was a major turning point in the history of the human sciences: Nietzsche died, Sigmund Freud published *The Interpretation of Dreams,* and Wilhelm Dilthey published a paper entitled "The Rise of Hermeneutics." Given the obscurity into which Dilthey has fallen in the intervening period, it is important to remember that in 1900 Freud was a somewhat obscure (if increasingly controversial) figure, while Dilthey was a prominent and widely respected thinker, even if Freud studiously ignored him.

The son of a Lutheran theologian, born in 1833, Dilthey studied theology at Heidelberg, then Berlin, where he shifted his attention to history and philosophy and attended the lectures of Leopold von Ranke, Jacob Grimm, Theodor Mommsen, and other famous scholars. He devoted much of his time to studying the life and work of Martin Luther, the Historical School of Law, and the Romantic hermeneutics of Friedrich Schleiermacher (1768–1834). These early efforts culminated in a two-volume biography of Schleiermacher, published in 1861 and 1863, and a voluminous study of the Renaissance and Reformation worldviews, published in 1914, three years after his death.

Schleiermacher was an important influence on Dilthey and emphasized the importance of achieving a deep *psychological* understanding of his subjects. But Schleiermacher applied hermeneutics to the elucidation of texts such as legal codes, treaties, encyclicals, newspaper editorials, business contracts, plays, novels, letters, and so on. Dilthey argued that hermeneutics is an interpretive discipline that can be applied in a more encompassing way to "Life." And "Life," as Dilthey explained, is first and foremost *Erlebnis* — an untranslatable German word that is usually rendered as "experience." However, *Erlebnis* does not merely refer to my *individual* experience, for a life — any life — always unfolds in historical time, in a particular cultural setting. Thus, *my* world is always to some extent a shared world, shaped by the prevailing cultural understandings of the world (Makreel 1975).

Contrast this (quasi-Hegelian) way of approaching experience with those we encountered in the previous chapter. As indicated earlier, Kierkegaard and Nietzsche's perspectives were predicated on the sharp categorical distinction between the individual and "the crowd" or "the mob." Indeed, in Kierkegaard's estimation, only individuals are actually, ontologically, real. Human collectivities, even the idea of the species as a whole, are illusions invoked to evade authenticity and responsibility for oneself. For Nietzsche, by contrast, human collectives are frighteningly real because they are inflected, indeed *infected,* with slave morality.

Whereas Kierkegaard and Nietzsche construed the relation between the individual and society in bleak, adversarial terms, Dilthey cherished a more balanced and finely nuanced idea of the relationship between the individual and society. Whether they know it or not, the most reclusive or aggressive individualists are still bearers of certain social relations that are embedded in the fabric of their lives. Indeed, the patterns of an individual's life are invariably reflected in the contours and content of his or her thought; on close inspection, the two form a seamless continuum, and you cannot fully understand the one without the other. (The term "situated subjectivity," so popular nowadays, is actually Diltheyan in spirit, if not in derivation).

Another difference between Dilthey, one the one hand, and Kierkegaard and Nietzsche on the other, concerns style and method. Deep indignation, devastating wit, irony, loneliness, and shattering epiphanies punctuated Kierkegaard and Nietzsche's work. By contrast, this confessional, deeply personal mode of address never intrudes on Dilthey's writings, where lively calm prevails. Moreover, as *Introduction to the Human Sciences* (1883), *Ideas Concerning a Descriptive and*

Analytical Psychology (1884), and many unpublished papers attest, Dilthey never produced a finished "system," but was deeply committed to conveying his methodological stance to readers in lucid, intelligible prose, without exhorting readers to make an extraordinary "leap of faith" or join in a Dionysian dance.

However, there are also significant areas of agreement among Dilthey, Kierkegaard, and Nietzsche. Like Nietzsche, Dilthey thought that the will, and not reason, is the faculty chiefly responsible for the emergence of individual self-consciousness. As Rudolph Makreel points out,

> Dilthey starts from the totality of psychic life and articulates the cognitive, emotional and volitional functions operative in it. . . . This is the background for understanding Dilthey's remark . . . that 'no real blood flows in the veins of the knowing subject constructed by Locke, Hume and Kant, but rather the diluted extract of reason as a mere activity of thought.' The more full-blooded approach of Dilthey's self-reflection sees the will's relation to reality as central to the foundation of the sciences, especially the human sciences. Whatever resists the will is immediately felt as a reality independent of it. On the basis of this experience, it becomes possible to differentiate a real self from the reality of the external world. The two realities — self and world — are equiprimordial poles of the totality of psychic life. (1975, 9)

Moreover, and in very a similar spirit, Dilthey was quite critical of Cartesian rationalism and took the unity of mind and body as his theoretical point of departure: the mental life of man is part of the psychophysical life unit which is the form in which human existence (is) . . . manifested. Only by means of abstraction is the mental life separable from the psycho-physical unit. The system of these life-units is the reality which constitutes the subject matter of the socio-historical sciences" (Dilthey 1989).

Finally, like Kierkegaard and Nietzsche, Dilthey was an antimetaphysical thinker who insisted that the breadth, depth, and variety of life can never be grasped in its entirety by the intellect alone. And in this, of course, he also resembled Pascal. Moreover, like Pascal and Kant — and unlike Nietzsche — Dilthey had a healthy respect for the rigor and dignity of natural scientific inquiry. However, Dilthey made a clear conceptual distinction between the different modes of intelligibility found in the *Naturwissenschaften* or natural sciences, and the *Geisteswissenschaften* or human sciences. The natural sciences, says Dilthey, explain the behavior of phenomena in causal, naturalistic (Galilean) terms, a process he designates by the German word *erklaren.* These disciplines seek knowledge in order to predict, to mitigate, or to control these phenomena, and with those objectives in mind, develop methodologies that accumulate data, formulate hypotheses, quantify, and experiment in ways that wrest things from their natural surroundings. And this is entirely appropriate, he says, because the entities in question have no personal volition and give no evidence of imparting meaning or value to the world. In short, they are not human.

Whereas the *Naturwissenschaften* explain the behavior of phenomena naturalistically, through a process of *erklaren,* says Dilthey, the *Giesteswissenschaften* approach their subject matter through a process of understanding, or *verstehen.* Since much of the material under study has already occurred, (is in the past), the goals of prediction and control that guide natural scientific inquiry are utterly beside the point. If the object of inquiry is contemporaneous, (for example, emerging trends in music, art, and architecture), it may still elude comprehension through quantification and experiment and remain obscure absent some elucidation of its historical development. Whether the phenomenon in question is in the past or the present, a cultural artifact or another human being, the human science approach attempts to render human thought and behavior intelligible in light of personal experience and social and historical context, using empathy and intuition as well as evidence and logic. Why admit squishy, ephemeral, and unreliable sources like empathy and intuition into our methodology? Because understanding another person's perspective, their way of being-in-the-world — be it through utterance, gestures, artifacts, writing, and so on — is essentially an act of *communion,* and not of detached observation or control. Indeed, said Dilthey, the capacity for communion with the other person is the *essential precondition* for all interpretive or hermeneutic research:

> the individuality of the exegete and that of the author are not opposed to each other like two incomparable facts. Rather, both have been

formed upon the substratum of a general human nature, and it is this which makes possible the communion of people with each other in speech. . . . Now inasmuch as the exegete tentatively transports his own sense of life into another historical milieu, he is able within that perspective, to strengthen and emphasize certain psychic processes in himself and to minimize others, thus making possible within himself a reconstruction of an alien form of life. (Makreel 1975, 250).

In other words, Dilthey thought of individuality as a unique kind of personal presence that emerges from a "general human nature" that renders interpersonal communication possible. But more than that, the fact that we share an underlying "substratum" enables the historian to grasp the fundamental experiences and intentions of the authors of texts who lived centuries or millennia ago by drawing on his own "inner experience." In addition to reconstituting the world from the author's original standpoint, hermeneutic understanding is blessed with the wisdom of hindsight, discerning patterns and relationships among ideas and events that were not yet evident to the author, and that sometimes exceed what language can readily express.[1]

However, the existence (or nonexistence) of unconscious mental processes and their bearing on the fate of the individual was a thorny problem for Dilthey. Without turning it into a noun — *the* unconscious — Kierkegaard and Nietzsche made ample allowance for unconscious mental processes in their reflections on the vagaries of "mass psychology." Moreover, several of Dilthey's well-known contemporaries — Nietzsche, Eduard von Hartmann, and Theodor Lipps — had made unconscious mental processes integral to their systems of thought.

Like most of his illustrious contemporaries — including Wundt, Franz Brentano, and Husserl — Dilthey rejected the idea of uncon-

---

[1] This process of reflective reconstitution — which Dilthey called *Nacherleben* — literally means to "re-experience," and it is often mistakenly conflated with mere empathy or intuition, in the exact etymological sense of "seeing into," or more simply, insight. In fact, it requires and presupposes both. Though neither term entirely captures what Dilthey was exploring, we have used the terms "empathy" and "intuition" so as not to confuse English-speaking readers.

scious mental processes as a non sequitur. But Dilthey's rejection of unconscious mental processes was neither as consistent or as categorical as theirs. Like them, he said that the idea of unconscious mental representations — first propounded by J. F. Herbart and adapted by Lazarus and Steinthal in their theory of language — is nonsense. But his remarks circa 1880–1890 are remarkably sympathetic and prescient in several ways. In chapter 9 of an excerpt from the *Nachlass* entitled *Foundations of Knowledge,* he wrote,

> The concept of the unconscious representation is often rejected at the outset as self-contradictory. . . . The difficulty is [that] . . . consciousness is the way in which a psychic content is there for the ego, insofar as it can be represented at all. Accordingly, an unconscious representation would be an act of being-aware of a psychic content that was not there for the ego . . . this is not self-contradictory given a stricter concept of awareness, but it has ramifications that are hard to conceive. Certainly an act of representing that did not involve a direct awareness of something is unthinkable. Thus a *representation* that is *unconscious* must nonetheless be *a direct awareness of a content.* By making this fact clear to ourselves, we find ourselves faced with the idea of a direct awareness which is not itself there for consciousness. This leads to a distinction between lower and higher modes of representing, according to which the ego adds a higher, unified mode of representing that appropriates the lower mode, which is initially not inwardly there for the ego [and] which can have its effect only from without, like an external stimulus. . . . [This] is . . . consistent with Pfluger's theory about the functions of the spinal chord and its relative autonomy. (Dilthey 1989, 310–11)

In other words, Dilthey noted that a theory of unconscious representation must posit a distinction between "higher" and "lower" modes of representation, the lower of which is not directly available to consciousness, but impinges on it from without in a quasi-autonomous fashion — a pretty fair adumbration of Freud's primary and secondary processes. Dilthey even tried to give this lower mode of representation a neuro-anatomical location in the spinal chord, while Freud abandoned the effort to localize psychic functions in this way after 1897 (Ricoeur 1970).

Still, though he met Freud halfway, anticipating ideas that were not yet in print, in the final analysis Dilthey opted for a position much like Sartre's, and like Harry Stack Sullivan's theory of "selective inattention":

> All those facts that are supposed to be explained by the hypothesis of unconscious representations or, more generally, unconscious psychic acts can be explained by psychic acts available as facts in experience whose effects can be confirmed by a variety of instances. These psychic acts are conscious, but not attended to, noticed, or possessed in reflexive awareness. Thus the existence of the unconscious representations or psychic acts cannot be proved on the basis of their effects. (Dilthey 1989, 311)

Despite this resounding refutation of the unconscious, Dilthey also claimed, "The final aim of hermeneutic procedure is to understand the author better than he has understood himself; a proposition which is the necessary consequence of the doctrine of *unconscious creation*" (in Connerton 1978, 116; emphasis added).

By Dilthey's reckoning, then, hermeneutic understanding is always unfinished, always incomplete. It yields insights that transcend the author's limited self-understanding, but in accordance with the maxim "individuum est ineffabile" — a maxim Dilthey was quite fond of — hermeneutics can never exhaust the plethora of meaning that pulses through the (historically interconnected) networks of human minds. But though he spoke, now and again, of "unconscious creation," Dilthey's hermeneutics was not an "unmasking psychology" (Jaspers), nor a "hermeneutics of suspicion" (Ricoeur) such as Nietzsche practiced in *The Genealogy of Morals*, or Freud advanced in *The Interpretation of Dreams*. Granted, Nietzsche treated religion as a "symptom," while Freud treated patients' dreams, symptoms, and parapraxes as so many "texts" awaiting interpretation. However, both their interpretive strategies were predicated on the idea of an unconscious censorship and a sharp distinction between a text's manifest and latent "contents." There is no hint of unconscious censorship in Dilthey. Moreover, and more importantly, Freud was an unwavering positivist who aligned psychoanalysis with "the natural scientific Weltanschauung." Indeed, without citing Dilthey by name, Freud scorned proponents of the *Geisteswissenschaften* who sought to develop distinctive research methodologies to approach cultural and psychological phenomena (Freud 1933, sec. 35).

What relevance does Dilthey have for contemporary psychotherapy? Dilthey never discussed the vagaries of mental disorder, treatment technique, or the like. But he was the first person to discuss psychology explicitly as a human science, and his emphasis on empathy and communion as a precondition for interpersonal understanding and the situated character of human subjectivity had a profound impact on Edmund Husserl, Karl Jaspers, Max Scheler, Martin Buber, and R. D. Laing, among others. That being so, therapists who embrace a "human science" perspective draw on his work whether they know it or not. Those encountering Dilthey for the first time can still profit from his reflections and share his insight that because of our cultural and historical embeddedness, we are always somewhat opaque to ourselves, and that a suitably trained and sympathetic interpreter may discern what we mean better than we do ourselves.

EDMUND HUSSERL

Edmund Gustav Albrecht Husserl was born to Jewish parents in Prossnitz, Moravia, in 1859. He graduated from Gymnasium in 1876 and went to the University of Leipzig to study physics, astronomy, math, and optics. In 1878, he went to Berlin for specialized studies in math and received his doctorate in 1883 for a dissertation entitled "Contributions to the Theory of the Calculus of Variations." The young Husserl was looking for a firm mathematical foundation for logic, and with it a reliable path to nonrelative truth. But that was not to be. Frustrated and perplexed, in 1883 Husserl dropped mathematics to study psychology in Vienna with Franz Brentano (1838–1917) in the hope of finding a firm foundation for logic there.

In 1886, at Brentano's urging, Husserl left Vienna to study with Brentano's student, Carl Stumpf, at the University of Halle, where he completed his habilitation. That same year Husserl converted to Catholicism and one year later married Malvine Steinschneider. Despite the consolations of his newfound faith, his Halle years (1887–1901) were among his most difficult. It was there he realized that the attempt to ground logic in psychological "laws" — as John Stuart Mill had previously attempted to do — was utterly misguided. Thanks to Gottlob Frege's cogent criticism of his first book, *Philosophie der Arithmetik* (1897), Husserl finally realized that psychology merely *describes how* we think, and occasionally sheds light on *why* we think that way, for better or worse. By contrast, logic actually *prescribes* criteria and specific rules and operations that either validate or correct our thinking, depending on circumstances. It addresses how we *ought to* think, irrespective of how and what we actually think in certain situations. Since psychology is a descriptive discipline, while logic is prescriptive, the attempt to ground logic in psychology can only lead to disaster. The two domains must be kept separate if we are to make any sense of either one (Moran 2000).

Husserl's failure to ground logic in psychology prompted him to ponder the nature of the experience that precedes all formal thinking and, in due course, to formulate the first principles of phenomenology. The first fruits of his efforts appeared in *Logical Investigations* (1901), which Dilthey and Bertrand Russell both greeted as one of the most important in modern philosophy. *Logical Investigations* brought with it a certain renown, and by 1905 Husserl — who moved to Göttingen in 1901 — was surrounded by a circle of ardent followers who devoted themselves to reforming philosophy, and who referred to Husserl reverently as "the master."

During his Göttingen period, Husserl attempted his first systematic account of his evolving theoretical perspective in *Ideas Pertaining to a Pure Phenomenology and a Phenomenological Philosophy*, the first volume of which was published in 1913. In 1916 he moved to Freiburg to assume the chair in philosophy and in 1919 was awarded an honorary doctorate in law by the University of Bonn. He lectured in London in 1922, and in 1928 went into semiretirement, lecturing occasionally. He went to Paris in 1930, where he finished writing *Cartesian Meditations*, which was published in 1931. This book was written in French and did not appear in German until after World War II. In 1933, the Nazis seized power and, because of his Jewish ancestry, Husserl was barred from teaching in Germany — a move that was supported by his former friend and follower, Martin Heidegger, who had recently been installed as rector of the university by the Nazi party. This did not deter Husserl from working diligently on *Transcendental Phenomenology and the Crisis of the European Sciences,* his last book, until his final illness in 1938.

Different philosophers tend to privilege specific perspectives as being central or overarching. For Kierkegaard, ethics took precedence over epistemology. For Nietzsche, as we saw, the esthetic standpoint took precedence over all others. For Husserl, who despised Nietzsche's irrationalism, *epistemology* was the real starting point for all philosophical reflection. Moreover, like Descartes, Husserl wanted to renew philosophy, to begin afresh, starting from the ground up. Indeed, he described himself as a "perpetual beginner" who was continually revising, refining, and, in truth, reinventing the fundamental premises and procedures that guide phenomenological inquiry. This curious trait renders his work difficult to summarize succinctly. It also baffled his students and totally defeated his own (considerable) efforts at systematization. There is something endearing, inspiring, and yet strangely self-defeating in all this. On his deathbed, Husserl was heard to remark, "*Now* I could begin" (Moran 2000).

Perhaps we should begin to explain Husserl in relation to Franz Brentano. Husserl always stressed what Brentano called the intentionality of consciousness — the fact that consciousness always refers to something, is always "consciousness of. . . ." Brentano and Husserl use the term "intentionality" to refer to the perception of external objects *and* so-called "inner experiences," namely aesthetic and moral judgments, feelings of attraction and aversion, and so on. And unlike mainstream empiricists, who treat such "subjective" experiences as off-limits to rigorous and unbiased inquiry, Husserl maintains that these "inner experiences" are also "objects" of consciousness and can be investigated in a rigorous and methodical fashion.

The difference between Brentano and Husserl resides in Husserl's ultimate refusal of the subject/object dualism. According to Brentano, consciousness often "intends" objects that exist independently of it in a world outside the mind. Like Dilthey, Husserl insists that we can never know for certain whether or not objects (or other people) really exist independently of our awareness of them, because we are only aware of them in and through our consciousness. Likewise, we are conscious of our dreams and fantasies, which evoke thoughts and feelings and can therefore be scanned and scrutinized phenomenologically, even though they may lack any reference to "external" reality.

To understand what Husserl was getting at, let us quote Dilthey, whom Husserl often credited with being the first phenomenologist. Dilthey tried to refute (1) the realist thesis that objects or entities exist independently of our knowledge of them, and (2) the argument that consciousness itself is ultimately reducible to physical processes that occur in the brain. In the *Introduction to the Human Sciences* (1989), for example, Dilthey writes:

> when I examine my earliest memories, I find that objects, much like those that surround me today, have always been there for me. My life stands within this relation to the external world that is independent of me . . . even most of the concepts and laws of science are only abstractions from objects, from physical bodies, representations of the relations of their elements.
>
> Nonetheless, the beginning of all serious and consistent philosophy is the insight that these objects, even the persons to whom I stand in relation, are there for me only as facts of my consciousness. Facts of consciousness are the sole material from which objects are constituted. The resistance that objects exert, the space they occupy, their painful impact as well as their agreeable contact — all are facts of consciousness.
>
> Thus I only *appear* to live among things that are independent of my consciousness; in reality, my self distinguishes itself from the facts of my own consciousness, formations whose locus is in me. My consciousness is the locus which encompasses this seemingly immeasurable external world; it is the stuff from which the objects that press on one another in that world are woven. (1989, 245–46)

Elsewhere in *Introduction to the Human Sciences,* Dilthey disputes the truth of any position that would presuppose an opposition between perceptual contents given within me and something independent of them. But such a distinction is by no means given in the self-presence and self-certainty of a state of consciousness. It *could be* the case that facts of consciousness result from another order of facts which did not fall within the sphere of our consciousness, which conditions the above mentioned order of facts. . . . [But] such a distinction becomes nonsense when applied to the facts of consciousness. . . . When we speak of what is real and its power, we mean first of all the facts of consciousness, as real lived experience — indeed, as life itself — which constitute that realm. They bask in the sun of consciousness, where any underlying order would be at best a shadow world. (Dilthey 1989, 251)

Dilthey's epistemology anticipates Husserl's. In effect, Dilthey asserts the *primacy of experience* and the corollary view that the natural scientific worldview is a product of monumental abstraction divorced from the immediacy of lived experience. But if that is so, ask skeptics, why does the phenomenological mode of "lived experience" seem so rarified, so remote from the day-to-day experiences of ordinary human beings? To this, Husserl replies that in their day-to-day lives, most people are enmeshed in one or two prephilosophical "attitudes" or orientations, namely, the *natural* or *theoretical* attitude. In the *natural* attitude, the individual is immediately engaged in "subjective" relationships with others and things, and with various personal projects and concerns. In this frame of mind, he or she judges the merit of ideas on a purely naive and pragmatic basis, according to whether or not they get results, bracketing the question of their "objective" or nonrelative truth. The theoretical attitude, by contrast, is based on a natural scientific or Galilean conception of the universe, in which "objective" truth is actively sought after. However, in the theoretical attitude, truth is usually defined as something that only can be grasped if the inquiring mind is methodically purged of all subjective qualities and experiences, that is, of the "inner" half of reality, through a careful study of the material structure and the measurable properties of objects and their various interrelationships.

While valid and necessary in their own right, says Husserl, neither the natural nor the theoretical attitude is genuinely *philosophical* or conducive to phenomenological inquiry. Therefore, his method (or methods) try to orient the mind *away* from the spontaneous inclinations of both the natural and theoretical attitudes. If we succeed in overcoming them, transcendental phenomenology affords us access to a world that is not obscured by the filters of custom and convention and which precedes the objectified and abstract world of natural-scientific inquiry. According to Husserl, this process is not an irrationalist exercise or an undignified surrender to the arbitrary whims and parochial perspectives of particular observers. On the contrary, he claims, rigorous phenomenological observation and description can clear away all that rubbish and yield surprisingly robust results.

Unfortunately, that is much easier said than done. By Husserl's reckoning, most of us oscillate unreflectively between the natural and theoretical attitudes. The only way to get around (or "beneath") these attitudes is through what Husserl called the "epoché" — a term coined by the ancient skeptics to denote the deliberate suspension of belief and disbelief. Alternatively, borrowing from mathematics, he called this reflexive exercise "bracketing" (Moran 2000, 150–52). According to Husserl, the first step in phenomenological inquiry consists in attending fully and faithfully to all the inflections of experience, including one's own feelings about what one thinks and perceives, while suspending (or "bracketing") all naturalistic preconceptions about the causes of phenomena and their various interrelationships. The Husserlian phenomenologist investigates consciousness and is agnostic on the issue of whether objects or other people actually exist outside of *his* consciousness. But while suitably trained persons can "bracket" naturalistic preconceptions — indeed, *all* preconceptions, says Husserl — they cannot bracket their own bracketing activity, or eliminate their own subjectivity entirely. That being so, he continues, in the act of bracketing, one can suspend belief and disbelief in others, in objects, and so on, but not in the existence of the *bracketer,* that is, one's self, the locus of experience and intentions toward the world. In Husserl's estimation, there is an irreducible residue of the ego whose existence — evidenced by its thinking activity — cannot be doubted (Husserl 1960). Shades of Descartes!

And here we come to another theoretical innovation. Though he rejects the subject/object dualism, Husserl acknowledges that consciousness is typically polarized in terms of an experiencer who experiences something and that which they experience. Following the Greeks again, Husserl called the "that" or the "what" of experience the *noema* (plural *noemata*) and called the "how" of experience, the act of perceiving *noesis*. According to Husserl, the "how" of experience and the "that" of experience, *noesis* and *noema*, only can be separated from each other by a process of abstraction that does violence to the actual content and qualities of immediate experience, though it takes a rigorous process of reflection and the *unlearning* of many old habits of thought to fully realize this. Once insight has been achieved on this path, however, both naive realism and Kant's dualistic distinction between the *phenomenal* world of appearances and the (hidden) *noumenal* world become untenable (Husserl 1962, 1964).

How does Husserl's perspective relate to psychology? Husserl's phenomenological psychology was strictly concerned with elucidating the meaning of experience, without recourse to naturalistic explanations that reduce consciousness to a simpler set of (nonconscious, material) phenomena. His program for phenomenological psychology sought to engage several cohorts of researchers in the patient and exhaustive enumeration of all the potential structures (or acts) of *noesis* — perceiving, thinking, wishing, willing, feeling, remembering, imagining, dreaming, and so on — along with their manifold *noemata*, or corresponding mental contents, accompanied by precise descriptions of their various meanings (*not* causes) and conceptual interrelations. Once this laborious project is complete, many lifetimes hence, presumably, one would know in a thorough and encompassing sense just what consciousness would be completely transparent to itself, and complete self-knowledge would be attainable (Stewart and Mikunas 1990).

Though Husserl dismissed Hegelian dialectic as pseudological nonsense, his program for the future of psychology was haunted by a Hegelian motif. Unlike the Cartesian rationalist or the average empiricist of days gone by, who maintained that consciousness is transparent to itself and localized in the individual, Hegel maintains that consciousness is still opaque to itself and can only become completely "for itself" through the concerted agency of a multitude of people operating in historical time. And even then, presumably, not everyone is equally equipped to partake of the fruits of reason. Similarly, in Husserl, expert introspectors working collaboratively will eventually render all the actual and potential processes and "contents" of consciousness thoroughly explicit. The difference is that in Hegel's scenario "the cunning of Reason" is an *unconscious* process unfolding behind our backs. Husserl describes it as a potential product of conscious and deliberate planning, if and when a suitably trained team of experts could be convened for the purpose.

Thus far, we detect strains of Cartesian and Hegelian rationalism in Husserl. But there is a Kantian dimension as well. Here, as before, the parallels are not exact. For example, Husserl's motto, *zu den Sachen selbst*, or " to the things themselves," seems to imply that things in themselves really are accessible to philosophical inquiry, and he never wavered from this conviction. Like Hegel — albeit for different reasons — Husserl insisted, over and against Kant, that reality is intimately knowable and that careful reflection on our own experience can disclose the essential truth of things.

Two aspects of Kant that Husserl retained, however, were (1) Kant's intriguing question "how is experience possible," and (2) Kant's equally intriguing answer to this question — that is, his theory of the *transcendental ego,* which Husserl adapted, with important qualifications. Remember that when Kant talked about the "transcendental ego," he was *not* talking about some supernatural entity or some mystical "overself" hovering outside our daily, mundane consciousness that occasionally intrudes on our philosophic reveries. The word "transcendental" may have these connotations in everyday, vernacular English. But in philosophical terminology, the term "transcendental" refers to the properties of the ego, or of the knowing subject, which are structurally necessary in order for *any* experience to be possible, and which therefore transcend the content or idiosyncrasies of this or that particular experience. Or, in slightly different words, it is that without which experience in general is not possible. So, for example, space and time are *transcendental* categories. All possible processes and objects of experience are situated by us somewhere in outer or "inner" space, and unfold in some sort of temporal sequence. Likewise, size, shape, and number are categories that philosophers deem constitutive, or necessary to sorting experience out in an intelligible fashion.

Like Kant up to a point, Husserl thus believed that reality is not merely given to us in sense perception. On the contrary, it is actively constituted by the mind. One can illustrate this process of "constitution" by describing how we integrate diverse perspectives of a house. The house is an entity that we can view from above, from below, from the back or the front, from either side, in day or at night, in bright sun, torrential rain, dense fog, and so on. Depending on our angle of vision, the time of day, prevailing weather conditions, and the like, the house itself, which has an invariant shape, size, design, and actually *looks* very different. Its colors and contours seem to vary, and if we confine ourselves to one particular perspective, at one particular time, our judgment of it might prove totally mistaken. Moreover, the house as a *totality* can never be viewed directly because of its many sides and facets. The house as a totality can only be conceived or "constituted" in consciousness through a synthesis of the diverse perspectives we have, and through our ability to *infer* its invariant characteristics, that is, its true size, shape, and so on. Since all objects, big and small, are multifaceted and present themselves to us in different ways at different times, similar processes of "constitution" are said to underlie our whole perceptual universe.

Unlike Husserl, however, Kant speculates that the mental operations that render the temporal flux of successive appearances into a relatively stable and coherent perceptual universe typically go on outside or in some sense prior to conscious reflection, that is, at an *unconscious* level. That being so, says Kant, we can never directly experience that part of our own mind. We can only infer it on the basis of its products, namely, consciousness itself. Consciousness is a product of a complex concatenation of unconscious processes to which we have no direct access. For Husserl, however, the processes of world-constitution that "precede" consciousness are merely "prethematic," meaning that with an appropriately directed effort they could be rendered explicit and subjected to careful scrutiny.

Husserl's "transcendental phenomenology" was fleshed out in a formidable series of books and articles culminating with *The Crisis of the European Sciences,* published posthumously in 1939. *The Crisis* is unusual in several respects. In his previous work, Husserl deliberately refrained from making comparisons between his ideas and those of earlier philosophers, and expressed a disdainful attitude toward others, like Hegel, who had tried to arrive at truth through some sort of dialectical synthesis of earlier thinkers' views. His motto, "To the things themselves!" implies (among other things) that the budding phenomenologist should ignore earlier thinkers and rely on his own experience once he has learned how to "bracket" properly. This ambition to start again from scratch, as it were, gave Husserl's earlier work a slightly Cartesian flavor, as Husserl himself acknowledged, and as the title *Cartesian Meditations* makes plain.

In *The Crisis,* however, Husserl reverses his customary emphasis, and declares that to understand the phenomenological approach one must first examine the works of earlier thinkers in detail and review them in historical sequence. In that spirit, Husserl took on Galileo, Descartes, Hobbes, Locke, Berkeley, Hume, Leibniz, Kant, and Wilhelm Wundt (Husserl 1970). Other partners in dialogue — silent partners, so to speak, because Husserl seldom mentioned them by name — included Hegel, Dilthey, Heidegger, and Jaspers. Their impact is evident in Husserl's shift in focus away from the monadological frame of reference, his focus on the ego and on consciousness, to a careful consideration of the "life-world," and the embeddedness of the world-constituting ego in a cultural and historical frame of reference. And it is precisely Husserl's notions of "life-world" and "intersubjectivity" (Husserl 1960) that spurred a generation of phenomenologically oriented clinicians to understand human behavior as always embedded in social and historical contexts (Theunissen 1986; Spiegelberg 1972).

In keeping with Husserl's newfound emphasis on the life-world, *The Crisis* was the first and only book in which Husserl overtly acknowledged the social context in which he lived and wrote, in which he acknowledged — and lamented — the prevailing disenchantment with the natural sciences and the loss of faith in the possibility of arriving at objective truth or objective values. Being mindful of the imminent crisis, Husserl loathed comparisons to Kierkegaard and Nietzsche, whose ideas were lauded by Jaspers, Scheler, and Heidegger. Indeed, while careful to differentiate phenomenology from the natural sciences, Husserl inveighed angrily against the decadence of the *Existenzphilosophie* of Jaspers, Scheler, and Heidegger (Husserl 1970).

There were serious problems with *The Crisis,* however. First, Husserl's "transcendental ego," which can "bracket" the existence of others but cannot bracket itself, is highly analogous to the Cartesian cogito. Indeed, Husserl's critics in and out of phenomenology have said that it was merely a novel restatement of it, rather than something genuinely new. Husserl responded by saying that, unlike Descartes, he did not ontologize the division between *res mens* and *res extensa.* Fair enough. But while he rejected the dualism of mind and matter that bedevils the natural and theoretical attitudes, he did not *transcend* it in a convincing way. Instead, he merely *collapsed* the latter into the former and insisted that consciousness can exist in complete independence of the body — another transparently Cartesian claim. Since he lacked empirical proof for this position, Husserl relied on logical and experiential grounds to justify it. Despite the eloquence and ingenuity he mustered in its defense, Husserl's metaphysical idealism was merely the inverse diametrical opposite of the kind of reductionism he abhorred among materialists.

Another cogent objection is the profound incongruity or disjunction between Husserl's monadology, as he sometimes called it, and his critique of the aspirations and pretensions of modern science, which had a decidedly intersubjective orientation. In *The Crisis,* Husserl maintains that the ideas and activities pursued within the theoretical attitude are ultimately embedded in and subservient to projects and perspectives derived from the natural attitude, that is, in our subjectivity and sociability. Scientific objectivity, argues Husserl, is always established consensually and intersubjectively using communally agreed upon methods of inquiry by people engaged in collaborative and competitive relationships with one another (Husserl 1970). Thus, whether they acknowledge it or not, scientists are always engaged in passionate and inherently social pursuits. On some level, subjectivity underscores everything they do (Scanlon 1992). (This viewpoint underscores the intersubjective turn in psychotherapy and psychoanalysis that we discuss in the final chapters.)

Husserl, however, still clung to his earlier "monadological" approach, in which the being of others and the world at large is acknowledged as a strong possibility, as it was in Descartes, but is nonetheless tentative and provisional from the standpoint of the experiencing "monad." Contrast Husserl's stubborn solipsism with the Hegelian version of egoic consciousness, in which my being for myself and my being for others are always inextricably intertwined. Husserl was aware of the difficulties posed by solipsism, so he acknowledged that the life-world is in some sense constituted collaboratively by a plurality of selves. In short, Husserl was equivocating. He wanted to affirm and to "bracket" the existence of others at the same time, but could not do so intelligibly and so shifted back and forth between positions depending on what issue he was addressing. To explain the scientific *Weltanschauung*, which was the dominant force in European civilization and a source of terror and admiration for him and his contemporaries, Husserl found a plurality of coexisting subjects who collaboratively co-constitute the world an indispensable precondition. But when it comes to first principles, that is, epistemology, the actual existence of these hitherto indispensable egos suddenly becomes moot. Perhaps Husserl would have replied that this objection reflects a lingering immersion in the natural or theoretical attitudes, that only when one is free of their subtle biases will this apparent contradiction promptly vanish. This brings us to the third and final problem, Husserl's appeal to so-called "esoteric experience."

In *The Crisis,* Husserl claims, for example, that the phenomenological reduction effects "a complete personal transformation comparable in the beginning to a religious conversion, which then, however, over and above this, bears within itself the significance of the greatest transformation which is assigned as a task to mankind as such" (quoted in Moran

2000, 161). Assigned by whom, one wonders? When someone conjures with religious metaphors like these, it is often as a prelude to a call for piety or humility toward the superior wisdom or the presence of the divine. And such calls are notorious for their ability to mute or silence criticism — even cogent, well-meant criticism. However, the real problem with this kind of rhetoric is not that it is religious or hyperbolic in tone; that constitutes grounds for suspicion, but not complete dismissal. Things only get truly out of hand when we realize that Husserl's rhetorical strategy renders the philosopher who has undergone this dramatic transformation a member of an epistemic elite, or a small circle of adepts who are uniquely attuned to a world that is experientially inaccessible to the rest of us. Since we have no knowledge or experience of this dimension of the mind, presumably, we cannot possibly criticize those who do. Moreover, since Husserl discovered the method and mentored the circle of adepts, he alone was able to judge which of his aspiring students were genuine phenomenologists or not. The fact that his account of the method was subject to frequent change reinforces the impression that, unbeknownst to himself, perhaps, Husserl was attempting to insulate himself against criticism that he did not welcome. From his exalted standpoint, Husserl only had to declare that his critic's misgivings bore witness to an impoverished or inadequate understanding, or an overall orientation that was "pre-philosophical" — as he did, for example, with Einstein's general theory of relativity, which he said was "incoherent."

While this magisterial attitude may be acceptable in theology, it is simply inadmissible in philosophical discourse. Modern philosophy is more democratic and refuses to give credence to claims like these. Though Husserl would have resented the comparison, there is a strong resemblance between Husserl's epistemic elitism and that of Brentano's other famous pupil, Sigmund Freud. Like Husserl, albeit from a different vantage point, Freud claimed to possess a method that gave us privileged access to domains of experience that were unavailable to ordinary mortals. Furthermore, he claimed that those who were not initiated into his method had no experience and therefore no right or ability to criticize his findings, since in a very real and important sense, they did not know what they were talking about. Finally, like Husserl, Freud suffered the unenviable fate of witnessing the desertion of many of the most gifted and exuberant minds in his circle from the movement he founded, who became sharply critical of some of his ideas.

Psychology of the Unconscious
Freud and Jung

Sigmund Freud was born on May 6, 1856, in Freiburg, now Pribor, which is in the Czech Republic. His family moved to Vienna when he was six years old, and with the exception of studying in Paris in 1885, and a year before his death in 1939, when he fled to London to escape the Nazis, Freud lived in Vienna for his entire life. He was the eldest son (and favorite child) of his father's second wife, and was raised in the midst of a large and complex extended family. Judging from his letters to Eduard Silberstein, a youthful correspondent, Freud contemplated a career in law and politics before devoting himself to medicine (Roazen 2000) and, in due course, to neurology, where he distinguished himself as a protégé of Ernst Brücke and Theodor Meynert, two leading exponents of the mechanistic materialism of Hermann Helmholtz.

Though Freud's first love was neurology, an interest in psychology surfaced alongside it. Indeed, every elective Freud took as an undergraduate was in psychology, which he studied with Franz Brentano. Clearly, the links between psychology and neurology intrigued him. His interest in neurology only dimmed sometime after his graduation, when Ernst Brücke informed him that the University of Vienna had hired its quota of Jewish professors for the foreseeable future, and that a post for him would not be forthcoming, despite his superior qualifications. To diminish the impact of this disappointment, Meynert secured a grant for Freud to study the treatment of hysteria in Paris under the leading French neurologist, Jean-Martin Charcot. Freud leapt at the chance. Though Freud rejected Charcot's views on the role of constitutional "degeneracy" in the etiology of hysteria, Charcot's use of hypnotism to produce and dispel the symptoms of hysteria on command convinced Freud that unconscious mental processes were implicated in the genesis of patients' symptoms (Ellenberger 1970).

On his return to Vienna, Freud commenced translating works by Charcot and Hyppolyte Bernheim (another French authority in hypnotism and hysteria), and collaborated with an internist named Joseph Breuer, with whom he co-authored *Studies in Hysteria* (1886). In the process of treating Bertha Pappenheim (known for posterity as "Anna O."), Breuer hit upon something called "the cathartic method" — what Anna O. had called the "talking cure." The cathartic method provided patients with renewed access to traumatic episodes from their (relatively recent) past — episodes that had been repressed and therefore had to be "relived" before the quantity of disturbed affect associated with them, which gave rise to neurotic and somatic symptoms of various kinds, could be dissipated and normal functioning could be restored. Despite the seeming novelty of their approach, Breuer and Freud were not as original as some have suggested. The idea that trauma is a potent factor in the etiology of neuroses was endorsed by Charcot and Bernheim, while J. F. Herbart had offered a cogent theoretical discussion of "repression" and the "dynamic unconscious" some decades before.

Though he embraced it initially, Freud soon abandoned Breuer's cathartic technique because it entailed the use of hypnotism, which Freud distrusted, and because Breuer refused to acknowledge the central role of sexual factors in the etiology of hysteria (Ellenberger 1970). Moreover, with the passage of time, Freud grew increasingly convinced that the relatively recent traumas reported by severely disturbed patients, while authentic in their own right, were usually "screen memories" designed to mask earlier traumas of various kinds, most of which involved precocious or premature sexual stimulation or even rape by a parent, older sibling, or caretaker.

As a result, Freud formulated the goal of treatment as the lifting of "infantile amnesia," or the patient recollection and reconstruction of traumatic episodes from infancy and early childhood that derailed the patient's mental development later, under the pressure of renewed suffering or privation of some sort. Freud called his new approach "psychoanalysis" to distinguish it from Breuer's cathartic technique, and from "psychotherapy," a term coined by French physician Bernheim in 1886, and adopted by contemporaries like Pierre Janet, who acknowledged the impact of childhood traumas, but downplayed their specifically sexual dimensions, and continued to incorporate hypnotic techniques into treatment methods.

In the 1880s and 1890s, Freud published numerous papers dealing with hypnotism and psychotherapy, but drew away from them in 1897 when he commenced his "self-analysis" (Tanner 2003) and prepared to publish his first major work, *The Interpretation of Dreams* (Freud 1900). Spurred by the discovery that many of his patients' "memories" of early childhood seduction or abuse were inauthentic, Freud started to place less emphasis on the role of actual trauma and more on the role of unconscious phantasy in the etiology of neuroses (Ellenberger 1970).

To avert misunderstanding, it is important to note that in Freudian literature the word "fantasy" — with an "f" — denotes a quality or content of *conscious* experience familiar to everyone, consistent with vernacular usage. If a patient daydreams about scaling Mount Everest or imagines his spouse betraying him, for example, these are instances of what is commonly called "fantasy." Fantasy fulfills a wish or expresses a fear, but there is nothing *unconscious* about it, and the feelings or desires that give rise to it are usually readily accessible to consciousness and therefore not difficult to interpret.

By contrast, unconscious phantasy — or just "phantasy," spelled with a "ph" — denotes a fear or wish-based flight into the imaginary which is *not* present to consciousness and not accessible to ordinary introspection or efforts at retrieval, but which shapes our experience and attitudes toward others and can only be rendered conscious through special techniques like free association, dream interpretation, word association tests, and so on (Burston 1996b).

The Interpretation of Dreams also introduced readers to two of Freud's clinical innovations — the analysis of dreams and the use of "free association" to access hitherto repressed or unconscious material. Free association is a state of lucid, self-conscious reverie in which any and every thought, feeling, memory, or mental image that emerges in the field of consciousness is duly noted, then relinquished to make way for the next mental "content." Before Freud stumbled on it, free association had been described by Francis Galton and others as an interesting thought experiment or as an aid to creative writing (Fancher 1996). However, Freud was the first to recommend specific rules for elucidating the meaning of "stream of consciousness" for clinical purposes.

The Interpretation of Dreams also introduced readers to the distinction between primary and secondary process thought, the former being alogical, timeless, driven by instinctual forces blindly seeking expression or release; the latter governed by reason, realism, and restraint (Freud 1900, 1911). In due course, Freud transformed primary and secondary process thought into the id and the ego, respectively (Freud 1923). In addition, an internal agency or "dream censorship" monitors the dreamer's emotional state in sleep and supposedly interdicts and disguises "the latent dream thoughts," or the dreamer's deepest fears and desires through the use of "mechanisms" such condensation, displacement, projection, reversal. This dream censorship was later endowed with the additional role of prohibiting and punishing the patient for harboring unruly passions, becoming the superego in Freud's later structural theory of the mind (Freud 1923).[1]

---

1. Since the distinction between primary and secondary processes is often touted as one of Freud's greatest "discoveries," not least of all by Freud, it bears repeating that the contrast between two different modes of mental functioning had been vividly anticipated by several theorists in our survey, including Pascal, Hegel, Nietzsche, and Dilthey. What rendered Freud's discussion of this idea distinctive was the way it was conjoined with (and perhaps burdened by) his evolving theory of "infantile sexuality."

To Freud's embarrassment, *The Interpretation of Dreams* sold poorly at first, but was followed promptly by *The Psychopathology of Every Day Life* (1901) and *Fragment of an Analysis of a Case of Hysteria* (1905), the first book to emphasize the necessity of analyzing the patient's "transference" to the analyst to bring treatment to a successful conclusion. That same year, Freud published *Three Essays on the Theory of Sexuality,* which describes a broad range of adult psychopathologies as the products of fixation at (or regression to) specific stages in an ontogenetic sequence of "psychosexual" development that commences at birth and ends in early adulthood (Freud 1905). In addition to the concepts of repression, regression, fixation, and transference, the concept of "libido" was central to Freud's thought. We will discuss libido later, but for now, let us clarify what Freud means by "repression."

According to Freud, thoughts, memories, or desires that evoke conflicted feelings are often rendered unavailable to normal efforts at introspection or "retrieval" in the interests of enabling people to maintain a neurotic equilibrium. A neurotic equilibrium enables someone to function in a reasonably intact fashion, but entails a measure of self-deception that conceals an unconscious conflict of some kind. As a result, if they exceed a certain threshold, repression (and the other "defense mechanisms") tend to distort our "reality testing" abilities in our vulnerable areas, falsifying our sense of self and the world. As a result, they start to hinder or obstruct our "adaptation to reality" in more dramatic ways, and our symptoms deepen or proliferate. That is why psychoanalysis situates normal, neurotic, and psychotic personalities on the same human continuum. For example, a mild neurosis is only barely distinguishable from normalcy, while a severe neurosis impairs our judgment so much that it borders on psychosis.

Unfortunately, for the most part, like Nietzsche before him, Freud analyzed strong emotional reactions in terms of processes that transpired inside the person, rather than *among* people. This emphasis on the *intrapsychic* dimension, and the relative neglect of the interpersonal one, is reflected in the complex theoretical languages Freud developed to describe and explain the processes, structures, and levels of unconscious functioning, while all interpersonal commerce between patient and analyst was subsumed under the somewhat questionable (and manifestly inadequate) heading of transference and countertransference.

Leaving techniques like dream interpretation and free association aside, the method that Freud used to familiarize himself with his patients' psychic interiors was the case history method. A typical case history begins with a brief description of the patient and his recollections concerning the events or experiences that preceded the onset of symptoms, along with any obscurities or contradictions pertaining to their emotional life that the initial inquiry phase gives rise to. This is usually followed by a narrative that summarizes the course of the treatment, which is based on the premise that the patient's symptoms have a symbolic or substitutive character that both gratifies and disavows furtive desires. By remembering or reconstructing crucial episodes from the past, and the conflicted feelings they engender, the patient will presumably gain mastery over his unconscious conflicts and no longer need derivative modes of gratification (Freud 1914).

Freud's steadfast reliance on the case history method was remarkable and, in a certain sense, symptomatic of his own inner conflicts because, on deeper reflection, psychoanalytic technique incorporates elements of the four *nonexperimental* methods for ascertaining truth that we discussed previously in relation to Descartes. It begins with naturalistic observation (on the therapist's part), encourages rational introspection (on the patient's part), which is promoted through Socratic dialogue (between patient and analyst). The therapeutic dialogue between patient and analyst is animated and sustained through an interpretive or hermeneutic process addressed to the patient's dreams and symptoms, which are read as a kind of text, or a running commentary on the patient's unconscious mental processes (Freud 1914).

While this situation is intriguing, it raises some curious methodological problems. Though he made a single, noteworthy exception in the case of Jung's word association experiments, Freud scorned the suggestion that experimental psychology had anything useful or illuminating to contribute to psychoanalytic theory (Roazen 2000). Yet the mechanistic materialism espoused by Freud's neurological mentors, Ernst Brücke and Theodor Meynert, and which Freud himself adhered to throughout his life, was legitimated entirely through a series of ingenious and ground-breaking experiments in physics and biology conducted by Hermann von Helmholtz (Fancher 1996). Despite this fact, and his own background as a medical researcher, Freud maintained that training in the humanities and social sciences was eminently suitable as a preparation for analytic training, supporting the practice of "lay analysis." But by his own estimation, at least, Freud was also an unwavering positivist who never doubted that one day a new generation of scientists would vindicate his ideas, providing a kind of Rosetta stone, or a demonstrably correct and reliable method for translating his major discoveries back into the language of physics and chemistry.

The cumulative impression one gets is that Freud wanted it both ways. He wanted to possess the aura, authority, and prestige of the natural sciences while theorizing in a way that defied or circumvented all their customary rules of evidence. He wanted to recruit and credential people from the humanities and social sciences while stubbornly insisting that they were really doing "natural science." The result, as Jose Brunner points out, are intractable ambiguities in the way classical psychoanalytic theory and technique are articulated — sometimes as a hermeneutic (or even an "archeological") enterprise, sometimes as a kind of pseudoexperimental procedure, and often, improbably, as a heady mixture of both (Brunner 2001). This fusion (and confusion) of methodological perspectives is sometimes fruitful and sometimes fatal to his enterprise. Nowhere is this more apparent than in Freud's approach to the problems of attraction and attachment, which he explained in terms of "the economics of the libido."

In the course of his case histories, and various theoretical papers, Freud explained conflicts concerning our relationships with others in terms of libidinal "cathexes" involving definite (but unspecified) quantities of a hypothetical energy that people "invest" in others. Conversely, ending a relationship with someone supposedly involves a process of divestiture, or diverting emotional energies elsewhere. Consider the woman who comes for therapy agonizing over whether she should return to her husband, whom she left, or to move in with a lover. Candid discussion discloses that despite her abrupt departure from the marital home her feelings are evenly divided in the sense that she has "invested" an equal amount in both relationships, which are both fraught with ambivalence and complications of various kinds. Since there are no children on the scene to "tip the balance" in favor of one partner or the other, the resulting emotional stalemate will probably be resolved on the basis of qualitative, rather than quantitative factors, and above all by the kind of future she imagines having with either partner.

Erich Fromm found talk of libidinal "investment" vulgar and misleading, because it describes our most tender and complex emotions from the standpoint of an alienated *homo economincus,* who treats his passions and affections as so much psychic "capital" (Fromm 1956, 1959, 1970). Fromm's critique has merit, but tends to obscure the fact that, according to Freud, libidinal "investments" are not always conscious choices or calculated to ensure our pleasure or safety. As often as not, they are completely involuntary and end in complete disaster.

Freud's emphasis on forces that determine our behavior outside of conscious awareness places him squarely in opposition to Descartes's cogito. For Descartes, the process of thinking — the action of our own minds — was the only thing we could be absolutely certain of. In contrast, the psychoanalytic notion that the ego is a passive effect of forces outside of its control is born out by Freud's statement, "Thus in relation to the id [the ego] is like a man on horseback, who has to hold in check the superior strength of the horse" (Freud 1923, 25).

At the same time, Freud's theory of mind retained a strongly Cartesian character. For while it undermines the cogito, classical analytic theory adheres to the constitutive dualisms of subject and object, internal and external experience, and never overcomes the ostensible division between body and mind. There is also a striking parallel between Freud's notion of libido and the emotions and physiological conjectures of Descartes, which hinge on their shared use of hydraulic models and metaphors. Descartes had speculated that different emotions were the product of different "animal spirits," or of tiny material particles of different kinds suspended in cerebro-spinal fluid which bathe our nerves, resulting in fear, anger, wonder, mirth, and so on. According to Descartes, the *quality* of the emotion we experience as a consequence is determined by the size and shape of the material particles that collide with the nerves, while the intensity of the feeling is determined by the *quantity* of such particles that course through our bodies and brains. In short, Descartes had a hydraulic or volumetric theory of emotions that approached them as fluid, changeable entities (Fancher 1996).

Similarly, Freud explained emotional states and relationships of one sort or another in terms of dammed-up quantities of libido, or of the "flow" of libido being diverted from one object onto another. The difference is that Freud did not recognize the existence of different kinds of "animal spirits," but of a single psychic energy (like capital, incidentally) that is fungible and as mobile as circumstances and opportunity allow. Consequently, Freud's discussion of emotional conflicts always tends to put hydraulic and quantitative factors first. The reason for this is because Freud was hard pressed to explain the specific *quality* of emotional attachments and experiences, and he tried to get around that difficulty by discriminating between different *stages* of libidinal development, which supposedly impart specific desires and attitudes to the attraction or attachment in question. Thus, oral libido is compliant, clingy, and yielding, and entails a strong need to be loved. It therefore imparts a different quality or mode of relatedness to others than anal libido, which is stubborn, sadistic, and prone to obsession. Phallic libido is intrusive, voyeuristic, and exhibitionistic, while urethral libido is impatient, laden with ambition and the urge to dominate. Only genital libido, properly sublimated, could be relied upon to promote a measure of genuine concern and reciprocity.

All this sounds quite impressive, of course, but few of Freud's theories (or interpretations based on them) could be verified or refuted by recourse to experimental methods. While the concepts he borrowed from physics and economics to explain our passions and aversions were quite useful, heuristically, Freud intended this new theoretical language to be understood in more than a merely metaphorical sense. Indeed, for many decades after his death, the degree of one's fidelity to Freud — and by implication one's standing with the movement's leadership — was assessed primarily in terms of how closely one adhered to his theory of libidinal development.

Carl Jung

In short, for a variety of reasons, Freud had a great deal "invested" in his libido theory — so much, in fact, that when it came to choosing between it and his "crown prince," Carl Gustav Jung, he clung to the former and disowned the latter, to Jung's profound disappointment. Jung was born in 1875 in Thurgovia, Switzerland, and died in Kusnacht, on Lake Zurich, in 1961. Though born in a rural village, Jung and his family soon moved to Basel. Jung was the only child of a retiring Calvinist minister named Paul Jung, and a severely disturbed mother named Emilie Prieswerk, who spent several months in a sanatorium during his third year of life (Ellenberger 1970).

Despite her disorder, or perhaps because of it, Emilie was the dominant personality in the Jung household, and by early adolescence Jung concluded that his mother really had *two* personalities — one conventional, polite, and submissive, the other assertive, impatient, and somewhat ruthless, with a ribald sense of humor and an unerring ability to spot people's weak spots and hypocrisies (Jung 1961). Furthermore, because of her strange behavior and uncanny intuitions, Jung *feared* his mother much more than his father, which accounts for Jung's skepticism regarding Freud's claims about the Oedipus complex. After all, Freud claimed that the father is the parent who is most powerful and most feared, and that ambivalence toward the father is the source of most religious ideation. Jung was decidedly ambivalent toward his father, but chiefly because he lacked the courage of his convictions and a deep spirituality to ground his faith (Hogenson 1983).

When Jung was in his early teens, his father read a book by Hippolyte Bernheim, which had just been translated into German by a relatively unknown Viennese specialist named Sigmund Freud. Like most psychiatrists in his day, Bernheim had an anticlerical agenda and purported to explain all cases of faith healing as instances of hysteria. Paul Jung found Bernheim's arguments quite persuasive, which precipitated a loss of faith and a deep depression from which Jung's father never entirely recovered (Ellenberger 1970). In old age, Jung would describe his father as his first psychiatric patient, because his father confided in him — to no avail, finally (Jung 1961).

In 1895, as his father was dying, Jung received a scholarship and registered at the Medical School of Basel University. During the course of medical studies, he became passionately interested in the works of Emanuel Swedenborg, Anton Mesmer, Cesare Lomboroso, Arthur Schopenhauer, and Friedrich Nietzsche. At age 23, Jung joined a group of students who were investigating a local medium named Héléne Preiswerk, a cousin of Jung's (on the maternal side). The notes from these sessions formed the basis of his doctoral dissertation (Jung 1961).

FREUD AND JUNG: FROM FRIENDSHIP TO ESTRANGEMENT

In December 1900, Jung became the assistant to Eugen Bleuler, director of the famous Burghölzli clinic in Zurich. Under the supervision of Bleuler, who coined the term "schizophrenia," Jung read *The Interpretation of Dreams* and one year later, in 1903, wrote an appreciative review. In 1904, Jung published his famous word association experiments, the only psychological experiments that Freud greeted with unbridled enthusiasm. In these experiments, patients were asked to say the first word that occurred to them in response to specific "stimulus" words and were timed to see how long it took them to produce a response. Average reaction times were calculated by taking the patient's reaction times to all 50 stimulus words and dividing them by 50. Jung then noted the words that prompted a lengthy or unaccountable delay and inferred that these delays, the mishearing of the stimulus word, or a total failure to respond indicated the existence of an unresolved — and often unconscious — inner conflict.

Jung then compared all the words that elicited a delayed or abnormal response to see if they suggested any coherent pattern. Usually they did, and Jung was soon able to guess the nature of his patients' inner conflicts with astonishing accuracy, even among some who were deliberately secretive or frankly psychotic. Sexual, aggressive, and guilt-related themes surfaced frequently, as did background preoccupations with money, fame, and personal losses or death. Borrowing from Janet, Jung called these conflict-laden themes or clusters of associations "complexes" (Jung 1904).

Freud was delighted because the credibility accorded to these experiments by the scientific community enhanced the prestige of his own enterprise. Moreover, up to that point, the overwhelming majority of his followers were Viennese Jews, and Freud feared that psychoanalysis would be dismissed by the Gentile world as a "Jewish science." In 1907, Freud invited Jung and his young assistant, Ludwig Binswanger, to spend a weekend with him in Vienna. The friendship between Freud and Jung grew quickly, and Freud soon named Jung his successor and made him the first president of the International Psychoanalytic Association, founded in 1907. When Freud died, presumably, Jung would assume the leadership of the psychoanalytic movement — or so Freud hoped. As their correspondence attests, Freud and Jung went a considerable distance down this road together, sharing ideas and mutual encouragement. But in 1911, Jung became more reticent and withdrawn, and in 1912, to Freud's deep disappointment, he refused to shoulder the burden of succession (Hogenson 1983).

As Jung later recalled, Freud rigidly insisted that all psychic energy — libido — is derived in the first instance from the sexual instincts (Jung 1961), while Jung accorded equal or greater significance to the instincts of self-preservation (Jung 1910). Moreover, Freud's libido theory was tied to a whole host of deterministic assumptions derived from the mechanistic materialism of Helmholtz, Brücke, and Meynert, which justified his relentless focus on early childhood, while Jung emphasized the "prospective function," which propels the psyche toward genuinely new situations and conflicts to facilitate growth. In addition, Freud wanted to privilege one complex — the Oedipus complex — as the nuclear or "core complex," which presumably underlies all mythology and religious belief. Jung entertained very different ideas about myths and symbols and their implications for clinical practice. In 1912 Jung published *Transformations and Symbols of the Libido* (1916/1956), cementing his divergence from the psychoanalytic school of Freud; the book soon became his most widely known and influential work. Finally, Freud claimed (somewhat disingenuously) to be uninterested in the paranormal and the occult, which interested Jung continuously until his death (Burston 1999).

When the two men finally parted company in 1913, the International Psychoanalytic Association, of which Jung was still the nominal president, split into the Vienna school and the Zurich school, respectively. Around 1920, Jung named his evolving approach "analytical psychology" (to distinguish it from psychoanalysis), and in due course founded the International Association of Analytical Psychology (IAAP) in 1947 (Kirsch 2000). Meanwhile, to explain (or excuse) their mutual estrangement, Jung privately accused Freud of having an unresolved and overweening father complex, and of infantilizing his followers by punishing expressions of intellectual independence (Burston 1999), while Freud accused Jung of harboring anti-Semitic sentiments and repressed parricidal impulses (Maidenbaum 1991). For our purposes, it makes more sense to situate their differences in cultural, historical, and philosophical perspective.

Although Freud and Jung clashed over the sexual etiology of neuroses, the primacy of the Oedipus complex, and so on, these contentious issues become more intelligible when they are examined in the light of a larger, more encompassing conflict between rationalist and irrationalist sensibilities. To illustrate this contrast, consider that for Freud, by and large, the function of symbols in dreams and myths is to disguise the aims and operations of the instincts, to make them acceptable, though indecipherable, to consciousness, and thereby subvert or circumvent the purposes of the rational ego. Jung regarded dream symbolism less skeptically than Freud, as both a repository of "complexes," and a reality-oriented and life-enhancing force that compensates for the ego's blind spots. Rather than "unmasking" the unconscious, or robbing it of its power to falsify or deform conscious awareness through interpretation, Jung's approach to dream work attempted to elicit a mixture of openness and respect toward the symbol so that the conscious ego, with its limited powers of observation, will heed this communication from the depths of nature and alter its outlook accordingly (Burston 1997).

For example, take a patient — call him "Steven" — who is angry and disappointed with his analyst for seeming bored and indifferent toward him. One night, Steven dreams that he arrives at his next analytic appointment, where his analyst greets him warmly. As he enters her office, it turns into an elegant dining room, where they share a lavish meal she has prepared for him, to the accompaniment of music and laughter. What does Steven's dream mean?

A classical Freudian analyst might say that the unconscious phantasy that prompts Steven's dream is an oral one, and belies an unconscious desire to be fed, yearnings to be held and admired, and so on. By this reckoning, Steven's feelings toward his analyst are indicative of a mother-fixation transference, which entails fears of starvation and abandonment that will surface, no doubt, as the analysis proceeds. In short, they are a repetition of early childhood experiences at the mother's breast.

A classical Jungian analyst, being less interested in the infantile templates for adult attitudes and experiences, would probably emphasize the *compensatory* function of the dream. Steven's unconscious is saying, in effect, that his feelings of disappointment are unwarranted and colored by his complexes — that the analyst's attitude to him is friendlier, her efforts more sincere, and that he is "nourished" more by their relationship than he is consciously willing to acknowledge. Rather than sulking about his analyst's lack of concern, he may as well get down to business and tackle the challenges of the analytic work.

Now, dreams are often open to multiple interpretations, and we are not defending or rejecting either hermeneutic strategy. The point is that Freud viewed the unconscious rationalistically, as being tied to the infantile, atavistic side of our nature. He said so clearly in an essay entitled "Formulations on the Two Principles of Mental Functioning," in which the vagaries of phantasy were aligned with "primary process thought," while reason, judgment, and restraint were aligned with "secondary process thought" (Freud 1911). And for Freud, only reason affords us some leverage against our inner demons.

By Jung's account, however, reason is a limited and imperfect instrument that can scarcely fathom and seldom match the wisdom of the unconscious, and the real function of dream symbolism is not to lead reason astray, but to convey to consciousness what consciousness is not yet ready or able to comprehend. For Jung, in other words, the unconscious is not like an animal or an enemy to be subdued, but like a peculiar sort of friend whose communications range from the oblique and fanciful to the blunt and confrontational. Either way, dream symbolism often conveys the truths of which the ego is perforce quite ignorant (Burston 1997).

THE GOALS AND TECHNIQUES OF THERAPY

When asked to state what the goals of psychoanalytic therapy were, Freud replied: "lieben und arbeiten." In other words, the goal of treatment is to enable patients to love and to work. Few would quarrel with this appraisal, or with the underlying assumption that adult human beings *need* to love and to work to safeguard their mental health. Having said that, this pithy statement is alarmingly short on specifics. Just what is entailed in this prescription? How did Freud conceive of love and work and the relationship between the two? And how does analytic treatment promote them?

According to classical psychoanalytic theory, the ability to love and to work depends on a quality called "ego strength." Therefore, the purpose of psychoanalysis is to strengthen the ego by unifying it as much as possible. As Freud states, "the neurotic patient presents us with a torn mind, divided by resistances. As we analyze it and remove the resistances, it grows together; the greater unity which we call his ego fits into itself all the instinctual impulses which before had been split off and held apart from it" (Freud 1919, 161). The enlargement of the ego takes place through the facilitation of the ego's communication with, and integration of, the instinctual forces that it previously defended itself against using free association and dream interpretation. The expanded unity of the ego is achieved not simply through establishing mastery over the id, but through the integration of the id's impulses within itself. For classical psychoanalysts, this amounts to the pursuit of autonomy and emancipation through the growth of self-knowledge — a process that is never fully completed.

However, autonomy and self-knowledge, however limited in scope, are not achieved without considerable struggle. In Freud's estimation, inner and interpersonal conflict are ubiquitous because human beings are endowed with a vast surplus of sexual energy, over and above what they require for simple reproduction. That being so, the central problem of human existence is to find the optimal degree of libidinal satisfaction consistent with civilized existence. But civilization, in turn, depends on hard work, that is, a tolerance for frustration, concentrated planning and effort, and a willingness to renounce private pleasures in favor of collective gains of one sort or another. By Freud's reckoning, then, the "optimal" degree of sexual satisfaction (from a civilized perspective) does not mean the "maximum" degree possible because the development of human reason and of sociability depends on the individual's capacity to sublimate or renounce a significant amount of their sexual desires (Freud 1905, 1930).

Initially, then, the goals of psychoanalytic treatment were:

(1) to bring repressed traumas and emotional conflicts to light;
(2) to facilitate the dissolution of harmful libidinal fixations or regressions, thereby
(3) to free energy for a more gratifying love life;
(4) to renounce sexual impulses that "cost" the patient more suffering than they were worth, and
(5) to sublimate the surplus of sexual energy remaining after steps 1 through 4 were accomplished in culturally syntonic activities and interests.

This classical approach to analytic treatment entails a complex reallocation of resources and priorities within the "economics of the libido," with the libido being liberated, rechanneled, and in some instances, simply "renounced" to resolve paralyzing inner conflicts and produce a mature person. The treatment also engendered confusion among practitioners and lay people because of an absence of clarity about the meanings of certain terms. The term most shrouded in obscurity is "sublimation," which, unlike "renunciation" — a conscious, deliberate decision, taken after sober reflection, on the "costs" of entertaining certain desires — is a spontaneous and involuntary "mechanism" that silently averts conflicts and provides powerful incentives for "adaptive" behavior. While analytic patients were sometimes urged to "sublimate" their desires in a certain direction, the fact remains that sublimation is really an *unconscious* process whereby libidinal energies that were originally directed toward private or personal satisfactions are channeled into the acquisition of skills that benefit society as a whole, and for which the individual is socially rewarded. In this way, impulses that would otherwise estrange the person from the community are rendered serviceable, giving the person a "stake" and a well-defined role in his or her cultural setting.

Thus, for example, someone with strong "oral" tendencies could sublimate their interest in food into becoming a respected restaurant critic. Alternatively, she may earn her livelihood by studying and writing about nutrition or the ecological benefits of organic farming practices. A patient with "anal sadistic" impulses to tear the flesh of others, or to see them bleed, for example, may acquire surgical training, transforming his antisocial tendencies into lifesaving strategies of various kinds, gaining knowledge, realism, and respect in the process. A woman with "phallic-exhibitionist" tendencies sublimates her need to be the center of attention and to dazzle, amuse, or offend others into a successful theatrical career, and by taking challenging roles — Shakespeare, Ibsen, Shaw, and so on — she gains a greater understanding of human nature (her own included). Finally, a nun sublimates her desire to bear and raise children into the rehabilitation of orphans, transforming their lives (and her own) in the process.

So despite his reputation to the contrary, in some quarters, Freud was not a sexual revolutionary. He demanded greater honesty and tolerance in sexual matters than Victorian culture generally allowed. But beyond that, he said that the sources of inner and interpersonal conflict are intractable and inscribed, so to speak, in the human condition. A certain Stoicism is therefore necessary for mental health, though everyday unhappiness becomes bearable in light of the blessings conferred by love and work — in the final analysis, by our own efforts, and the expenditure of energies that benefit others as well as ourselves.

In other words, in terms of our typological constructs, Freud was not just a rationalist, but also a profoundly *anti-utopian* thinker. Though he rejected the charge that he was misanthropic, Freud never denied that his view of human nature was deeply pessimistic. Like Thomas

Hobbes, he saw the basic relation of one person to another as being predatory in nature, and his maxim — "Homo homini lupus" — supports this view. In keeping with his rationalistic bias, Freud saw civilization as based on a "social contract," and insisted that some sacrifice of instinctual freedom is necessary — that unless aggression and sexuality are subdued, civilization deteriorates and human life becomes debased.[2] Finally, Freud was profoundly irreligious. While effort, austerity, reason, and love all contribute to our welfare, in Freud's worldview there is no room for grace or transcendence, and patients who cherished religious beliefs or had religious experiences were likely to be baffled or insulted by the kinds of interpretations he gave for their beliefs or experiences.

Freud used certain techniques to achieve the goals of analytic treatment The first technique is the basic rule of psychoanalysis, which obligates the patient to say anything and everything that comes to mind, no matter how far-fetched, irrelevant, embarrassing, or painful it may seem at the moment. If the patient will "free associate," or relinquish his conscious self-censorship, the hope and expectation is that his *unconscious* self-censorship will also abate in due course, allowing hitherto repressed material access to consciousness (Freud 1913). To help the patient in this process, Freud had his patients lay on a couch and recommended that they come in for sessions five days a week. For optimum effect, the material elicited in this manner should be interpreted in three ways: in terms of broad thematic preoccupations and convergences that are more or less self-evident, and readily acknowledged by the patient; in terms of latent (or repressed) themes that are tracked by the analyst for the patient's benefit, which the patient may or may not own up to at present; and in light of any abrupt interruptions to

---

2. Lou Salome was not the only one to compare Freud to Nietzsche, of course. Several of Freud's erstwhile followers — including Jung, Otto Rank, and Wilhelm Reich — compared Freud to Nietzsche after they severed their ties with "the Professor," hinting that he was either inferior to Nietzsche, or that his ideas were derivative. Whereas Freud greeted Lou's remark as a compliment, he greeted this comparison among former disciples with cold hostility.

the flow of associations, which betokens the existence of an inner conflict, the emergence of a "resistance," or perhaps, indeed, a "transference" reaction (Freud 1912a, 1915).

While free association sounds easy enough to the uninitiated, it often takes time to achieve, especially when you consider that the analyst is, in the first instance, a perfect stranger who is not under a comparable obligation to share his spontaneous thought processes with the patient. Indeed, if a Freudian analyst were as honest and unguarded as his or her patient is expected to be, this would undo their chances of helping the patient gain leverage against their own problems. Though Freud would have rued the comparison, his "basic rule" sounds remarkably like a secular equivalent to the Catholic rite of confession. After all, in "normal" communication between adults, the kind of frank, unguarded honesty expected of the analytic patient is usually an expression of deep trust, which is only elicited by a fair degree of reciprocity, or confidences shared and mulled over for a considerable period of time. (One does not normally confide in strangers in this way, nor does one speak one's mind that freely if the other will not reciprocate in kind.)

Alternatively, the kind of honesty enjoined by the basic rule may be an expression of (or defense against) despair — a desperate sense of having nothing to lose, and perhaps something to gain, by reposing trust in a person who somehow represents a "power" that can dispense understanding or forgiveness. Such an attitude is perfectly intelligible if the patient's trust in others (and a capacity for candid self-disclosure) has been seriously eroded. Such circumstances may facilitate greater honesty in the short run, but will eventually strain the working alliance between analyst and patient, when issues of "basic trust" and the capacity for intimacy with others (that is, outside the therapeutic setting) emerge later on.

Either way, Freud's basic rule, while quite simple on the face of it, places complex demands on the relationship between patient and analyst and indirectly raises issues of trust and the patient's capacity for authentic self-disclosure. Freud himself never addresses these issues in quite so many words, but recommends that the analyst greet the patient's free associations in a spirit of "neutrality." The term "neutrality" is ambiguous, however. One the one hand, it prescribes "evenly hover-ing attention," or careful listening, and a nonjudgmental attitude, both of which are commendable. On the other hand, it prescribes a clinical posture in which the therapist is enjoined to emulate a "blank screen," becoming an impassive and inscrutable presence who delib-erately suppresses any spontaneous expressive gestures, ostensibly with a view to encouraging the patient's projections and transferences and disguising the analyst's own unconscious responses to the patient, or "countertransference," provoked in the process.

Whether therapists should deliberately try to provoke or elicit trans-ference or projection, or let nature take its course, is a highly contentious issue. But Freud's recommendation that analysts should emulate a blank screen is clearly quite misguided and manifestly at odds with how he acted with his own patients. In a sustained therapeutic dialogue, patients always pick up significant clues regarding the therapist's thoughts and feelings from their tone of voice, the content of their interpretations, and so on, even when they are not meant to. Moreover, patients who have suffered from depersonalized or depersonalizing treatment at the hands of others, who need to address themselves to (and to be addressed by) a genuinely concerned human being in order to regain their bear-ings, will only be retraumatized by this sort of treatment (Guntrip 1961, 1968; Laing 1960, 1985). Beginning with the "active analysis" of Sándor Ferenczi in the late 1920s, these issues provoked the emergence of several "revisionist" schools of psychoanalysis that abandoned this practice, as did many clinicians (including Binswanger) who started their careers as psychoanalysts, but veered afterward toward existential phenomenology.

Finally, it is one thing for therapists to conceal certain facets of their family and personal lives, and to declare them off-limits, as far as patients are concerned. That is quite legitimate. But it is something else entirely if a therapist *pretends* not to think, to feel or to imagine certain things in response to a patient's candid avowals of frustration, desire, despair or inner turmoil of one sort or another. This engenders an absurd situation in which the patient is instructed to practice perfect honesty and to abandon all restraint, while the analyst must maintain an *appearance* of indifference, a kind of schizoid withdrawal, which can easily be misinterpreted by patients as indifference, if not covert hostility. Sustaining a pretense like this over hundreds of hours of conversation is profoundly inauthentic and engenders a suffocating sense of boredom, which requires further efforts at dissimulation to conceal. The result is pervasive "bad faith" (Sartre 1941).

As critics of classical psychoanalysis suggest, after cultivating an inexpressive countenance for hundreds of hours, the bored psychoanalyst must pretend *not* to be bored, and "interprets" the patient's reproaches to that effect as the expression of the patient's unresolved transference issues. But truth will out. As many analytic patients will attest, the old joke about analysts falling asleep in the middle of the analytic hour — or even sooner, toward the end of a long day — is not a rare occurrence, and due in part to this dubious technical precept. Greater candor on the therapist's part — modulated tactfully, with a good sense of judgment and timing — is obviously much preferable.

While classical analytic technique turned into a rigid, ritualistic dogma after Freud's death, the fact remains that Freud's "blank screen" recommendation was seldom strictly adhered to, least of all by Freud himself (Roazen 1971). By his own admission, Freud often illustrated his interpretations of patient's dreams with Jewish jokes, and judging from his patients' subsequent reports, made candid avowals of his pleasure, irritation, or disappointment with a their progress (Wortis 1950). In short, there was a vigorous (if infrequent) emotional exchange between Freud and his patients in many of his sessions, technical rules notwithstanding. Moreover, and more to the point, perhaps, the blank screen rule was abandoned by revisionist psychoanalysts, who encourage varying degrees and modalities of therapist self-disclosure. An extreme example of this was D. W. Winnicott, who once claimed that one of his difficult young patients profited from the therapist's frank expression of "hatred."

If nothing else, this example serves to remind us that one rationale for prescribing the blank screen rule in the first place was Freud's desire to contain and to mitigate the therapist's countertransference reactions. And rightly so, up to a point. Many therapists recognize themselves and the conflicts they struggle with in their patients' recurrent problems. And sometimes it is the stark contrast, rather than the similarity, between the therapist's experience and attitude to life and that of the patient that provokes a strong reaction. Many therapists report feeling that, in ways that stubbornly elude their conscious apprehension, their patients' transference provokes or elicits complementary roles or reactions that have been unconsciously "scripted" by the patient, which set them up for failure, or confirm their patient's worst fears, or seduce the therapist into an attitude toward the patient that clouds their judgment in some way. In instances like these, it is devilishly difficult to discern the difference between countertransference and a perfectly authentic emotional response to the patient. Regardless of the specifics, a sensible therapist will always carefully scrutinize his or her feelings before deciding how (and how much) to share with the patient.

In any case, once the blank screen precept is abandoned as unfeasible and potentially harmful to the patient, and therapist self-disclosure is allowed or encouraged, interminable discussions about how much therapist self-disclosure is desirable automatically ensue. Not surprisingly, the issue of the analyst's self-disclosure remains a controversial topic for contemporary psychoanalysts. Attempts to resolve this issue by recourse to a simple, straightforward formula are all likely to fail because every therapist, and every patient, is different. Though there may be some general guidelines to follow, the thoughts, feelings, or personal experiences a therapist discloses to a patient always depend to some degree on the therapist's personality and judgment, and on the needs of the particular patient.

While Freud and his followers debated the blank screen issue for most of the twentieth century, it was utterly irrelevant to Jung and his circle. As early as 1907, Jung engaged a patient at the Burghölzli, Otto Gross, in what he termed a "mutual analysis." Admittedly, Gross, though a patient, was also a psychiatrist, so elements of their encounter could be construed as "peer supervision" (Heuer 2003). According to Jung, patients can be harmed by an analyst who attempts to be an anonymous cipher, and can benefit considerably from relating to a therapist who expresses himself candidly, without pretense or evasion.

Jung's words were prophetic, in some respects, but were not heeded by Freud and his circle. Although Jung's "mutual analysis" with Gross ended badly, this did not deter Jung and followers from conducting subsequent mutual analyses (Kirsch 2000). Indeed, many therapists — including Martin Buber, Erich Fromm, and Leslie Farber — reported firsthand experiences in which the analyst was transformed by his encounter with a patient, and where the effort to wrestle with the patient's problem elicited some very frank self-disclosure from the analyst that helped rather than burdened or befuddled the patient. But after his break with Freud in 1913, Jung was in no position to make such claims credible because he had slipped into a prolonged period of disorientation and demoralization, when he frequently feared for his sanity, and dropped his teaching and clinical practice.

Judging from his memoir, *Memories, Dreams, Reflections,* (1961), from 1913 until the end of World War I, Jung suffered from an agitated depression with acute psychotic features. In retrospect, however, Jung construed this lingering season of torment as his first adult encounter with the "collective unconscious." In an attempt to gain insight and leverage against his ungovernable moods and phantasies, Jung experimented with a variety of new therapeutic techniques that he used on himself and later introduced into the treatment of his patients. These included active imagination and amplification, among others (Casement 2003).

While a detailed discussion of these therapeutic techniques is beyond our purview here, one way in which they differed from Freud's basic rule was that they allowed and encouraged patients consciously to embellish on their fantasy constructions. They also were calibrated to penetrate beneath the patient's "personal complexes" to put them in touch with the archetypal or "mythic" layer of the psyche. Archetypes are part of the collective unconscious and form the basic content of religion, myth, art, and legend. Underlying Jung's approach to technique were two fundamental differences in the way Freud and Jung regarded human nature. The first concerns the role and meaning of religious symbolism.

According to Freud, religion is nothing but a perpetuation of infantile trends in the psyche that have long outlived their usefulness (Freud

1927). According to Jung, however, next to the survival instinct, the search for transcendent meaning is the most powerful "instinct" in human nature. Indeed, Jung speculated that the repression of sexuality pales in comparison to the repression of "the religious instinct" in twentieth century society, and that many mass movements with an overtly secular orientation — including Marxism and psychoanalysis — were really secular surrogates for genuine religious faith that disguised their underlying mythological bases with scientific jargon. The Freudian tendency to devalue mythology, or to translate it into purely scientific terms, is the result of an impoverished understanding of human interiority. As Anthony Storr (1973) points out,

> A great deal of the difference between the two points of view hinges upon different conceptions of the inner world of the psyche. Psychoanalysts consider that the inner world and its images are infantile phenomena; admittedly powerful determinants in man's idea of the external world, and therefore of his behavior, but actually a hindrance in adaptation to reality. The mythological level of the psyche is, in this view, a misconstruction which ought to be outgrown or overgrown if a person is to be properly oriented . . . in an adult way. . . . Jung, on the other hand, puts the inner world of myth and archetype on an equal footing with the external world. He sees the ego poised, as it were, between the inner and the outer, between subjective and objective, with an equal need to relate to each world. The idea that the inner world is in any sense infantile or pathological appears to be alien to him. (68)

Indeed, in contrast to Freud, Jung's emphasis is squarely on the archetypical, or "inner" nature of the psychical experience, and as a result Jungians have traditionally privileged the "internal" perspective over all others. As a part of the collective unconscious, Jung tells us that archetypes emerge in the individual psyche through dreams and visions. Archetypal figures in dreams are not the archetype itself, but are representations of it. The appearance of an archetype in a dream points to the connection between the personal and collective unconscious, and often has a numinous quality. One of the central objectives of Jungian analytic psychology is the growth of the individual psyche through connection to the collective unconscious in a process known as individuation. Through individuation, the wisdom and wealth of our inner worlds become known to conscious experience.

Another fundamental difference between Freud and Jung, closely related to the first, concerns their attitude toward the ego. Put simply, Freud's *Ich,* or ego, is equivalent to the self, and this ego/self, by Freud's account, is a "slave" to the id (or instincts), to the "outer world," and, finally, to the superego. That being so, the goal of classical psychoanalysis is to strengthen the ego. This is done, presumably, by liberating the patient from infantile fixations and neurotic conflicts while fostering renunciation and sublimation — which, unlike repression and the defense mechanisms, anchor the individual in reality and do not squander psychic energy unnecessarily.

While cogent enough on the face of it, this way of formulating the goals of therapy only makes sense if you accept the tacit equation between the ego and the self. And Jung emphatically did not. Drawing on Asian philosophy — Vedanta and Taoism, above all — Jung thought of the self as a deeper, more encompassing entity than the ego. The self is the true center of our existence, which an overidentification with the ego is likely to obscure. As Jung understood it, the ego is the instrument (or "organ") of active or willful adaptation to the environment; one that seeks to control the flow of events and experience in accordance with its own narrow (personal) objectives (Storr 1973). As a result, however, the rational ego is precluded from fully participating in Being and always lacks a sense of wholeness. To do that requires that the self first *relinquish* control and stop identifying itself with the willful ego; or in Heideggerian terminology, to embrace *Gelassenheit,* and to let Being be. Jung was cheerfully (perhaps shamelessly) eclectic in borrowing from the world's religious traditions, so his descriptions of the therapeutic process might be reminiscent of a Taoist commending surrender to the nameless Way, or a Christian preacher enjoining us to stop trying to achieve salvation through our own efforts and to surrender to God's inscrutable will.

In any case, Jung did not shrink from describing the goal of psychotherapy as the provision of a "religious experience," or restoring *homo religiosus* to his rightful place in the center of the psyche. Although he always counseled patients to become reacquainted with their own indigenous faiths, he was not interested in fostering a conformist or complacent attitude, or an intolerance toward other faiths. On the contrary, while he said that rediscovering one's own religion is usually a sine qua non to spiritual recovery, he encouraged patients to explore mystical and heterodox tendencies within their own faiths, and to familiarize themselves with other wisdom traditions as well. Indeed, the Eranos circle, which Jung founded in 1924, and is a multidisciplinary forum for exploring the all the world's religious, theological, and mythological orientations (McGuire 1982).

We will say more about Freud and Jung in the chapters that follow. For now, it is enough to note that the two movements they founded influenced one another in unusual and unexpected ways. Beginning in the late 1940s, Michael Fordham, a British Jungian, began to explore the ideas of Melanie Klein and British object relations theory, and to incorporate their developmental and diagnostic formulas into his approach to treatment. In the intervening years, this trend has continued apace, with the result that many Jungian analysts today are deeply versed in one or two post-Freudian approaches to psychotherapy, as well as Jung's classic texts. This makes for a very lively intellectual ferment, and a mind-boggling profusion of new schisms and approaches (Kirsch 2000).

Jung has also had a strong (if indirect) influence on many of the more creative and controversial figures in post-Freudian revisionist psychoanalysis, including Erik Erikson, Erich Fromm, D. W. Winnicott, Charles Rycroft, R. D. Laing, and many others. In many instances, this influence was never acknowledged openly, or was simply denied because of the profound antipathy that existed between he followers of these two men until the end of the twentieth century. Nevertheless, in general, one might say that any theorist who (1) accords primacy to patients' struggles with the maternal imago, rather than to Oedipal issues, (2) rejects the blank screen rule, allowing or encouraging a fair amount of therapist self-disclosure, (3) takes a conciliatory attitude toward religious experience and belief, or (4) refuses to equate the ego and the self, is following in Jung's footsteps and might be described as "post-Jungian" or "post-Freudian" with equal justice.

To speak of Freudians or Jungians today is therefore to refer to networks of therapists whose theory and practice have moved well beyond what Freud and Jung actually said. While some of the general ideas developed by Freud and Jung continue to be important to clinicians, many of their specific theories have been discounted. For example, the emphasis each placed on essential and universal traits and behaviors no longer holds water in today's pluralistic society or heterogeneous practice setting. Indeed, Freud and Jung's perspectives on the feminine and on the psychological differences between men and women are not only old-fashioned, they are offensive. In contrast, many post-Freudian and post-Jungian therapists seek to explore the wider social, cultural, and political contexts of human experience, demonstrating the indelible connections between psychical life and social reality, without privileging one over the other.

Today, post-Freudian psychoanalysis generally consists of four schools: classical or drive-defense analysis, ego psychology, object relations, and self-psychology (J. A. C. Brown 1964; Mitchell and Black 1996). In addition to these four schools, there are three main revisionist trends in psychoanalysis: interpersonal, intersubjective, and relational, each of which we will examine in future chapters. In turn, contemporary post-Jungian analytical psychology has three schools: classical, developmental, and archetypal psychology, which is associated primarily with the work of James Hillman (Samuels 1985; Withers 2003). The developments in post-Jungian analytical psychology are particularly relevant given the continuing debate over Jung's activities just prior to World War II.

In 1933, Jung was appointed by Matthias Göring (and the incoming Nazi regime) as the president of the International General Society for Psychotherapy to oversee the provision of psychotherapy services to German-speaking citizens. One of the organization's roles was to ensure that psychotherapy was not contaminated with Jewish, that is, Freudian, ideas or practices. From then until his abrupt resignation in 1936, Jung said and did things that to some suggest anti-Semitic and racist bias (Cocks 1991). Though he later repudiated the Nazis vigorously, Jung's actions seemed to justify Freud's misgivings about his latent anti-Semitism. Thus far, Jung's denials have had little effect on post-Freudian appraisals, but Jungians themselves are reexamining this era of Jung's life more critically (Samuels 1993b; Maidenbaum 2002). Most importantly, in contrast to Jung's unwarranted privileging of an internal perspective over all others, much contemporary post-Jungian scholarship seeks direct engagement with the realms of social and political experience (Samuels 1993a; Hauke 2000).

Phenomenology and Human Experience
Scheler, Jaspers, and Heidegger

During his years at Göttingen and Freiburg, Husserl trained or mentored many well-known philosophers, including Max Scheler, Eugene Fink, Alexander Pfänder, Alfred Schutz, and Martin Heidegger. Sadly for him, as their work unfolded they developed in directions that differed from his original vision. While Husserl was disappointed with several of them, the one truly tragic story in this sad saga concerns Martin Heidegger. Husserl had hoped that Heidegger would replace him as the leader of the phenomenological movement, much as Freud had hoped that Jung would replace him. It was not until 1928 that Husserl read Heidegger's opus, *Being and Time,* carefully, and realized that Heidegger had embarked in a totally new direction. In retrospect, it is difficult to discern how much of Husserl's misjudgment was the product of wishful thinking and self-deception, and how much was due to dissimulation on Heidegger's part. But Husserl felt betrayed, and with some justification. Even Hannah Arendt, who was on intimate terms with Heidegger when these events transpired, construed Heidegger's behavior as evidence of a "death wish" toward Husserl (Moran 2000).

Next to Heidegger, Husserl probably felt Scheler's "defection" most acutely. And though he lacks Heidegger's commanding stature in contemporary philosophy, Max Scheler was once a force to be reckoned with. Indeed, at his funeral in Frankfurt in 1928, Heidegger declared Scheler one of the greatest minds of the twentieth century — an odd tribute, when you consider that Heidegger never cited Scheler in any of his major works, except in passing. In any case, Scheler was the first in a long series of existential phenomenological thinkers who subjected Freud's ideas to sustained and sympathetic scrutiny, creating a fertile climate of discussion at the interstices of philosophy and psychotherapy.

MAX SCHELER

Max Scheler was born in Munich in 1874. His mother was Jewish and his father Lutheran. By contrast, young Max was drawn to Roman Catholicism and converted at age 14. He became a lecturer at the University of Jena in 1901, but was dismissed in 1907 because of his extramarital affairs. After a bitter divorce, Scheler joined Husserl's group in Göttingen, where his eloquence and erudition won him a large and faithful following — one that extended Husserl's sphere of influence but posed the threat of potential rivalry between himself and Husserl, especially as they drifted apart.

Meanwhile, however, Scheler was quite prolific. *The Nature of Sympathy*, published in 1913, was the first book to explore interpersonal relations and the problems and processes of mutual understanding from a phenomenological perspective. *Formalism in Ethics and Non-Formal Ethics of Values*, arguably his most famous book, was published in 1916, while "Ordo Amoris," a major paper written in 1914–1915, was only published after his death. In addition to philosophy and psychology, Scheler had a lively interest in politics and sociology. The range of Scheler's interests served him well. Despite several career setbacks prompted by his aggressive promiscuity, Scheler carved out a niche for himself as Catholicism's premier intellectual spokesman, and he was given the ironic title of "the Catholic Nietzsche" by historian Ernst Tröltsch after the publication of *Ressentiment* in 1915 (Scheler 2000).

Scheler wrote most of his major works before 1917, when he left Göttingen and became a diplomat for the German Foreign Office in Geneva. In 1919, however, Scheler became a professor of philosophy and sociology at Cologne, only to be dismissed for fresh indiscretions a few years later, when Scheler divorced again. Once a forceful and articulate spokesman for Catholicism, Scheler was now in frail health and had lost the sympathy and support of the Catholic Church. He seemed to be drifting toward pantheism, or even atheism. An old interest in Schopenhauer surfaced in *Man's Place in Nature* (1928), posthumously published, which was fused with ideas gleaned from Dilthey, Freud, and Henri Bergson.

Our interest in Scheler is restricted to his reflections on Nietzsche and Freud. After all, 15 years before Freud dwelt on "the pathology of civilized communities" in *Civilization and Its Discontents* (1930), Scheler's *Ressentiment* (1915) attempted to effect a Nietzsche/Freud synthesis, bridging the gap between clinical research and social psychology, all under the aegis of phenomenological philosophy. Four years earlier, Scheler had published a paper entitled "On Self-Deceptions" in the first issue of the journal *Zeitschrift für Psychopathologie.* It was later edited and reissued as "The Idols of Self-Knowledge" in a two-volume collection of essays, *Abhandlungen und Aufsatze,* published in 1915. Though largely ignored in the psychoanalytic community, "The Idols of Self-Knowledge" took up the issues of suppression and repression, illusions, hysteria, and self-deception with great clarity and sensitivity (Scheler 1973). For example,

We understand by "repression" not a causal hypothesis, but an actual phenomenon which frequently appears in acts of inner perception. It consists in an instinctual looking away from the stirrings of imagination, of feeling and longing, of loving and hating, from such stirrings as would result in a negative value judgment if fully perceived (a judgment coming from one's own "conscience," or a social judgment based on a code of rules we acknowledge). It would be very wrong to limit this phenomenon to the memory of earlier experiences. Memory only offers it a particularly rich field. However, it is also at hand in the inner perception of present experiences. Someone will ask: How, then, is "repression" possible in that case? For "repression" is strictly distinguished from ethical self-control (suppression), that is, a conscious and voluntary obstruction of *fully seen* experiences. What distinguishes them is both the fact that (in repression) the experiences are indeed there but not *seen,* and the fact that they are not altered by conscious acts of the will but are simply placed out of sight by an instinctive drive. Is it not necessary that the experience already be inwardly perceived if it is to be "repressed"? Let me recall what was said earlier. The aroma of value (*das Wertparfum*), so to speak, of an earlier experience, of a stirring of feeling, or striving, is already present to inner perception, even if the experience itself, especially the content to which the striving or feeling, love or hate, is directed, is *not* yet present. The drive reacts to this initial value of the stirring and keeps the experience from crossing the threshold of inner perception. In this way, the experience remains barred not only from the sphere of judgment . . . but also from the sphere of inner perception itself. It is an entirely different matter when an experience is perceived and pride, or shame, or motives of duty come into conflict with its inherent tendency and obstruct its translation into expressive movements or into actions. . . . Thus a clear dividing line runs between ethical self-control, or a real conflict of motives, and that looking away and closing one's eyes which is called "repression." (84–85)

Admittedly, Scheler's reference to "instincts, "drives," and so on sound wooly and archaic today. Nevertheless, the distinction he made between repression and ethical self-control is still useful. What Scheler called "ethical self-control" is a ubiquitous psychic phenomenon, a form of *conscious* (or deliberate) self-censorship that obstructs the overt and outward *expression* of a feeling, impulse, or fantasy that is present to awareness. In Scheler's terminology, the phenomenon is "fully seen." Repression goes one step further. It not only inhibits the expression of a particular thought or feeling, but also prevents the experience of it from even crossing the threshold of conscious awareness in the first place. Ethical self-control (or conscious suppression of an impulse) is lucid and undeceived about its own motives. Only in repression is there an element of *self-deception*.

The preceding remarks apply equally to normal and neurotic people. For like Freud, Scheler believed that "normal" people repress a great deal, too. Hysteria, says Scheler, entails a more vivid and intense form of this normal phenomenon. Indeed, what was distinctive about hysteria is that both deception and self-deception are present, fostering a pervasive theatricality:

the intensity of the expression of the affects is not in proportion to the inner state (for instance, the individual appears much angrier than he really is, or much sadder, to judge from his moans and effusive tears, so that the uninitiated will always be deceived). . . . The patient's concern for the impression he makes on the spectator, for example, the doctor, or for the "social image" he presents, immediately and, as it were, automatically induces the discharge of affect. . . . Thus *the deception of the observer is always the result of an antecedent self-deception,* and this fact distinguishes hysterical behavior from any comedy or simulation which begins in the conscious sphere of will and judgment and aims directly at the observer. (Scheler 1973, 78; emphasis added)

Today the term "hysteria" has been expunged from the diagnostic lexicon. But Scheler's characterization of this bygone disorder is still an apt description of the "historionic personality disorder" in the *Diagnostic and Statistical Manual of Behavioral Disorders,* 4th edition (DSM-IV). Moreover, Scheler was not content to transpose Freudian perspectives on mental disorder into a phenomenological frame of reference. He attempted to broaden and expand the scope of analytic inquiry, particularly regarding the psychology of "normal" people. For people who are not manifestly disturbed, cognitive distortions in the realm of "inner perception" — or our ability to apprehend our own feelings, attitudes, and motives without recourse to self-deception — are not merely the result of repression or an intrapsychic censorship. Often, the very language we use for the description and classification of "inner" (emotional) states and processes turns us away from certain feelings and motives that we cannot adequately describe or represent. A language that has a word for "shame," but not for "guilt," for example, constricts the individual's capacity to experience and express guilt feelings consciously. Similarly, languages that do not discriminate between irony and sarcasm, between fear and anxiety, or between envy and jealousy, for example, obscure important features of human experience and motivation. Absent the words to describe them, to ourselves or others, people are oblivious to what Scheler terms "inner" experiences:

It would be a great mistake to think that language, the tool of communication, has simply the meaning and function of communicating experiences which have already been perceived. In fact, the influence of language reaches much further. The traditional words referring to psychic states have a wide-reaching impact on what we *generally perceive* in our own and other's experiences. An experience for which there is no special word, or a particular quality of an experience for which there is only a quite general and undifferentiated term, is for the most part not perceived by the individual who goes through the experience or is perceived only to the extent that it corresponds to this term. . . . (Ibid., 86–87)

Inner perception first shows us only that aspect of experience which corresponds to the traditional forms and modes of experience current in the family, in the people, and in the other forms of society of which we are members. . . . Only an ongoing emancipation from the traditional focus of inner perception, from the historical system of categories within which inner perception takes place, enables us to grasp the psychic experiences of the individual. . . . (87)

Only a slow process of coming to know ourselves as individual essences, a process accompanied by hindrances of every kind, allows us to separate what we ourselves experience from what is only forced upon us . . . and does not belong to "us." Generally speaking, only a systematic *historical critique* is capable of breaking the power of tradition and freeing the authentic life of the epoch concealed behind the sham life of tradition. (88)

Scheler's reference to "the sham life of tradition" and his call for a "historical critique of tradition" as a vital prerequisite to genuine self-knowledge are intriguing. Admittedly, Scheler's belief that we each have an "individual essence" that is separate from language falls short of the later Heidegger's emphasis on the primacy of language, which plays as large a role in Heidegger as labor plays in Marx's ontology. But Scheler's reflections on the "historical system of categories" embedded in language redirects psychoanalysis toward the kind of cultural and genealogical inquiry favored by Nietzsche, for example.

Whatever its shortcomings, however, "The Idols of Self-Knowledge" represents an early and crucial step beyond Freud, for whom the self's opacity to itself is primarily a matter of individual self-censorship. When individuals render their emotional lives intelligible in light of words and categories that are rooted in language, culture takes up residence in the most intimate interstices of the psyche. While a form of routine censorship is entailed in the cultural alexythmia Scheler describes, it does not emanate from a single psyche, nor an agency within the psyche, but represents the *impersonal* effect of cultural templates on personal experience. It is no longer merely self-deception, but also the social construction of reality — "inner" or "subjective" as well as "outer reality — that is at issue here.

Ressentiment, published in 1915, was Scheler's longest meditation on Nietzsche and addressed the problems of envy, malice, and self-deception as they bear on the origins of religion and ethical value systems. Though he quarreled with Nietzsche regarding the nature of Christianity, Scheler agreed wholeheartedly with Nietzsche that *ressentiment* (or slave morality) is not confined to oppressed or marginalized groups, or even to declining elites dreaming of their former glory. Like Nietzsche, Scheler said that this warped, subaltern mentality infuses the whole spirit of modernity.

Following Nietzsche, Scheler used *ressentiment* to denote the presence of malice, vindictiveness, and a thirst for revenge, not as transient states or impulses, but as abiding traits of character that warp our judgment and rob our life of companionable pleasure. And again, like Nietzsche, Scheler stipulated that these hateful impulses are seldom present to consciousness among those so afflicted because they are repressed and rationalized as righteous indignation, engendering a pronounced tendency to disparage or devalue others, whether in a subtle deprecations or vicious, all-out attacks. But unlike Nietzsche, who situated the core disturbance in a person's relationship to his own instinctual urges, as Freud would have, Scheler insisted that *ressentiment* is an inherently *social* phenomenon involving (1) the process of comparing one's actual power and status with the status one feels entitled to, and/or (2) the process of comparing oneself unfavorably to other individuals of one's own reference group. And though Scheler did not quite express it in so many words, the context makes it clear that the former process of comparison implicates one's sense of corporate identity, as it is embodied or expressed in one's ethnicity, gender, or class-consciousness. For example, Scheler points out that in medieval society, people seldom cherished fantasies of upward social mobility. Power and status were hereditary and deemed natural and necessary in the scheme of salvation, thereby mitigating whatever envious impulses occurred spontaneously. Industrial democracies, by contrast, replaced the traditional yearning for salvation in the afterlife with the clamor for affluence in this world, breeding extravagant needs and expectations, and upending traditional class and caste divisions by creating new wealth for the lower orders and unexpected hardships for the aristocracy. It also bred fierce competition among individuals and different social groups, fostering envy and *ressentiment* among those who remained relatively disadvantaged in the struggle to thrive and succeed.

By contrast, Scheler notes that the second category, the process of comparing oneself to others within one's own reference group, is natural and ubiquitous and by no means necessarily harmful. After all, unless we know how others differ from ourselves we cannot possibly appreciate or understand them as individuals. Moreover, and more importantly, someone whose self-esteem is intact can compare themselves to others endowed with greater gifts or material wealth without feeling that their own dignity or worth is diminished or impugned by the competence, intelligence, vitality, or good fortune of others.

In other words, said Scheler, a person who possesses a calm and unselfconscious sense of his or her own worth weathers such comparisons without repressing his or her feelings or allowing them to warp their judgment. Rather than responding to the presence of a prodigy or someone favored by fortune through a reflexive tendency to devaluation, the healthy person sees superior gifts in another person as cause for celebration or, indeed, for love and esteem. Following Nietzsche and Georg Simmel, Scheler called this mode of relatedness the "noble" mentality and described it as characteristic of aristocrats in days gone by. By contrast, said Scheler, the envious, vindictive person has a "slavish" cast of mind. He suffers from (repressed) feelings of impotence, inferiority, and worthlessness, and uses devaluation and self-deception to compensate for his hidden injuries.

Having said all that, however, Scheler also claimed that in the twentieth century, *ressentiment* flourished among the privileged and powerful as well as among the downtrodden, because no matter how fortunate or privileged they are in other respects, someone who is fundamentally unloved will always be prone to making invidious comparisons between themselves and others. They will always be envious, insecure, and potentially hateful because they lack a wholesome self-love or self-respect, which Scheler, unlike Nietzsche, distinguished carefully from mere egoism. Scheler then took a decisive step beyond Nietzsche and said that the diffusion of *ressentiment* in our time is caused, not by repression of the instincts, or some nebulous will to power, but by *the pervasive decline of love.* But love, as Scheler depicts it, is not a function of desire or of the experience of absence, as it was for Freud, Sartre, and Lacan, but an expression of strength, abundance, of generosity of spirit, all of which are vitiated by *ressentiment,* whose underlying cause is a feeling or experience of *impotence,* or powerlessness. Moreover, according to Scheler, the disinterested love that affirms the worth and dignity of the other person is always based on a robust sense of one's own worth — a capacity for self-affirmation. According to Scheler, affirming (or loving) oneself and affirming others are not mutually exclusive, but actually interdependent, as Erich Fromm would later insist (Fromm 1956).

Scheler's emphasis on the centrality of love to human existence, and the decline of love under capitalism, sounded a new and important note in the development of existential phenomenology. It also anticipated some of the central ideas of Martin Buber, Ludwig Binswanger, and above all, Erich Fromm. However, serious problems with Scheler's thesis also warrant discussion. Despite the century that has elapsed between Scheler's day and ours, we are still apt to think of self-confidence coupled with great generosity of spirit, the capacity to admire others without feeling diminished in the process, as a "noble" trait. But we are not inclined (as Nietzsche and Scheler were) to conjure with dubious philological conjectures, or to reify our concepts with essentialist overtones. In short, we do not share Scheler's need to attribute nobility of character chiefly to nobility in feudal times, which prejudges the whole issue along class lines and betrays a strong tendency to idealize the Middle Ages.

Despite his stated intention of approaching this phenomenon phenomenologically, Scheler qualifies his reflections on *ressentiment* with assertions about the relationship between character and social structure, which places considerable emphasis on (unspecified) *biological* factors, and therefore strays well outside the phenomenological frame of reference: "the manner in which *ressentiment* originates in individuals or groups, and the intensity it reaches, is due primarily to hereditary factors and secondarily to social structure. Let us note, however, that the social structure itself is determined by the hereditary character and the value experience of the ruling human type" (Scheler 2000, 42). At this point, a potential problem emerges. On the one hand, Scheler presents *ressentiment* as an intrinsically *social* phenomena, engendered by specifically social processes of comparison. On the other hand, Scheler claims that these social processes are actually the expression of other, specifically hereditary factors, that is, of biology, rather than of politics, history, and economics, which merely provides an arena for the unfolding of these latent, biologically based dispositions.

Unfortunately, this last assertion undercuts his initial description of the phenomenon, robbing it of cogency and power. After all, if the process of making invidious comparisons between oneself and others (and seeking neurotic compensation for the feelings aroused in the process) is the result of hereditary factors, why bother with such a detailed description of its social roots and ramifications? And in addition to this oddly self-canceling quality, there is an incipiently *circular* character to this argument, which derives character from social structure, and social structure from character.

Of course, the threat of intractable ambiguity can only be averted by according primacy or priority to either environmental or hereditary factors. As it turns out, Scheler opts for the latter, issuing in the following explanatory schema: nobility of character (or the lack of it) derives from a chiefly social structure, which in turn derives chiefly from (unspecified) biological factors. Having asserted the primacy of hereditary factors in chapter 1, Scheler also goes on to characterize women as "the weaker and therefore more vindictive sex" by virtue of their biological makeup, and he discussed female prudery and prostitution in the modern era in what can only be described as crudely essentialist terms. Jews are accorded similar treatment. In chapter 5, footnote 27, Scheler remarks, "In Sombart's opinion, the 'Jewish spirit' is one of the chief causes of development of the capitalist social structure. It is quite in agreement with my thesis that this spirit, which has had a lien on *ressentiment* for a long time, plays a major role in this process" (Scheler 2000, 165). In fairness to Scheler, the hereditary perspective that he brought to bear on social psychology echoes Nietzsche's own prejudices. But Nietzsche insists that Christianity is a continuation of "the Jewish slave revolt in morals," and that early or "primitive" Christian communism is a forerunner of contemporary socialism or of other movements that promote equality. Just as Nietzsche went to great lengths to "prove" that Christianity is the product of Judaism, Scheler went to great lengths to prove that it was not. He never refuted this contention in quite so many words, however. Instead, by endorsing Werner Sombart's fascist ravings about the "Jewish spirit" and the development of capitalism, he *implies* that Judaism harbors values that are antipathetic to ones he cherishes, and therefore, is a historic adversary of the Christian faith. In addition, Scheler castigates Nietzsche for conjuring with "dim analogies" between modern socialism and early Christian communism and the spirit of Saint Francis. Like Kierkegaard and Nietzsche before him, and Ortega y Gasset shortly afterwards, Scheler despised collectivism of any kind, arguing that genuine Christianity is never collectivist, but inherently hierarchical and aristocratic in character.

It is instructive to note that while divagating on these issues, Scheler commends Nietzsche for his theoretical "anti-humanism," arguing that humanism is nothing more than an ideological justification for class hatred, or a fundamental lack of patriotism. And he makes the novel claim that this "humanist" mentality can be traced back to Stoic philosophy:

> On a historical scale, this is the source of the "love of mankind," the "cosmopolitan" affect, which is so noticeable in the writings of the later Stoics: it spread in the aging Roman Empire when the individual, severed from the nourishing and sustaining force of the city-state, felt lonely and deprived of all support. Exactly the same motive underlies "modern humanitarian love." It came about mainly as a protest against patriotism and finally turned into a protest against every organized community. Thus it is the secondary result of a repressed hatred of one's native country. (Scheler 2000, 99–100)

Why this attack on Stoicism? Perhaps because of its link with "slave morality." Epictetus, the greatest Stoic philosopher between Seneca and Marcus Aurelius, was actually born a slave. (His name derives from the Greek word *epiktetos,* which means "acquired"). Despite abundant evidence that Epictetus and Marcus Aurelius's teachings prefigure or parallel early Christian doctrine on many important points, Scheler stubbornly insisted that the Stoic emphasis on the oneness and kinship of the human species is essentially un-Christian. According to Scheler, the leveling, universalistic, and humanistic tendencies that Nietzsche thought he detected in Christian thought, and which he attributed retroactively to the Jews, are really expressions of Stoic *ressentiment,* which the Church first embraced for purely propagandistic purposes, only to succumb to its own poison with the passage of time.

Though it purports to be a study in (analytically informed) phenomenological sociology, *Ressentiment* surprisingly became the occasion, or perhaps a pretext, for an apology for the Christian and, specifically, the Catholic faith. Christianity in general (and Catholicism in particular) could not exist without the concepts of free will and the fundamental unity of the human species, and the fact that Judaism and Stoicism were the historic bearers of these concepts in pre-Christian times vitiates Scheler's overwrought polemic, which totters on the brink of incoherence when these elementary facts are taken into account. And while tenable before World War II, when there was still considerable room for ambiguity on this score among theologians, the whole spirit of Scheler's polemic is profoundly at variance with Catholic social thought after Vatican II.

Though compromised by his intemperate desire to undermine modernity and to vindicate medieval Christianity, Scheler's project of synthesizing Nietzsche and Freud, clinical and social psychology, remains intriguing. In terms of our typological schemata, Scheler was a religious irrationalist with a decidedly anti-utopian orientation. Strictly speaking, he was neither modern nor postmodern, but perhaps premodern or anti-modern. His animosity toward capitalism and democracy combined elements of traditionalism and antitraditionalism, and by virtue of their Nietzschean background and implications, foreshadowed many ideas of Heidegger, as we shall see.

KARL JASPERS

Karl Jaspers was born in Oldenburg, Germany, in 1883, and died in Basel, Switzerland, in 1969. He was a sickly child and adolescent, and suffered from bronchial and heart problems throughout his adult life. He began his university studies in 1901 and, after two years at law, shifted to medicine, which he pursued for six years in Berlin, Göttingen, and Heidelberg. He was registered as a doctor in 1909 and became a volunteer research assistant at the University of Heidelberg psychiatric clinic — a position he held until 1915. Because he was not paid, he was able to work at his own pace, seeing only the patients that interested him, and producing *General Psychopathology,* published in 1913, when he was only 30. *General Psychopathology* drew extensively on the ideas of Kierkegaard, Nietzsche, Dilthey, and Husserl, and made occasional references to Hegel and Scheler. He then took a degree in philosophy and was given a position in the faculty of philosophy at Heidelberg in 1916, where he became the head of the Heidelberg School of Psychiatry. He was cross-appointed to a chair in philosophy in 1921. Meanwhile, *General Psychopathology* had become a classic textbook in psychiatry and was revised in 1946 and translated into English in 1965. His other publications are too numerous to list separately; however, they address themes and thinkers from ancient, medieval, and modern philosophy, political theory, art, literature, German war guilt, the prospects for world peace, and so on.

Jaspers's early interest in philosophy and the social sciences brought him in close contact with diverse members of the German intelligentsia, including Max Weber, whom he sometimes referred to as "the Galileo of the social sciences." Weber was a neo-Kantian who deplored irrationalism in culture and politics, and as one might expect from an admirer of his, Jaspers framed his philosophy of *existenz* in a way that made ample allowance for reason and objectivity. Indeed, many experts claim that Jaspers's approach to phenomenology is really more indebted to Kant than to Dilthey or Husserl (Walker 1995).

At the same time, however, Jaspers was profoundly indebted to Kierkegaard and Nietzsche. While well aware of their differences, he preferred to stress their commonalities, arguing that Kierkegaard and

Nietzsche philosophized from the core of their personal existences, ignoring the fashions and conventions of academic discourse. In truth, Kierkegaard and Nietzsche mistrusted professional philosophers whose careerism made them risk-averse, inauthentic, and detached from real life. Jaspers agreed with their assessment of academic philosophy although, like Weber, he was a member of the mandarin caste of German intellectuals who reigned in the German universities before the Nazis seized power, who professed to be "above" politics.

Like many of the mandarins, Jaspers did not take the Nazi threat seriously at first and was shocked by Martin Heidegger's willingness to support their cause. Until 1933, Jaspers thought Nazism was too fragmented to coalesce and seize power, and as a result of his error he spent most of the war in hiding because his wife, Getrud Mayer, was Jewish, and his refusal to surrender her rendered him an enemy of the state. Though his wife eluded the Gestapo, Jaspers defiance did not go unnoticed, and in 1945 he learned from an authoritative source that he was scheduled for deportation to Auschwitz on April 14. Fortunately, fate intervened, and the Allies took Heidelberg on March 30.

Prior to the Second World War, Jaspers shared Max Scheler's lofty, aristocratic disdain for democracy. At the end of the war, however, Jaspers became an outspoken promoter of democratic ideals and was sought by the allies to assist them in the process of "de-Nazifying" German universities. At the request of the Allied authorities, Jaspers wrote a letter to them regarding Heidegger's collaboration with the Nazis in December 1945, and recommended that Heidegger be pensioned and forbidden to teach. Jaspers's attitude toward Heidegger can only be described as profoundly ambivalent. On the one hand, Jaspers admired Heidegger's originality and likened him to Max Weber — a comparison that would only have baffled or antagonized Heidegger. On the other hand, Jaspers mistrusted Heidegger's reticence, his insincerity and opportunism, and his animus toward the natural sciences, which he found misguided and politically dangerous. It is not difficult to see why. When Jaspers brought up the Jewish question to Heidegger in 1933, Heidegger insisted that there was "a dangerous international alliance of Jews" menacing Germany. When Jaspers asked how an uneducated man like Hitler could rule Germany, Heidegger responded, "It's not a question of education; just look at his marvelous hands!" (Wolin 1993, 145). Statements like these make a profound impression.

If politics were largely irrelevant to Jaspers before the Second World War, they dominated his concerns afterwards. Though he did his best to foster the democratization of Germany after the war, he became deeply disenchanted with the de-Nazification processes since many of his colleagues had collaborated, like Heidegger, were eventually reinstated. In 1948, he accepted a professorship in Basel, Switzerland, becoming a Swiss citizen in 1967, two years before his death.

Jaspers's approach to psychotherapy was based, like Sartre's, on an appeal to human freedom and responsibility — though like Buber, Tillich, and other religious existentialists, Jaspers made ample allowance for the experience of transcendence, and he cultivated a lively dialogue with theologians. Though decidedly anti-utopian in tone, and modern, rather than postmodern in outlook, Jaspers's view of history and the human condition is extremely difficult to classify according to our other criteria, being neither rationalist nor irrationalist, religious nor irreligious, but *both* in some sense. Jaspers's attitude toward Freud and psychoanalysis was as ambivalent as his attitude toward Heidegger, though for entirely different reasons. In Jaspers's estimation, Freud was not an original thinker. Moreover, methodologically speaking, Freud confounded the elucidation of meaning (in a hermeneutic sense) with the identification of a causal nexus (in the natural scientific sense). According to Jaspers, therefore,

> psychoanalysis is . . . a confusing mixture of psychological theories . . . it is a philosophical movement or a creed which has become a vital part of certain people's lives. . . .
>
> As a cultural, historical phenomenon, psychoanalysis is a popular psychology: What Kierkegaard and Nietzsche had achieved at the highest level of culture was again achieved at a lower level. . . .
>
> Psychoanalysis therefore is partly responsible for a lowering of the cultural level in psychopathology as a whole.
>
> It can be said that psychoanalysis appeared with shattering truthfulness in a hypocritical age. This is only partly correct. . . . It unmasked a bourgeois world which lived without faith within the conventions of

a society that had definitely relinquished religion and morality with "sexus" as its secret god. But the exposure was no less false than what it unmasked. Both were bound to sexuality as their supposed absolute. (Jaspers 1965, 359–60)

While he dismissed Freud as a popularizer of Nietzsche — somewhat unfairly, perhaps — Jaspers welcomed Scheler's *Ressentiment*. At the same time, however, he qualified his praise of Scheler by noting the existence of a form of self-deception in the realm of values that is widely distributed among the ruling elite — a phenomenon he termed *attachment to the value of social status*. Though never intended as a critique of Scheler, at least not explicitly, Jaspers remarks are a useful corrective. He does not assume, for example, that the suppressed or underprivileged strata of the population are uniquely susceptible to value distortions. The privileged are as impervious to truth as the underprivileged:

> The individual for whom things go well, who is fortunate in his birth and belongs to the ruling classes, tends not to ascribe this to luck but to his own innate superiority and merit. The privileged position is not seen in the first place as a challenge, but simply as the individual's due. In addition to everything else underprivileged people have to bear, he maintains that their suppression is right because they are inferiors. Full of self-regard, he takes affluence, power, superiority as a sign of aristocratic nobility, and health, strength and good spirits as a sign of his ultimate worth. He does not let himself see the accidental nature of his own position and the roots of ruin in all this. He cannot stand modesty, humility or any knowledge of the realities which brought him to his advantages. He wants to avoid any threat of fall and decline and to escape the responsibilities of his position. He therefore makes use of the rightness of his status as a protective screen so that he can be free of his obligations and enjoy his possessions in peace. Thus suppressor and suppressed alike both falsify their scales of value in a complimentary manner, just as a sense of the realities, truthfulness and open-mindedness are possible for them both. (Jaspers 1965, 325)

MARTIN HEIDEGGER

Martin Heidegger was born in Messkirch, Germany, in 1889. Like his erstwhile friend and adversary, Karl Jaspers, he was a sickly child and youth who showed great promise in his studies. Heidegger attended Gymnasium in Constance and Freiburg where he became engrossed in the work of Franz Brentano, whose paper "On The Manifold Meaning of Being in Aristotle" (1862) set him to thinking about the issues that occupied him for the remainder of his life. In 1909, Heidegger began studying theology with the Jesuits in Tisis, Austria, and then at the Albert-Ludwig University in Freiburg. However, Heidegger soon shifted from theology to general philosophy, and in 1913 he completed his doctoral dissertation, entitled "The Doctrine of Judgment in Psychologism," under Heinrich Rickert. He completed his postgraduate studies with a habilitation dissertation on "The Doctrine of Categories and Signification in Duns Scotus" in 1915.

In 1917, Heidegger married Elfriede Petri, and shortly thereafter was called up for service, but after less than a year was discharged due to ill health. In 1919, Heidegger became Husserl's assistant at the University of Freiburg, where he taught courses on Augustine and neo-Platonism, Aristotle, Descartes, and Husserl's *Logical Investigations*, among other topics. And though he renounced Catholicism in 1919, during the 1920s Heidegger taught several courses based on his friend Rudolf Bultmann's hermeneutic reading of the New Testament. Like Bultmann, Heidegger referred habitually to the "Greek-Christian mentality," or the "Greek-Christian world," effectively divorcing Christianity from its Jewish origin — much as Scheler tried to do.

From 1923 to 1928, Heidegger was professor of philosophy at the University of Marburg where he met and began an affair with his student, Hannah Arendt. Following the publication in 1927 of his chief work, *Being and Time,* he assumed the chair in philosophy vacated by Husserl at the University of Freiburg in 1928. Among his colleagues during this early period in his career were Bultmann, Nicolai Hartmann, and Paul Natorp, and his students included Hans-Georg Gadamer and Karl Löwith. From 1928 to 1932, Heidegger primarily lectured and wrote about Leibniz, Kant, and metaphysics.

In 1933, following the election of National Socialism in Germany, Heidegger became rector of the University of Freiburg and a member of the Nazi party. Although he never resigned his membership, he stepped down from his post as rector in 1934 after ten months. Heidegger retreated from active politics and devoted himself to commentaries on Lao Tzu, Schelling, Holdlerin, Nietzsche, and Heraclitus. It was also around this time that Heidegger's philosophy underwent a "turning," or *Kehre,* in which he abandoned his project of fashioning a fundamental ontology, and turned instead to the study of the relation of language and Being.

If 1936 indicated the beginning of his philosophical transformation, 1946 was marked by multiple personal and professional upheavals. That year, Heidegger applied for emeritus status from the University of Freiburg, which was initially denied. As a result of the stress, Heidegger spent part of the spring of 1946 at the Haus Baden sanatorium in Badenweiler, where he was treated by the psychiatrist Viktor von Gebsattel, a colleague of Ludwig Binswanger's. Awarded a modest pension by the university senate, Heidegger retreated to his beloved mountain hut in Totnauberg in the Black Forest and wrote a book on Anaximander, a lecture to commemorate Rilke, and started a translation of Lao-Tzu into German.

In 1946, Heidegger also wrote his famous "Letter on Humanism" to Jean Beaufret. In this, and in subsequent publications, Heidegger developed a thoroughgoing critique of humanism and developed an approach to philosophy that would provide the foundations for postmodern thinking. In 1949, Hans-Georg Gadamer organized a festschrift to celebrate Heidegger's sixtieth birthday, and in 1950 he was reinstated as a professor at Freiburg, much to Karl Jaspers's dismay. From 1950 to 1957, Heidegger traveled and spoke extensively in France, Germany, and Austria, and from 1959 to1969 conducted a series of intensive seminars for psychiatrists with Medard Boss in Zollikon, Switzerland. By the time he died in 1976, Heidegger was one of the most famous philosophers of the twentieth century, a standing that would soon be marred by the debate over his political past.

Heidegger is a controversial figure in the history of philosophy. As we shall see in the following chapters, he fundamentally impacted the development of theory and practice in psychotherapy. Yet we cannot responsibly talk about Heidegger's role among psychiatrists, psychoanalysts, and psychotherapists without addressing his stance on National Socialism in more detail. Certainly the facts speak for themselves: Heidegger was a member of the Nazi party and carried out the policies of the regime in the context of higher education during the course of his rectorship. Moreover, he never subsequently repudiated anything he said or did at the time.

Heidegger's politics is a complex issue and has spawned numerous commentaries (Farias 1989, Friedman 1994, Ott 1993, Rockmore 1995, Wolin 1993), often polemical in nature. Recent scholarship (see Wolin 2001) has focused on Heidegger's relationship with his famous Jewish students: Arendt, Hans Jonas, Herbert Marcuse, and Löwith. Their dual support and critique of Heidegger captures the complicated nature of the debate.

In 1925, for example, Heidegger began an affair with Arendt that spanned many years. To his intimates, Heidegger later confessed that Arendt was the great love of his life, a fact that distressed his wife, who was a known anti-Semite. In 1941, Arendt fled Paris, where she had moved in 1933, for the United States. Arendt went on to become a leading intellectual and professor at the New School for Social Research in New York. As repayment for Heidegger's abiding love, and to the puzzlement of many, she used her growing reputation in the English speaking world to rehabilitate Heidegger's intellectual standing after World War II.

Meanwhile, in 1925, two more Jewish pupils approached Heidegger — Herbert Marcuse and Hans Jonas. Though less famous than Marcuse, Jonas became an early and important figure in the philosophy of biology and bioethics (Jonas 1966), whose prescient thesis on Gnosticism (supervised by Bultmann) elucidated Heidegger's affinities with this ancient, heretical movement in considerable depth and detail (Jonas 1963). After World War II, Jonas went on to teach at the New School in New York, where he remained close to Arendt and her circle.

Unlike Jonas, whose politics were somewhat conservative, Marcuse tried to synthesize Heideggerian phenomenology with Marxism — an effort which, by his own admission, was doomed to failure (Kellner

1984). Nevertheless, his early efforts in this direction brought him to the attention of Max Horkheimer, director of the Frankfurt Institute for Social Research, which he joined in 1934 when it was in exile in New York. After *Reason and Revolution* (1947), a masterful study of Hegel, Marcuse went on to achieve great fame in his own right. Though disillusioned with Heidegger, he defended him against the aggressive critique of his Frankfurt school colleague, Theodor Adorno, whose *Negative Dialectics* (1966) and *The Jargon of Authenticity* (1973) were scathing dismissals of Heidegger's work.

The issue is whether there is a link between Heidegger's philosophy and his political engagement with National Socialism. In 1933, after the Nazis took power, and to the astonishment of many of his students, Heidegger was elected rector of the University of Freiburg. Efforts to dissuade him proved fruitless. Heidegger's now infamous inaugural speech, entitled "The German University's Self-Affirmation," ended with a quote from Plato, but as Löwith recalled, the speech was profoundly ambiguous. One the one hand, Heidegger affirmed the autonomy of the German university, but denounced the liberal idea of academic freedom. The university must be free — free to integrate itself seamlessly into the Nazi social order. The rector, said Heidegger, must be the spiritual leader of the faculty and students, and must therefore be animated by the historic mission of "das Volk," which was decreed by "fate," followed by rhetoric about the individual finding his authentic self, his true vocation, through self-sacrifice and submersion in the destiny of the people (Wolin 1993). When he met Löwith again in Rome in 1934, Heidegger denied that his speech was at variance with his philosophy.

As the work of Friedman (1994), Rockmore (1995), and others has shown, the relationship between Heidegger's philosophy in *Being and Time* and his allegiance to National Socialism raises essential questions about Heidegger's fundamental ontology. Was Heidegger's turn to National Socialism indicated by his philosophical position? Did the emphasis on *Dasein*'s possibilities, which must be realized in opposition to all tendencies to fall into the anonymity of the They (*das Man*), make Heidegger's thought susceptible to totalitarianism? Or is it the case that Heidegger's actions are not contingent upon his philosophical position and that his political misadventures do not reflect the inherent values of his thought? Certainly the fact that Heidegger's philosophy continues to maintain its dominance, despite the debate over his political activities, speaks to its considerable influence on current theory.

In fact, after his initial support, Heidegger's relations with the Nazi party grew strained toward the end of 1934, when he resigned his position as rector. Among other things, Heidegger refused to submit to party pressure to appoint Nazi stalwarts and functionaries to key administrative posts. Moreover, in his seminars, he expressed open disagreement with the Nazi ideologues Alfred Baumler and Alfred Rosenberg on racial genetics, and accordingly was placed under constant surveillance by the Gestapo, and ridiculed and misquoted in the Nazi press (Ott 1993). Though he never resigned his party membership, Heidegger soon retreated from active politics.

Immediately after the war, in 1945, Heidegger was asked by the de-Nazification commission to justify his actions as rector. Jaspers, who in 1937 had been prohibited by the Nazis from teaching and publishing, was asked by the commission to provide an assessment of Heidegger. On the basis of Jasper's recommendation, the university senate decreed in 1946 that Heidegger be deprived of his teaching license and removed from his post with a reduced pension (Safranski 1998, 341).

Jaspers' misgivings about Heidegger seem to have been well founded, because in 1953, in *An Introduction to Metaphysics*, Heidegger reprinted a lecture from 1935 that praised "the inner truth and greatness" of the Nazi movement (Habermas 1993, 1997). To the end of his life, Heidegger believed that Germany had a unique (if quite vague) historic mission to reorient the Western world to Being, and he was deeply mistrustful of democracy. During his Zollikon seminars in the 1950s and 1960s, Heidegger's colleague, Medard Boss, admonished the participants not to ask the philosopher about his involvement with the Nazis (Stadlen 1999). Clearly, Heidegger wanted to deal with his Nazi past on his own terms.

In 1966, Heidegger finally granted an interview to *Der Speigel*, which was published posthumously in 1976. In it, he characterized Hitlerism as the historical expression of a "structural" sickness in humanity, and expressed concern that it would take some time to eliminate the problem (Wolin 1993). Predictably, perhaps, his remarks were fraught with ambiguity. Heidegger's friends and advocates construed them as a clear renunciation of his Nazi past, while critics found them slippery and evasive because they seemed to shift the blame for the ravages of Nazism and lacked a clear acknowledgment of his personal involvement in Nazi politics.

Regardless of whether one is an advocate or a critic of Heidegger, the relevance of his philosophical concepts cannot be overlooked, not least because they provide the basis for many contemporary philosophical currents such as hermeneutics (via the work of Gadamer) and post-structuralism (via the work of Derrida). In order to appreciate his pervasive influence on the domains of theory and practice in psychotherapy, we will focus on several concepts: being-in-the-world, the problems of consciousness, embodiment, *Befindlichkeit* (affect), temporality (historicity), authenticity, and conscience. Although hesitant at first, Heidegger (2001) eventually acknowledged the connections between his fundamental ontology and psychology. Yet he also cautioned interested psychologists that his inquiry into the question of Being is "ontological" in nature and must not be seen as equivalent to the "ontic" investigations of psychology (Frie 1997). As he states in *Being and Time,* "The existential analytics of *Dasein* is prior to any psychology, anthropology, and (above all) biology" (Heidegger 1962, 71).

Heidegger dedicated *Being and Time* to Edmund Husserl, but his philosophy took a different direction. As Husserl depicts it, phenomenology is a radical epistemological critique, a way of reorienting our thinking about experience and cognition. Another way of putting this is that the desire to elucidate the contents, the qualities, and the structures of consciousness are what *drive* transcendental phenomenology. By contrast, consciousness takes a backseat in Heidegger's existential phenomenology. Unlike Husserl, who took consciousness as his starting point, Heidegger was interested in the meaning of Being (*Sein*) as different from beings (*Seiende*). He proceeds by a phenomenological examination of a particular being, namely the human being that he refers to as *Dasein*. According to Heidegger, *Dasein* is preoccupied with the meaning of Being. *Dasein* reveals itself a phenomenon whose nature it is to be-in-the-world. Heidegger examines first what is meant by world and then what it means to be in such a world. *Dasein* relates to the world through care (*Sorge*) in such as way that its practical involvement with creatures and things is never fully conscious or present to itself. As such, Heidegger sought to move beyond phenomenology to fundamental ontology (or inquiry into Being) in which consciousness is a transient quality and a secondary, rather than a primary datum. As a result, consciousness is an ever-present possibility, but never the sine qua non of Being. Indeed, the word "consciousness" (*Bewusstsein*) scarcely even appears in *Being and Time*.

Without doubt, Heidegger's central contribution to the practice of psychotherapy is the notion of being-in-the-world. By situating human existence in relation to the world, and not in relation to the internal workings of the individual mind, Heidegger overcomes both the dilemmas of solipsism and the Cartesian paradigm of consciousness. He also creates a radically different focus than Freud's theory of intrapsychic processes. For Heidegger, the customary division of internal experience from external behavior is an artifact of Cartesian thinking, which obscures our fundamental situatedness in the world. At the same time, Heidegger provides the means to understand and conceptualize human relations not in terms of the interaction of two subjective monads, á la Husserl, for example, but as the interrelation of two beings in the world through the concept of "being-with." We will explain these ideas in the following chapter on the impact of Heidegger's philosophy on the psychotherapeutic approaches of Binswanger and Boss.

To put Heidegger's philosophical innovations in historical perspective, remember that Husserl's transcendental phenomenology purported to be a rigorous inquiry into the structure and possibilities of consciousness, and that despite its distance from Enlightenment positivism, shared the rationalist contention — found in Descartes and Hegel — that consciousness can be completely transparent to itself, that full and complete clarity and self-knowledge is an achievable goal. By contrast, as noted previously, Heidegger said that complete self-transparency is impossible. Depending on the nature of our project, and our level of practical engagement with the world at any given moment in time, certain regions of our being are always necessarily opaque to us. A second point of divergence between Heidegger and Husserl was that Husserl allowed for the possibility of a consciousness that is utterly detached from the body, or of a *disincarnate* intellect, while Heidegger argued that *Dasein* is always being *in* the world.

Third, and most importantly, perhaps, Husserl aspired to a mode of inquiry that is entirely free from presuppositions, while Heidegger said that in order for things to "appear" or manifest themselves in the first place, we must notice them in the course of our practical engagement with the world and therefore from a specific perspective and through the prism of certain preconceptions. Perspectivity, said Heidegger, is a function of our "thrown" condition — the fact that we emerge in reality into conditions and situations that are not of our own choosing. Today the concept of thrownness is used less often than the notion of "situated subjectivity," whose derivation is as follows.

According to Heidegger, we never encounter the world in an entirely unprejudiced fashion. But unless we reflect carefully, we are often unaware of our prejudices and preconceptions, and the way they color or shape what we see. And one way of accessing or illuminating our tacit understandings of reality is a process of self-attunement, or patient sensitivity to our changing *moods*. Heidegger's discussion of moods and affect falls under the heading of *Befindlichkeit*, a term he coined from the German word *befinden*, which means situated, located, or attuned. The nearest equivalent in English might be "situated," though this merely expresses the sense of spatial location in relation to other entities and neglects to convey the reflexive dimension implied by the German phrase *sich befinden*, which means literally "to find oneself." Heidegger's idiosyncratic usage combines both senses — the discovery of one's situation and the awareness of one's emotional responses to it.

From the perspective of psychotherapy, it is important to note that like his forebears, Kierkegaard and Nietzsche, Heidegger does not address feelings of sadness, anxiety, boredom, or depression, for example, as inherently pathological states. On the contrary, said Heidegger, they are urgent reports from the depths of our own nature, and if we attend to them respectfully, they disclose important information about our relationship with our environment. Instead of seeking to banish them, or to objectify and "analyze" their irrational underpinnings, we should seek to understand them as reflections of existential actualities that have bypassed our conscious thought processes. Indeed, moods often reflect existential actualities more faithfully than our conscious cognitions: "The possibilities of disclosure which belong to cognition reach far too short a way compared with the original and basic disclosure of moods" (cited in Gendlin 1988, 55). And again, "Even if Dasein is assured in its belief . . . if in rational enlightenment it supposes itself to know . . . all this counts for nothing as against the phenomenal facts of the case" (ibid., p. 55).

Yet the notion of *Befindlichkeit* encompasses more than moods. According to Heidegger, one always finds oneself thrown, so to speak, into a particular situation that is a specific social and historical conjuncture. Unlike Dilthey, however, Heidegger did not use the term "historicity" to denote the rootedness of the present in the past. The historicity of *Dasein*, said Heidegger, breaks radically with the past. Like Scheler, Heidegger distinguished between the terms "heritage" and "tradition," and emphasized that authenticity entails an ability to take up one's "heritage" freely in ways that break with "tradition." In fact, a break with tradition is a vital prerequisite to self-determination, since the self can only know itself through the gradual unfolding of its latent possibilities, which emerge continuously in the present, flowing freely into the future, unconditioned by the past. The temporality of consciousness, as Heidegger would say, is *futural*, much as it was for Hegel and Marx. Heidegger even gave an oblique acknowledgment of this fact in his "Letter on Humanism," where he commended Marx for his awareness of the alienation or homelessness of "modern man," declaring that this rendered "the Marxist conception of history . . . superior to all others" (Friedman 1994, 262).

Heidegger's reflections on Marx, while intriguing, are also a little odd, because he approached the problem of alienation from a completely different angle. Moreover, as Marcuse once remarked, Heidegger never actually *read* Marx. Indeed, Heidegger only heard about Marx's theory of alienation from pupils like Marcuse, which casts doubt on the sincerity of this statement, which may have been intended to ingratiate Heidegger to his growing French readership, who because of Alexandre Kojève and Sartre, took Hegel and Marx very seriously. In any case, unlike Hegel and Marx, Heidegger did *not* conceive of human history as a cumulative, unified, or linear process, nor did Heidegger think of society as being comprised of different classes. The role of class dominance in deforming human subjectivity simply does not register in his accounts of human historicity, though it figures centrally in Marx.

Instead of class conflict, in *Being and Time* Heidegger describes a diffuse but intractable conflict between the "resolute individual" and *das Man,* or the "public world," which is characterized by ambiguity, idle talk (*Gerede*) and curiosity (*Neugier*). To the extent that the self becomes absorbed in the public world or "the They," says Heidegger, it "falls" into *lethe,* forgetfulness or oblivion — a basic unconsciousness of our thrown condition. However, when *Dasein,* or the fundamental structure of human subjectivity, shuts out the noise of the public world, it enters a state of *Unheimlichkeit* or the uncanny, in which *Dasein* is freed up to experience its own inner nature as "thrown." As Heidegger says in *Being and Time,* "Uncanniness is the basic kind of Being-in-the-world, even though in an everyday way it has been covered up." And again, "In uncanniness, Dasein stands together with itself primordially" (1963, 323, 333).

Heidegger's notion of *Unheimlichkeit* strikes many people as counterintuitive. After all, when you or I talk of feeling "alienated" from someone or something, we usually mean that we feel ill at ease in their presence, or at variance with their way of being. Yet the German term *Unheimlichkeit,* and its synonym *unzuhause,* which are translated as "uncanny," mean literally, "un-at-homeness," the sense of not being at home or at ease in the world. In order to grasp what Heidegger is saying, it is important to remember that Heidegger is not a therapist and is therefore not concerned with whether or not the person feels at ease. In fact, by his account, the sense of being "at home" or comfortable in the public world is a symptom of our "fallen" condition.

According to Heidegger, the sense of *Unheimlichkeit* or the uncanny only occurs when the self is deeply attuned to itself, to its essential thrown-ness (*Geworfenheit*) and possibility (*Möglichkeit*). A sense of uncanni-ness and alienation from the public world — *das Man* — heralds growing self-knowledge and self-awareness, and absent the requisite estrangement from others, genuine self-knowledge cannot be achieved. Active absorption in others prompts *Dasein* to lapse (or "fall") into inauthenticity or a denial or unawareness of its own contingency (mor-tality) and, above all, its finitude and eventual death. This marks an important difference from Marx, who looked forward to a definitive transcendence of alienation in a postrevolutionary social order. Nothing in Heidegger suggests that any amount of social change can funda-mentally alter the terms of the self and its ongoing dispersal in and recov-ery from "the world."

To put it a little differently, in Marx's theory of alienation, self-estrange-ment and alienation from others usually go hand in hand. To mitigate or abolish either one, you have to address the other as well. By con-trast, in *Being and Time*, Heidegger implies that being "at home" with oneself and with others simultaneously is ultimately impossible:

> Dasein, as a being-with which understands, can listen to the Others. Losing itself in the publicness and idle talk of the "they," it fails to hear its own-self in listening to the They-self. If Dasein is able to get brought back from this lostness of failing to hear itself, and if this is to be done through itself, then it must first be able to find itself — to find itself as something which has failed to hear itself, and which fails to hear in that it *listens away* to the they. This *listening away* must get broken off. (Heidegger 1962, 315–16)

Heidegger thinks that our "listening away" to others invariably envelops the Self in "the They" — that the true call of conscience is precisely the opposite of that "chatter." For example, he says, "In con-science Dasein calls itself. . . . The caller is unfamiliar to the everyday They-self; it is something like an alien voice. What could be more alien to the 'they,' lost in the manifold world of its concern, than the Self which has been individualized down to itself in uncanniness and been thrown into the 'nothing' "? (ibid., 321–22). And further, "The call of conscience, existentially understood, makes known for the first time what we have hitherto merely contended: that uncanniness pursues Dasein and is a threat to the lostness in which it has forgotten itself" (ibid., 322). That being so, says Heidegger, existential guilt is not to be confused with the idea of indebtedness to others, or of guilt for any act or omission that injures another.

Existential guilt is essentially a failure to actualize all of one's innermost possibilities. It is a state of self-betrayal occasioned by our inability to live out all of our deepest potentials. By this definition, everyone is already guilty, if only we have the wisdom to realize it. This renders reproaches that call us to account for specific misdeeds trivial or beside the point, especially if they plead or condemn on the basis of moral norms and obligations that are supposedly "objective" or socially constructed. For example, Heidegger says,

> And yet, if the caller — who is nobody, when seen after the manner of the world — is interpreted as a power, this seems to be a dispassionate recognition of something that one can come across Objectively. When seen correctly, however, this interpretation is only a fleeing in the face of the conscience — a way for *Dasein* to escape by slinking away from the thin wall by which the They is separated from the uncanniness of its Being. This interpretation of conscience passes itself off as recognizing the call in the sense of a voice that is "universally" binding, and which speaks in a way that is "not just subjective." Furthermore, the universal conscience becomes exalted to a world-conscience, which still has the phenomenal character of an it and nobody, yet which speaks — there in the individual subject — as this indefinite something. But this public conscience — what else is it than the voice of the They? (Ibid., 323)

Public conscience, an "indefinite something," an it and a nobody — what is it but Freud's superego, the internalization of ethical precepts and prohibitions that accompany socialization? Granted, Heidegger had not read Freud when he wrote these words, and makes no reference to internalized parental imagos. He was probably inveighing against Kantian ethics and the categorical imperative. But in every other respect, "public conscience" fits the superego's profile rather neatly. Evidently, Heidegger felt that genuine conscience is something fundamentally different, which immunizes the Self to the admonitions and reproaches of others.

In *The Gnostic Religion,* Hans Jonas calls attention to the gnostic tropes in *Being and Time.* An alien voice recalling the individual from his dispersal in collective false-consciousness is one theme. Another is the suggestion that the sense of dread, of the uncanny, is a prelude to (or corollary of) the soul's discovery of its basic situation, and that the general run of humanity try to avoid or evade an authentic self-awareness by immersion in the *lethe* or oblivion of the crowd. Finally, there is the *antinomian* thread in Heidegger's discussion of conscience, where he opposes the authentic conscience of the individual with an inauthentic (public) conscience. Like the gnostics, and like Nietzsche, Heidegger seemed to feel that the epistemic elite, those truly "in the know" about the human condition, are not bound by the same moral precepts that govern the rest of us. They are answerable to themselves alone (Jonas 1963).

While *Being and Time* aspired to being a systematic analysis of fundamental ontology, Heidegger dropped this project in the mid 1930s and shifted dramatically toward a more poetic and aphoristic style. The words "authenticity" and "resolute" almost disappeared from Heidegger's vocabulary, replaced with a new emphasis on receptivity and openness to the world. According to the later Heidegger, humans have a distinctive way of "being in the world" characterized as "ek-static," in which we may function as decentered, nonanthropocentric witnesses to Being. By Heidegger's reckoning, we are mere "clearings" in and through which Being probes its own depths, mediums for the disclosure of Being to itself.

Moreover, while the word "resolute" implies vigilance and disciplined effort, in short, human agency, the later Heidegger harbored a deepening mistrust of human agency, embodied in his various writings on technology and in his enigmatic musings on the "will-not-to-will." In *The Life of the Mind* (Arendt 1978), Arendt construed the "will-not-to-will" as emblematic of *die Kehre* — the "reversal" or "turning" that Heidegger underwent circa 1936–1940, when he was composing his two volumes on Nietzsche. On Arendt's reading, Heidegger's "will-not-to-will" represents a repudiation of Nietzsche's will to power, and his own involvement with the Nazis two years previously (Arendt 1971, 172–74). To buttress this argument, Arendt points out that the term *Sorge* — "care" or concern — originally denoted a lively apprehension or vigilance on behalf of oneself and those to whom one is closely attached. But in the later Heidegger, she contends, *Sorge* denotes an active devotion to the preservation of Being rather than an essentially *self-preservative* impulse (ibid., 183). It therefore entails a shift from a self-centered to an other-directed mode of attunement, expressed, among other things, in Heidegger's new emphasis on the relationships between language and Being.

In fairness to Arendt, in this period of Heidegger's work, human agency is regarded warily, at best, and the attuned and responsive person is described variously as a "guardian" or "servant" or "shepherd" of Being, ever on the alert for encroaching threats, ever ready to witness, to facilitate or lend a hand. The kind of activeness at issue here does not appear to be striving on its own behalf. It does not initiate, interrogate, transform, or create on its own behalf. Nor does it seek self-fulfillment or self-expression in the creative act. It simply watches and protects and is "obedient" to Being. It does not speak, but is "spoken" by language.

Unlike Scheler and Jaspers, who read and responded promptly to Freud's ideas, Heidegger only read some Freud in the 1950s, and then only at the request of his friend, the Swiss psychiatrist and psychoanalyst Medard Boss. Heidegger's reaction to Freud, and to psychoanalysis in general was not positive. Indeed, according to Boss, Heidegger "couldn't believe that such an intelligent man could write such stupid things, such fantastical things, about men and women" (cited by Craig 1988, 34). Freud himself remained unfamiliar with the philosopher, though one can justifiably ask whether he would not have been similarly mystified by Heidegger's work. In contrast to Freud, the French psychoanalyst Jacques Lacan had a strong interest in Heidegger, going so far as to translate Heidegger's *Logos* essay during the early 1950s. But Lacan's interest was not reciprocated. In a letter to Boss, Heidegger (2001, 279–80) refers to Lacan's chief work,

Ecrits, as "obviously baroque," and quips, "I think the psychiatrist needs a psychiatrist!"

Heidegger's relationship with Ludwig Binswanger is more complicated. Binswanger was an early student of Freud, but was interested in the application of philosophy to psychotherapy and maintained a critical stance toward psychoanalysis. After *Being and Time* appeared in 1927, Binswanger sought to apply some of Heidegger's ideas about *Dasein* to the practice of psychotherapy, calling his approach *Daseinsanalysis,* which we will explore fully in the following chapter. Heidegger initially greeted Binswanger's approach with enthusiasm. Of Binswanger's chief — and still untranslated — book, *Basic Forms and Knowledge of Human Existence* (1942), Heidegger states, "Your work is so broadly conceived, and so rich in phenomena, that one would think that anyone who can see must recognize where you locate the entirety of psychopathology. However, because it deals with something so simple, most readers will have overlooked . . . the feat that you have accomplished in taking the step from the subject object relation to being-in-the-world. I thank you for the existence of your great work" (Frie 1999c, 250). Despite the tone of Heidegger's remarks, a productive interaction between the two men was not to be. In 1947 Heidegger received a visit from Boss, who was introduced to the philosopher's work by Binswanger. Boss and Heidegger soon became close friends and colleagues and as a result of their cooperation, Heidegger distanced himself from Binswanger's reading of his work (Boss 1957; Heidegger 2001).

At the invitation of Boss, Heidegger made trips to Zollikon, Switzerland, to speak to a group of some 50 psychiatrists over a period of ten years (1959–1969). Heidegger's *Zollikon Seminars* (2001) offer a course on some of the fundamental concepts of *Being and Time* as well as a number of newer themes and are significant because they reflect the philosopher's interest in conveying the relevance of his work for a wider, clinical audience. In the course of these seminars, Heidegger's views on Freud become clear. Heidegger's main critique focuses on Freud's notion of the unconscious, which he sees as the underside of the Cartesian conception of consciousness and utterly rejects. More important, perhaps, are Heidegger's views on the notion of embodiment.

The body had been almost entirely overlooked in *Being and Time*. Heidegger clearly distinguishes between body as *Körper* and the body as *Leib* and sees the limit of the former as one's skin and the limit of the latter as the horizon of the world for *Dasein* as being-in-the-world (2001, 86). His elaboration of embodiment allows for more detailed consideration of the affective dimension. Some of the sharpest critique, however, is directed at Binswanger, who, as we will see in the following chapter, took issue with Heidegger's notion of care (*Sorge*). But before we ponder the relationship between Heidegger, Binswanger, and Boss, we should size up Heidegger in terms of our heuristic schemata.

Heidegger was so vehemently opposed to anything Cartesian, so wary of science and technology, that he can only be classified as an irrationalist. His political stance was predicated on the assumption of unceasing tension between the individual and society, or the call of conscience and "the They," at least initially, and was profoundly anti-utopian. However, there are fleeting hints of a utopian sensibility in the later Heidegger, and some evidence for a global shift in his thinking during the course of the Second World War. The early Heidegger was a modernist who emphasized the active role of the subject in shaping his or her own destiny, while the later Heidegger was an incipient postmodernist, emphasizing a decentered subject who is not an actor so much as acted upon, whose virtue resides in an openness to Being.

While often commended for his originality on this score, the fact remains that Heidegger's critique of humanism after *die Kehre* was not particularly original. In fact, it was essentially a restatement of Taoism. But the intriguing thing about it is that despite their quietist and manifestly conservative tone, Heidegger's antihumanist rhetoric was taken up by left-wing, poststructuralist intellectuals like Louis Althusser, Foucault, Derrida, and others, ostensibly as a tool of ideological "subversion." Next to Nietzsche's transformation from a fascist icon to the darling of the Left, the transformation of Heidegger's antihumanism from a right-wing to a left-wing phenomenon is the most improbable story in the history of twentieth century philosophy.

The difficulty with the contemporary French poststructuralist interpretation of Heidegger is that it overlooks the importance of reading

Being and Time as a philosophical anthropology. The later Heidegger sought to distance himself from the works of Binswanger, Sartre, and others because they emphasized the role of *Dasein* as a human being. Yet it is precisely the notion of the human being as situated in a world of shared understanding that provides the basis for psychotherapy. In Heidegger's later theory, the concept of a decentered subject to which being simply reveals itself does not account for the grounded nature of our experience. Nor is there a place for an ethics of choice, which resides in our agency. Ironically, perhaps, it is Heidegger's anthropological notion of being-in-the-world that furnishes a concept of the human subject as agent that is necessary to counter the political swings in his philosophy. The human being is not only acted on, she is a grounded subject, an actor who must account for the nature of her actions.

Heidegger is most difficult to gauge in the religious dimension. He renounced Catholicism in 1919, and with Nietzsche inveighed against Platonic and Christian otherworldliness. But Heidegger also denounced the "worldliness" of *das Man,* and sounded distinctly like a religious moralist when he did so. As Jean-Paul Sartre once pointed out, the "moodedness" of these passages masks an unmistakable ethical judgment, despite the claim that the distinction between authenticity and inauthenticity has nothing to do with ethics. Indeed, Heidegger's contempt for inauthenticity and the "worldliness" of *das Man* and the "public conscience" is unmistakable. Heidegger's refusal to acknowledge this fact could only be sustained by self-deception. When Sartre had the misfortune to suggest that Heidegger was an atheist, Heidegger recoiled angrily, arguing that he did not rule out a possible transcendence at some indefinite point in the future. That being so, it is impossible to classify Heidegger as either a religious or irreligious thinker. We must settle for the odd and ambiguous conclusion that he was both, in some sense.

Modes of Relatedness
Buber, Binswanger, and Boss

MARTIN BUBER

Martin Buber was born in Vienna in 1878 and was raised by his paternal grandparents. His grandfather Solomon, a wealthy philanthropist, was steeped in rabbinic commentary on the Hebrew Bible, while his grandmother, Adele, was versed in Moses Mendelsohn, the German Enlightenment, and efforts to modernize European Jewry. So Buber's childhood environment tugged him in different directions — back toward the medieval sensibilities of his grandfather, and forward into modernity and the emerging Zionist milieu. Buber's secondary education gave him a strong background in the classics — so much so that his Jewish identity became quite tenuous during adolescence. During his university studies in Vienna, Berlin, Leipzig, and Zurich, Buber studied Hinduism, Buddhism, and Taoism and eventually wrote a doctoral dissertation comparing two Christian mystics, Nicholas of Cusa and Jacob Böhme, under Wilhelm Dilthey's supervision (Buber 1973).

As his university career came to an end in 1900, Buber found himself looking for ways of affirming and expressing his Jewishness in a secular, nonreligious frame of reference, when Theodor Herzl invited him to edit the Zionist weekly, *Die Welt*, in 1901. That same year, Buber married Paula Winckler and began a lengthy immersion in Hasidism, which resulted in publications that introduced this eastern European Jewish movement to a wider Western audience. He also became familiar with Achad Ha'am, a Zionist leader whose orientation was less secular than Herzl's, more mindful of Jewish faith and spirituality, and more receptive to the possibility of Arab-Jewish dialogue. In 1916, Buber met Franz Rosenzweig (with whom he began translating the Hebrew Bible in 1925) and pointedly broke with Herzl, whom he felt lacked a deep feeling for Judaism. That same year, he founded a new journal, *Der Jude,* which promoted Arab-Jewish reconciliation and a binational Israeli-Palestinian state, until 1924.

In 1923, Buber published his most famous book, *Ich und Du* (Buber 1983), which is often (incorrectly) translated as *I and Thou* (Buber 1970). Long before it claimed the attention of psychologists and psychotherapists, the work gained a sympathetic audience among Protestant theologians. Walter Kaufmann, who produced the most recent translation of *Ich und Du,* blames these same theologians for the mistranslation of the book's title as "I and Thou." The German *Du* simply means "you," but unlike "thou" — which is translated by the German *Sie* — it is intimate and informal, the way one would address a friend or a lover. Apparently, Christian theologians could not bear to address God in such intimate terms, even though eastern European Jews did so routinely in prayer, though not in print, which has iconic properties.

In 1933, Buber reopened the Freies Jüdisches Lehrhaus, an institute for general Jewish adult education in Frankfurt that Rosenzweig had opened by in 1920, and which was closed at his death in 1929. Many celebrated Jewish intellectuals — Gershom Scholem, S. Y. Agnon, Ernst Simon, Erich Fromm, and others — studied or taught there before the Second World War. This organization flourished under Buber for two years until the Nazis shut it down. In 1936, at 60 years old, Buber emigrated to Palestine, where he accepted a professorship at the Hebrew University in Jerusalem, and continued working on his Bible translation, which appeared in 1961.

In 1947, the British ended their turbulent occupation of Palestine, and the United Nations mandated the creation of two national entities, one Jewish, one Arab, in what is now the State of Israel. This was a blow to Buber, who had hoped for a binational state based on principles of mutual recognition and respect, a pluralistic society where Arabs and Jews together lived in peace and fellowship. Buber never relinquished his dream of such a state, and he advocated efforts to initiate direct dialogue with Israel's Arab neighbors throughout the cold war era — so much so, in fact, that a delegation from the Arab Student's Organization in Israel laid a wreath on his grave after his death in 1965.

Buber's reflections on dialogue, meeting, and encountering "otherness" have had an enormous impact on leading psychotherapists, including Ludwig Binswanger, Frieda Fromm-Reichmann, Erik Erikson, Leslie Farber, Hans Trub, Carl Rogers, Rollo May, R. D. Laing, and Maurice Friedman. To grasp Buber's impact on twentieth century psychotherapy, bear in mind that Heidegger's analysis of human existence hinged on the distinction between two different *modes of being* — inauthentic and authentic. Authenticity is only achieved by a turning away from the public world: a deliberate "breaking off" of the "listening away" to *das Man*. But as Buber often noted, this way of bifurcating human existence implies that our "being-for" and "being-with" others obscures or obstructs our self-realization, which is only achieved in solitary reflection, or a resolute "being-for-oneself."

By contrast, Buber's existentialism hinges on two different *modes of relatedness to others,* the I-Thou and the I-It orientation. The I-Thou is based on the principles of openness and affirmation, and engages the whole person, who addresses the other with respect and concern, even in difficult circumstances, or in the midst of anger. Communion and conflict can both be encompassed in the I-Thou mode of relatedness, provided that the whole person is engaged and addresses the other with full ethical responsibility. The I-It orientation engages but a fraction of ourselves — our intellect, our lust, our curiosity — and leaves the rest of us disengaged or indifferent to the other person's fate. Moreover, it openly or implicitly depersonalizes others, and it allows for mutual accommodation or conflict, but precludes genuine meeting or communion.

Buber's views on science and reason also warrant close attention. Though it aspires to omniscience, said Buber, reason divorced from the heart — and by implication, from human subjectivity — is intrinsically limited because reality can never be completely sorted out in any

definitive juggling of concepts and categories, however complexly articulated. Meanwhile, said Buber, love is also a valid path to knowledge,
not merely of other people, but of reality as a whole. In *Pointing the
Way,* for example, Buber says,

> What the most learned and ingenious combination of concepts denies,
> the humble and faithful beholding, grasping, knowing of any situation
> bestows. The world is not comprehensible, but it is embraceable:
> through the embracing of one of its beings. . . .
>
> The loving man is one who grasps non-relatively each thing he
> grasps. He does not think of inserting the experienced thing into rela-
> tions with other things; at the moment of experience nothing else exists,
> nothing save this beloved thing, filling out the world and indistin-
> guishably coinciding with it. . . .
>
> True science is a loving science. The man who pursues such science
> is confronted by the secret life of things which has confronted none before
> him; this life places itself in his hands, and he experiences it, and is filled
> with its happening to the rim of his existence. (Cited in Friedman 1994,
> 104–5)

Buber had studied Kräpelinian psychiatry for three semesters and
participated in psychological experiments in Wilhelm Wundt's laboratory in Leipzig while a university student (Buber 1973). If the above
remarks are any indication, Buber must have found the experience very
frustrating. Though he does not cite them by name, it is clear from
the context that, in Buber's estimation, neither Emil Kräpelin nor
Wundt provided access to the secrets of the human heart. But then,
neither did Freud — at least where Buber was concerned. Like most
of us, Freud used the word "love" more or less synonymously with
"libido" or "desire," and following Plato likened the process of falling
in love to psychosis. By his account, being in love entails a "sexual over-
estimation" or idealization of the beloved that distorts one's judgment
profoundly. Freud spoke of love in privative terms, as a response to an
experienced lack or deficit, or a transference process in which long
repressed yearnings for the parent of the opposite sex are unconsciously
reenacted. Such passions do not enhance our love of truth or our grasp
of reality. If anything, they diminish them. So to speak of a "loving

science," as Buber did, makes no sense at all from a Freudian perspective.

Freud describes love as a phenomenon rooted in scarcity, a lack, a search for tension-reduction. Buber, like his erstwhile friend, Max Scheler, describes love as a phenomenon of abundance, of generosity of spirit. And whereas Freud says that love impairs our judgment, Buber says that it deepens it. Finally, while Freud treats love as a completely involuntary and irrational process, Buber treats it as a voluntary process of witnessing, affirming, bestowing a sense of worth and recognition on others, analogous to gift-giving. The question then arises: Are we talking about the same phenomenon? Are attraction, desire, attachment, and love truly synonyms? Or are attraction, desire, and attachment actually deformations, impediments or obstructions to love?

No matter how we define it, Buber clearly overstates the importance of love for the natural sciences, which flourish even in its absence. But by the same token, a *human* science *not* guided by love (in Buber's sense) is likely to go astray. Despite his agreement with Scheler on this issue, Buber differed dramatically from Scheler in his overall assessment of Freud. For example, Scheler argued that repression is an everyday phenomenon that can be understood phenomenologically, and endorsed Freud's assertion that love and spiritual life are built upon the repression and sublimation of our vital instincts. In *Between Man and Man* (1965a), however, Buber argues that,

> it is not inherent in spirit, as Scheler contends, to arise by repression and the sublimation of the instincts. Scheler . . . takes these psychological categories from Sigmund Freud. . . . But though these categories have general validity, the central position which Freud gives them, their dominating significance for the whole structure of personal and communal life, and especially for the origin and development of the spirit, is not based on the general life of man but only on the situation and qualities of the typical man of today. But this man is sick, both in his relation to others and in his very soul. The central significance of repression and sublimation in Freud's system derives from the analysis of a pathological condition and is valid for this condition. (232–33)

Nevertheless, Buber allows that Freud's ideas are valid for our time, and for others that evince a similar "pathological condition." However, even there, says Buber, the core pathology of civilized communities is not an intractable conflict between our instinctual endowment and the requirements of civilization, but a pervasive lack of trust. When people trust the communities they live in to provide social and spiritual support, to allow and encourage them to be genuine, the average person

> must often . . . adapt his wishes to the commands of his community; but he must not repress them to the extent that the repression requires a dominating significance for his life. They often coalesce with the needs of his community, which are expressed by its commands. . . . Only if the organic community disintegrates from within and mistrust becomes life's basic note does the repression acquire its dominating importance. The unaffectedness of wishing is stifled by mistrust, everything around is hostile, or can become hostile. Agreement between one's own and others' desires ceases . . . and the dulled wishes creep hopelessly into the recesses of the soul. . . . The divorce between spirit and instincts is here, as often, the consequence of the divorce between man and man. (1965a, 233)

In other words, Freud's ideas only pertain to the broad generality of people in a society afflicted with spiritual malaise. Where trust is absent or eroded, repression intensifies to a considerable extent, and both sexuality and spirituality become disfigured by the furtive manifestations of unfulfilled desire. Freud's reflections on "the pathology of civilized communities," based on the study of disturbed souls, generalize indiscriminately from the present to the past and future and do not furnish the basis for a genuine understanding of human society. There is no inexorable conflict between the promptings of nature and the requirements of civilization. The "divorce between spirit and instincts" is the result of a social malaise, the "divorce between man and man" — and not, as some insist, between man and God.

Buber occupies a unique position among the philosophers we have examined so far. Kierkegaard, Nietzsche, and, more covertly, early Heidegger, were all radical individualists. To a large extent, mistrust of collectivism is what drove their philosophies. Like Freud somewhat later, albeit for different reasons, they believed that the interests of the individual and the community at large are *necessarily* antagonistic. Buber disagreed. Following in the dialogic tradition of Friedrich Heinrich

Jacobi, Ludwig Feuerbach, and Marx, Buber states that an "organic community" does not promote conformity, nor attempt to erase difference. The attempt to reduce the other to one's own terms, to level or abolish differences in an indifferent sameness, is the expression of a reifying I-It attitude rather than the I-Thou orientation. Buber concludes that *both* individualism and collectivism are one-sided ideologies, which obscure the intrinsically relational character of human existence.

However, though he accords it a different role and a different meaning than Heidegger does, solitude remains an intrinsic and invaluable element in Buber's account of human experience. Genuine subjectivity cannot flourish when the "I" is submerged in the anonymity of the crowd. But neither can it remain fixed in solitude or inwardness, as Kierkegaard or Heidegger suggest. In *I and Thou*, Buber says,

> the "I" that steps out of the relational event into separation and consciousness of separation does not lose its reality. Its sharing is preserved in it in a living way. . . . This is the province of subjectivity in which the *I* is aware with a single awareness of its solidarity of connection and its separation. Genuine subjectivity can only be dynamically understood as the swinging of the *I* in its lonely truth. Here, too, is the place where the desire is formed and heightened for ever higher, more unconditioned relation, for the full sharing in being. In subjectivity the spiritual substance of the person matures. (Cited in Freidman 1994, 162)

In "Distance and Relation," published in 1951, Buber amplified on this theme:

> "Becoming a self with me" . . . is ontologically complete only when the other knows that he is made present by me in his self and when this knowledge induces the process of his inmost self-becoming. For the inmost growth of the self is not accomplished, as people like to suppose today, in man's relation to himself, but in the relation between one and the other . . . in the making present of another self and in the knowledge that one is made present to his own self by the other. (Buber 1965b, 71)

What are the implications of Buber's philosophy for the practice of psychotherapy? Unlike Heidegger, who left it to others to infer how best to apply his philosophical precepts to psychotherapy, and was often unsatisfied with the results, Buber addressed psychotherapists directly in his writings. But even when he was not discussing Freud or psychotherapy specifically, some general conclusions may be gleaned from his remarks. For example, at various points, Buber notes that an I-It orientation may be culturally congruent and may foster smooth adaptation to one's social surroundings. In any given situation, it may be easier to treat the other person as a means (or as an obstacle) to the fulfillment of my own desires rather than an end in himself or herself, especially when the stakes are high and the outcome of events uncertain. Alternatively, the structure of authority or my social role as employer, administrator, lawmaker, or law enforcer may compel me to treat the other person as the embodiment of a heuristic abstraction, an ethnic, class, or gender category, rather than a unique individual. Or again, as a scientific researcher, I can regard the other person naturalistically, as an organism whose behavior is void of personal meaning or intention, and regulated by impersonal natural laws or as a particularly striking specimen of a psychopathological syndrome — a "typical" hysteric, obsessional, or schizophrenic.

In other words, exploitation, classification, and control are ubiquitous in human society and frequently go hand in hand, making a predominantly I-Thou orientation difficult to sustain in our day-to-day lives. Buber is quite conscious of this. But if the goal of therapy is to enable to the patient to be fully alive, and fully responsible, it makes no sense to frame the goal of therapy as narrowly as the removal of "target" symptoms, or as "adjustment" or adaptation to society. For Buber, psychotherapy is — among other things, but above all — an *ethical* dialogue, and rich, enlivening contact with others is impossible in the absence of (inner and interpersonal) honesty and responsibility.

The preceding remarks render some of Buber's quarrels with Freud and Heidegger, and Buber's concept of "existential guilt," more intelligible. Buber acknowledges the existence of a super-ego, which is the embodiment of parental and societal ideals and prohibitions. Transgression against its normative principles causes inner conflict. But Buber also seeks to distinguish between "neurotic guilt" and real, ontological guilt, complaining that most psychotherapists, following Freud, trivialize real conscious guilt feelings by treating them as the by-products of an intrapsychic disturbance, a symptom to be analyzed and excised, rather than an *existential* and therefore interpersonal problem. "[T]here exists real guilt, fundamentally different from the anxiety-induced bugbears that are generated in the cavern of the unconscious" (cited in Friedman 1994, 393). Psychotherapists often collude with their patients' desire to avoid owning their responsibility and addressing real, existential guilt by dwelling on early childhood antecedents to their actions and experiences. Or they dwell on furtive desires and fantasies that accompany them, all of which may be guilt- or anxiety-inducing in their own right, but which obscure, rather than illumine, the core of the problem. Instead of pointing to a distant and forgotten past, says Buber, unresolved guilt feelings often point to an unaccomplished task for the present and the future. Now the therapist's task, he said, is

> first, to illumine the darkness that still weaves itself about the guilt . . . not to illuminate it with spotlights but with abroad and enduring wave of light; second to persevere, no matter how high he may have ascended in his present life above that station of guilt — to persevere in that newly won humble knowledge of the identity of the present person with the person of that time; and third, in his place and according to his capacity, in the given historical and biographical situations, to restore the order of being injured by him through the relation of an active devotion to the world — for the wounds of an order of being can be healed in infinitely many other places than those at which they were inflicted. (Cited in Freidman 1994, 394)

Though couched in existential language, Buber's therapeutic prescriptions clearly derive from Jewish sources. Rabbinic Judaism emphasizes that the only proper way to atone for sin is through "active devotion to the world," and argues that after a period of grim inner reckoning, a return to the path of righteousness leads to reconciliation and renewed hopefulness. Buber also borrows from the Kabbalah, the Jewish mystical literature that stretches from the eleventh to eighteenth centuries. According to this tradition, sin is not merely a transgression of a divine command; it is an event with cosmic repercussions because, in Buber's words, it violates "an order of Being." Genuine repentance or *tikkun olam* does not merely justify the individual in the eyes of God, but helps to put the entire cosmos back in harmony and hastens the eventual arrival of the Messiah, enhancing the common good. Indeed, until the process of *tikkun* has healed the manifold wounds of Being, say the kabbalists, the Messiah will tarry and the messianic age will remain beyond our grasp. So while we may cherish God's love and forgiveness, our redemption ultimately depends on us and our deeds, not on any act of supernatural grace.

Now, contrast Buber's notion of "existential guilt" with Heidegger's. Heidegger conceived of existential guilt as an intrinsic and ineradicable aspect of the human condition, rather than a pathological intrusion on our lives. But he depicted it as a form of self-betrayal, or a failure to actualize one's innate potential — in short, as a deficiency or deformity in our relationship to ourselves, rather than to others and the world at large. This prompted Buber to criticize Heidegger's concept of existence in *Between Man and Man* (1965a) as being "monological" rather than "dialogical." In a manner strikingly akin to Ludwig Binswanger, Buber says,

> Heidegger's "existence" is monological. And monologue may certainly disguise itself ingeniously for a while as dialogue, one unknown layer after the other of the human self may certainly answer the inner address, so that man makes ever fresh discoveries and can suppose that he is really experiencing a "calling" and a "hearing"; but the hour of stark, final solitude comes when the numbness of being becomes insuperable and the ontological categories no longer want to be applied to reality. When the man who has become solitary can no longer say "thou" to the "dead" known God, everything depends on whether he can still say it to the living unknown God by saying "thou" with all his being to another living and known man. If he can no longer do this either, then there certainly remains for him the sublime illusion of detached thought that he is a self-contained self; as man he is lost. The man of "real" existence in Heidegger's sense, the man of "self-being," who in Heidegger's view is the goal of life, is not the man who really lives with man, but the man who knows a real life only in communication with himself. . . . Heidegger isolates from the wholeness of life the . . . situation of the radically solitary man, and wants to derive the essence of human existence from the experience of a nightmare. (Cited in Freidman 1994, 225)

What else can we learn from Buber's philosophy for psychotherapeutic purposes? The terms "abstinence," "empathy," and "confrontation" come to mind. The term "abstinence" was coined by Freud to denote the analyst's deliberate refusal to gratify what she or he perceived to be the patient's attempt to elicit expressions of love or respect from the analyst. Gratifying the patient's wishes or demands in this regard, said Freud, would only impede the patient's transference or increase their dependency needs. Rather than treat the request as an appropriate or realistic one, classical Freudians tended to *interpret* it as the deferred or derivative expression of some early but unmet need that is being reenacted in the transference. Again, Buber disagreed. He did not dismiss the idea of transference or a neurotic demand for love, but like Ferenczi, Fromm, and other analytic dissidents, said that there are many instances when the therapist's refusal to affirm the patient's worth is tactless or positively harmful.

Buber also differed from classical Freudians in the realm of confrontation, which occurs when a therapist calls attention to attitudes or inconsistencies in a patient's conduct or beliefs that betray an element of insincerity or self-deception. In such circumstances, there is also a discrepancy between how the patient views himself or herself, and how the therapist sees the patient. *How*, then, does the therapist address these disparities? In most therapeutic modalities, confrontation is usually tactful, sympathetic, and low key. It is timed and calibrated carefully not to overwhelm or embarrass the patient, and presupposes a good deal of "accurate empathy," which is a therapist's ability to see the patient as she sees herself.

In some therapeutic modalities, however, confrontation can be quite spirited and demanding. Steeped in the prophetic literature, Buber regards anger as something that, in certain circumstances, is appropriate, and motivated by what Paul Tillich calls "ultimate concern" rather than what Freud terms "counter-transference." Therefore, says Buber, the expression of anger may be vital to establishing or sustaining the authenticity of the relationship between therapist and patient. Alternatively, one could frame the issue as a therapist's refusal to collude with a patient's efforts to authenticate a false self, as R. D. Laing later did. Either way, what Carl Rogers terms "unconditional positive regard" is not deemed practical or therapeutic in the long run (Buber 1965b, appendix).

If this approach sounds radical to some, bear in mind that many of Buber's therapeutic prescriptions also seem distinctly conservative. In Buber's estimation, a completely reciprocal I-Thou relationship between therapist and patient is precluded by the nature of the therapeutic contract. In other words, strange as it sounds, the healer of souls seeks to promote an I-Thou orientation by evoking an awareness, a desire, and a capacity for fully reciprocal I-Thou relationships, but without expecting or even encouraging the emergence of such an attitude toward himself or herself.

Because an effective therapist, no matter how empathic, must maintain a certain distance with respect to the patient, the therapist must approach the patient with disinterested concern, and without entertaining the hope or expectation of meeting his own needs, even after the patient has made significant progress. Buber's emphasis on distance — which is not to be confused with "neutrality" — has another obvious implication. In the course of the therapeutic dialogue, the patient is expected to disclose a great deal about herself, including issues and experiences that may be fraught with shame, guilt, anger, pain, perplexity, and so on. In Buber's view, the therapist should not respond in kind, or do so in a selective and judicious manner. Buber sought to maintain the asymmetrical character of the therapeutic dialogue and saw it as a prerequisite to a therapist's effectiveness, rather than an instrument of power or domination, as Foucault, for example, did. On the face of it, Buber prescribes two different, if not contradictory attitudes: take risks, but keep your distance. However, these prescriptions only sound contradictory. Clinical judgment determines whether one approach or the other is more appropriate at a potentially critical juncture. The trick is to know which is which.

How does Buber's work stand up in light of the heuristic schemata we have employed thus far? On the whole, Buber was an irrationalist with strong religious and utopian tendencies. Moreover, though he construed Freud and Heidegger's ideas as symptomatic of the malaise of modernity, and reflected at length on the importance of dialogue and difference in human affairs, he would likely eschew postmodernism because of his emphasis on personal agency in his concept of "existential guilt." That being so, we have no alternative but to classify him as a modern thinker.

Ludwig Binswanger

Ludwig Binswanger was born in Kreuzlingen, Switzerland, in 1881, to a family of prominent psychiatrists. Binswanger attended the universities of Lausanne, Heidelberg, and Zurich, and he received his medical degree from Zurich in 1907. He trained as a psychiatrist under Bleuler and Jung at the Burghölzli Hospital in Zurich and was offered the directorship of the Burghölzli when Bleuler stepped down, but chose to remain director of his family's Bellevue Sanatorium in Kreuzlingen, which was founded by his grandfather in 1857. Under his stewardship, Bellevue Sanatorium became a famous center for psychiatric treatment. Among its patients were such well-known personalities as the Swiss artist Ernst Ludwig Kirchner, the Russian dancer Vaslav Nijinsky, and the German sociologist Max Weber. Among the prominent philosophers and psychoanalysts who visited Binswanger in Kreuzlingen were Freud, Husserl, Heidegger, Buber, Löwith, Cassirer, Pfänder, and Scheler. Binswanger retired from clinical work in 1956, but remained an active writer, publishing his last work just one year before his death in 1966.

Binswanger bridged the divide between psychiatry, psychoanalysis, and philosophy with relative ease. In 1907, he accompanied Jung to Vienna to meet Freud, and developed a friendship with him that survived the rupture with Jung in 1911–1912 and was sustained through personal visits and correspondence until the Freud's death in 1939 (appendix A). Meanwhile, as his interests in philosophy grew, Binswanger entered into correspondence with Husserl, Heidegger, and Buber. He never became a follower of a particular thinker or school of thought; nor did he found a school of his own. Nevertheless, his work influenced many famous clinicians, including Viktor von Gebsattel, Eugène Minkowski, Erwin Straus, and Roland Kuhn, who, following Binswanger's lead pioneered studies of the experience of space and time in schizo-phrenia, mania, and severe depression. Henri Ellenberger, a French Canadian psychiatrist and psychoanalyst, was another of Binswanger's pupils, as was the young Michel Foucault, who found Binswanger's work an attractive alternative to classical Freudian theory. (Foucault, however, broke with Binswanger in 1956, rejecting all forms of philo-sophical anthropology as retrograde and repressive.)

Binswanger was first introduced to English-speaking audiences in the late 1950s by Rollo May, Henri Ellenberger, and Ernst Angel in *Existence: A New Dimension in Psychiatry and Psychology* (May, Angel, and Ellenberger 1958). A few years later, Jacob Needleman translated some of Binswanger's essays and case studies in *Being-in-the-World: The Selected Papers of Ludwig Binswanger* (Needleman 1963). During the sixties and seventies, Binswanger achieved a measured popularity within humanistic psychology, but is now relatively unknown in the Anglo-American world because his writing is deemed too abstract or too distant from the concerns of contemporary psychology. Besides, most of Binswanger's writings have not yet been translated into English. Thus, what we do know of Binswanger is based mostly on dated com-mentaries and translations that are frequently imprecise. For this rea-son, our discussion draws on untranslated works. The situation is quite different in current-day Germany and Switzerland, where there is con-tinued interest in Binswanger's work. This is apparent in the recent publication of his *Selected Works* (Binswanger 1992, 1993a, 1993b, 1994) and a series of monographs and articles that examine the significance of his psychology (compare Herzog 1994; Hoffman 1997; Holzhey-Kunz 1990).

In *Freud: Reminiscences of a Friendship,* Binswanger (1956) remarks that his scientific development was determined by his effort to formulate a philosophical as well as scientific basis for psychoanalysis. In 1909, while working at the University of Jena, Binswanger published the first psychoanalytic case study at a German university psychiatric clinic. In 1910, he became president of the Zurich Psychoanalytic Society. However, even in this early period, Binswanger was critical of the neurological and physiological assumptions on which Freud's models of the mind were based, and sought to develop an account of human nature that was not reductionistic. This project culminated in his first book, *Introduction to the Problems of General Psychology* (1922). Though dedicated to "my teachers, Bleuler and Freud," it marked the turn toward philosophy that characterized Binswanger's later work. At this point, Husserl's transcendental phenomenology provided Binswanger with a useful way to address the "visual reality" of his patients.

While Husserl introduced Binswanger to phenomenological inquiry in the early 1920s, Heidegger's *Being and Time,* published in 1927, influenced him even more profoundly. According to Binswanger, Heidegger's fundamental ontology provided an analysis of the primary structures of human existence and constituted a necessary foundation for the human sciences. In *Being and Time,* Heidegger calls for the return to the meaning of Being as such. *Dasein* questions the meaning of Being and is neither autonomous nor self-contained, but always already situated in the world. As interpreted by Binswanger, this means that we are not isolated, encapsulated egos, but beings who are always in relation to other humans and the world around us. And correlatively, there is neither a subject-object dichotomy nor a division between subjective and objective experience. Heidegger's conception of world — the matrix of relations in which *Dasein* exists and discovers meaning — provides the clinician with a powerful tool for understanding and describing human experience.

Building on Heidegger's philosophy, Binswanger distinguished among three simultaneous modes of being-in-the-world: the *Umwelt,* constituting the environment within which a person exists; the *Mitwelt,* or world of social relations; and the *Eigenwelt,* the private world of self. According to Binswanger, the three modes of being-in-the-world constitute the basis for a person's "world design" — the general context of meaning within which a person exists (Binswanger 1955, 1993c). Binswanger's reading of *Being and Time,* which for a time set the standard for interested psychologists and psychiatrists, was not entirely faithful to the philosopher's text. However, Binswanger's creative misreading of Heidegger does not diminish his importance as a thinker.

Long before Boss and Heidegger conducted the Zollikon seminars, Binswanger addressed the central defect in Freud's metapsychology.

Freud and his followers attempted to render disturbed or disturbing behavior intelligible by elucidating the impact of the patient's "inner" world of unconscious representations on his conscious experience of (and attitudes toward) his "external" world, that is, his physical and social surroundings and vice versa. Thus, behavioral anomalies were explained as the result of conflict, distortion, and disequilibrium in the patient's inner world, which in turn, could be catalyzed by events or relationships in the external world, and so on.

Unfortunately, this method of interpretation replicates the Cartesian split between "res mens" and "res extensa." This dualistic way of mapping experience fails to capture the fundamental coinherence of "person" and "world" — being-in-the-world — that Heidegger highlighted, and that Binswanger, in turn, sought to rectify with his concept of world design. Accordingly, from 1927 onward, Binswanger no longer interpreted patients' experiences in terms of a mental apparatus, or the dynamic interchanges between structures or systems in the psyche.

In "Freud and the Magna Charta of Clinical Psychiatry," published in 1936, Binswanger completely broke with this way of thinking. Binswanger saw Freud as he saw himself, and wanted to be seen by others — as an unwavering positivist. And in that spirit, Binswanger embarked on a thorough assessment of Freud's debt to nineteenth century theorists who speculated on the "dynamic unconscious," tracing Freud's theory of instincts and unconscious representations back to Johann Friedrich Herbart, Wilhelm Griesinger, Gustav Theodor Fechner, Ernst Brücke, Carl Wernicke, and Theodor Meynert, among others. "Freud and the Magna Charta of Clinical Psychiatry" was perhaps one of the earliest attempts to situate Freud in the history of psychiatry, and no doubt inspired Henri Ellenberger's monumental study, *The Discovery of the Unconscious* (1970). Leaving Freud's intellectual antecedents aside, however, the fact remains that, from a phenomenological standpoint, "person" and "world" are always inextricably intertwined.

Applying Binswanger's perspective to clinical work obligates the clinician to understand the human being in the totality of his or her existence, which includes his or her relationship to others. Thus, the aim of psychotherapy is not to make the unconscious conscious, in the traditional Freudian sense, but to free patients from distorted modes of relating to others and the world around them. Much as he dismissed Freud's metapsychology, however, Binswanger did acknowledge the role of unconscious processes in human behavior. In his view, "the unconscious" refers to an aspect of the human mind that is not present to consciousness. But it does not exist as a world of its own, nor does it relate to itself through a world (Binswanger 1955). Rather, the unconscious can be understood more along the lines of what the interpersonal psychiatrist and psychoanalyst Harry Stack Sullivan (1953a) refers to as "unformulated experience" — experience that has yet to be articulated, elaborated, or fully understood, and remains unattended to.

Likewise with Freud's libido theory. Although the concept of libido was reformulated several times in the course of Freud's career, it always referred to instinctual or sexual energy, and was articulated in terms of the hydraulic metaphor. In Freud's metapsychology, other people primarily take the role of "objects" for the gratification of instinctual desires. Interpersonal relations thus have their origin in the discovery that other people aid in the reduction of tensions. Binswanger rejected this outright. In Binswanger's conception of the I-Thou relation, which was inspired by Buber, the other person is *not* simply a means to an end, libidinous or otherwise. On the contrary, in the dialogic discovery and affirmation of selves, the other person becomes a vital *participant* in the process of self-realization. Accordingly, Binswanger notes, "The monstrous difference between the *genetic derivation* of all forms of love from a single source and the disclosure of love as a unified anthropological originary phenomenon, forbids any attempt to even compare our concept with that of psychoanalysis" (Binswanger 1993a, 234–35). Binswanger states further that if love were simply an "*illusion,* in the explanatory sense of . . . Freud, then it would be difficult to conceive how love can constitute a 'reality'; a reality cannot be based upon something 'unreal'" (Binswanger 1993a, 135). In short, while it may account for much else, perhaps, Freud's theory of libido really fails to account for the nature of human love, which is central to the practice of psychotherapy.

Initially, Binswanger turned to Heidegger for a more satisfactory conception of human existence. However, just as he dismissed Freud's metapsychology and views on love, Binswanger found Heidegger's conception of interpersonal relations inadequate. The problem was not that Heidegger overlooked human sociality. The difficulty lay in the fact that *Dasein* achieved authenticity in isolation from others. As Binswanger says, Heidegger "sees only the inauthentic They-self besides the authentic self, and omits the authentic positive possibility of Being-with-one-another: that is, the being in one another of first and second person, of I and Thou, the We-self" (Binswanger 1993a, 217). Binswanger acknowledges that authenticity may follow from a candid confrontation with the inevitability of one's own death, but he believes that authenticity is also achieved through the I-Thou relationship.

The impact of Buber on Binswanger's theory of selfhood is most apparent in his chief and still untranslated work, *Basic Forms and Knowledge of Human Existence,* published in 1942 (See Binswanger 1993a). In fact, the preface to that text acknowledges an equal indebtedness to Buber's *I and Thou* and Heidegger's *Being and Time*. In addition to Buber, Binswanger's theory of self-realization is indebted to Hegel's dialectic of recognition. Indeed, Binswanger suggests that "recognition, in Hegel's sense, not only is very similar to love, it is . . . a special form of love. In this sense, what Hegel says about the unity of two self-consciousnesses, which continue to exist each for themselves, is definitive" (Binswanger 1993a, 390). In Hegel's master-slave dialectic (1977), the need for recognition conflicts with the need for absolute independence. The nature of this tension is paradoxical. Self-consciousness must not only win the recognition of the other, but also acknowledge the other as existing for himself or herself. Thus, for Hegel, each self-consciousness must exist for itself *and* for the other, with the result that both self-consciousnesses recognize themselves as mutually recognizing one another.

Relational psychoanalysts have recently taken up and expanded upon the Hegelian dialectic in order to explain the nature of analytic interaction (Benjamin 1988; Modell 1993). In an analogous fashion, Binswanger sought to demonstrate that the idea of mutual recognition is implicit to the I-Thou relation. He argues that within the we-dimension of love each partner has the need to recognize the other as both distinct from, and similar to, himself or herself. Similarly, Jessica Benjamin suggests that the need for recognition gives rise to a contradiction: "recognition is that response from the other which makes meaningful the feelings, intentions, and actions of the self. *It allows that self to realize its agency and authorship in a tangible way.* But such recognition can only come from another whom we, in turn, recognize as a person in his or her own right" (Benjamin 1988, 12). In other words, recognition must be accompanied by acknowledgment of difference. As Binswanger puts it, the "paradox between the 'relative' recognition of the singular and particular, and the moment of existence as we . . . implies that the being of love, the loving being-with-one-another, is thoroughly dialectical" (Binswanger 1993a, 459). Only thus can "the we" become a basis for the achievement of self-realization. It is this "we" that makes "possible myself and yourself in the sense of loving selfhood and autonomy" (Binswanger 1993a, 116).

Binswanger wrote little about therapeutic technique, and the objective of his case studies was chiefly to demonstrate the descriptive and explanatory power of "Daseinsanalysis." Binswanger's case studies stem primarily from the 1920s and 1930s, when schizophrenics were often viewed as medical objects to be studied, but essentially not treatable. Unlike many of his contemporaries, Binswanger viewed schizophrenics as sentient human beings who had lost their sense of relatedness, and he sought to restore it to them. As Binswanger states, "it is of the essence of being a psychiatrist, therefore, that he (or she) reach beyond all factual knowledge and the abilities that go with it, and that he (or she) reach beyond scientific knowledge found in the fields of psychology, psychopathology, and psychotherapy." For Binswanger, psychotherapy is properly to be understood not as a curative technique in the medical sense, but as a type of friendship. Seen from this perspective, Binswanger's approach to the therapeutic encounter has intriguing similarities to the work of recent interpersonal and relational theory. In what follows, we will sketch the ways in which Binswanger's concept of love and self-realization translates into a therapeutic context.

The mutuality and directness of the I-Thou relation is seen as crucial to the therapeutic process by many recent theorists. Thus, for example, the British object relations theorist, Harry Guntrip, argues that the vehicle for substantive change is a nurturing relationship. Guntrip states that

> Psychotherapy can only be carried on by those who are prepared to be exposed to all the subtle reactions that go on between two human beings who meet on an emotional rather than on an intellectual plane; and who are prepared to accept awareness of these reactions as essential to treatment. . . . What is therapeutic when it is achieved is "the moment of real meeting" of two persons as a new transforming experience for one of them, which is as Ronald Laing said, "Not what happened before (i.e. transference) but what has never happened before (i.e. a new experience of relationship)." (Guntrip 1969, 353)

The interpersonal psychoanalyst Darlene Ehrenberg refers to such moments as "the intimate edge" of therapy. She states that

> [therapeutic] work does not stop when contact is made or when each is truly touched in some profound way by the other and by their interaction; rather, it takes on new dimensions as the affective complexity of what gets activated in the moments of meeting can be clarified and explored in an endless progression. (Ehrenberg 1992, 40)

Like Buber, Binswanger saw the I-Thou relation, "face-to-face meeting" as both an end in itself and that which enables future meetings to take place with others *outside* the therapeutic arena. So in additional to reviewing, reliving, and reinterpreting the past, which is what classical analysis does, face-to-face "meeting" in the dialogic — or as Binswanger said, the dual — mode generates *new* experiences, and an awareness of new possibilities. Yet again, like Buber (1965b), Binswanger cautioned against the belief that the therapist can be entirely equal with the patient. Differences in terms of roles, functions, and power must be acknowledged throughout, and therapy is only possible if personal and professional boundaries are tactfully maintained. As Ehrenberg points out, "in effect, an authentic encounter can be facilitated by acknowledging the limits of what may be possible at any given moment, where ignoring these or pretending these do not exist precludes a more genuine and penetrating kind of engagement" (Ehrenberg 1992, 39).

Binswanger's elaboration of the I-Thou relation and therapeutic encounter thus presages a general shift in emphasis from the intrapsychic to the interpersonal dimension in psychoanalysis. Phenomena that were formerly interpreted chiefly as the result of isolated intrapsychic or instinctual processes are reinterpreted as having been formed in an interpersonal field. The role of therapy is to reach an understanding of such phenomena as they emerge in the interaction between therapist and patient.

In a manner akin to Harry Stack Sullivan and interpersonal psychoanalysis, Binswanger's emphasis on the primacy of relatedness also entails the conclusion that the loss of relatedness to others is the *central* feature in severe mental disorders. In regard to mania, for example, Binswanger states, "manic existence swings up to dizzy heights in which no stand is taken and no self-sufficient decision is possible. Love and friendship have, in these airy heights, lost their power. Human interaction is reduced to the level of psychiatric care" (Binswanger 1992, 245–46). Binswanger developed a similar argument in his exploration of schizoid and schizophrenic states. There, the descent into madness is characterized by what Erich Fromm, in *The Art of Loving,* later termed "existential aloneness" (Fromm 1956). Or, in Binswanger's words: "Dasein is withdrawn into mere interaction or traffic with itself alone, until even this peters out and becomes a sheer Medusa-like stare, a psychotically rigidified problem, an ideal, or the 'nothingness of anxiety'" (Binswanger 1992, 246–47). And in anticipation of R. D. Laing's *The Divided Self* (1960), Binswanger argues that schizoid or schizophrenic existence "is only possible where Dasein is 'despairingly' exiled from the home and eternalness of love and friendship . . . where it has isolated itself from interaction or traffic with others, and from the challenge and understanding that is only possible from such continued interaction."

In addition to the preceding parallels between Laing and Fromm, the loss of relatedness described by Binswanger is akin to Jacques Lacan's concept of "the Real," in which psychotic experience is characterized by the loss of meaningful speech (Lacan 1977a). Lacan suggests that the psychotic still resides within language, even if the ability to communicate is temporarily lost, while Binswanger maintains that the psychotic continues to exist as being-in-the-world, however delusionally distorted that world may be. For Binswanger, the psychotic is able to relinquish delusions only through the repair of his or her relations with other people and the world.

So, like Buber, Binswanger demonstrates that relatedness to others is crucial to human existence and to mental health. He notes that the psychotherapist is not simply "treating" an "illness," but sharing in the existence of the patient. However, his differences with Buber are noteworthy, too. Binswanger secularized Buber's I-Thou orientation, bracketing its theistic dimension, though he was not positively *irreligious,* like Marx, Nietzsche, or Freud. And while Buber said a great deal about interpersonal relations and psychotherapy over the years, his primary attitudes and commitments were social, political, and religious. As a philosopher concerned with the malaise of modernity, and with the challenges of faith, individuality, and the prospects for human solidarity and fellowship, Buber has more in common with thinkers like Leo Tolstoy, Max Scheler, Nikolai Berdyaev, or Gabriel Marcel than he did with Bleuler or Freud.

In contrast with Buber, but like his own psychiatric forebears, Binswanger was a dedicated clinician whose reflections on human relationships — though couched in existential idiom — seldom strayed outside the clinical arena to engage the broader social and historical forces that shaped the prevailing culture, except parenthetically. And unlike Buber, who described two modes of relatedness — personal and impersonal, humanizing and reifying — Binswanger distinguished among four different modes of relatedness (May, Angel, and Ellenberger 1958). The *dual mode* corresponds to Buber's I-Thou, or what Fromm termed a "core-to-core" relationship, which is characterized by reciprocity, respect, and openness, and a paradoxical but abiding sense of the beloved as eternally "present," even in their manifest absence. And whereas Freud likened love to psychosis, Binswanger said that the *dual mode* of relatedness is the most vivid expression of mental health.

The *plural mode* of existence, said Binswanger, is not lacking in passion, but lacks the core-to-core connectedness of the dual mode. Though love is absent here, relationships can be intensely personal, involving struggle and competition, domination and submission. The context for plural relations may be openly competitive, adversarial, or simply driven by a specific objective that needs to be met. But no matter how passionately engaged they are in confrontation or negotiation with one another, in the plural mode of existence people treat one another chiefly as instruments or obstacles to the realization of their own ends. Relations follow the I-It pattern, rather than the I-Thou.

The *singular mode,* by contrast, encompasses all aspects of a person's relationship to him or her self. This is a subtle and complex category, which includes psychopathological distortions that essentially exclude others: narcissism, autism, self-mutilation, and addiction. It is interesting to note that all these concepts — the dual, plural, and singular modes of relatedness — were outlined by 1942. It was not until 1949 that Binswanger posited the existence of a fourth mode of existence — the *anonymous mode.* The main difference between this and the plural mode is the greater degree of detachment and anonymity that prevails. In the anonymous mode, people engage one another in highly scripted or mechanical ways that are dictated by external circumstances.

While love and fellowship remain the same in Buber and Binswanger, the more instructive contrast here is actually between Binswanger and Freud. For Freud, the quality of interpersonal relatedness is patterned by specific expenditures or "cathexes" of libido characteristic of different psychosexual stages. For example, the oral stage is predominantly passive and dependent, the anal stage is primarily stubborn, defiant, and sadistic, the phallic phase is fickle, seductive, exhibitionistic, and so on. By contrast with Freud and his followers, Binswanger did not attempt to ground his modes of relatedness to others in a (hypothetical) maturational sequence and refused to assign any temporal priority to one over another. These modes of relatedness are always present, or potentially present, in each of us at all times. In existential terminology, they are "equiprimordial."

As was the case with Freud, there is, nonetheless, a normative dimension to Binswanger's views on human relationships. Of all the patterns of human relatedness, Binswanger privileges the dual mode as the only one that is potentially free of profound psychopathology. The others are not *intrinsically* pathological, perhaps, but Binswanger seems to imply that psychopathology is far more frequent and intense in these domains. As Binswanger grew older, and more detached from Freud, he saw psychopathology increasingly as a tragic constriction of human possibilities into one or more of these less desirable modes of relatedness. The aim of his therapy was to rekindle an awareness and a hope for creating and sustaining a loving way of being with others on the plane of human equality.

MEDARD BOSS

Born in 1903 in St. Gallen, Switzerland, Medard Boss grew up and lived in Zurich at a time when the city was a major center for psychological activity. He received his medical degree from the University of Zurich in 1928, taking time along the way to study in Paris and Vienna and to be analyzed by Sigmund Freud himself for thirty-odd sessions in 1925. After four years of working as an assistant to Bleuler at the Burghölzli hospital, Boss went on to study psychoanalysis in Berlin and London. Boss returned to Switzerland in 1938, establishing a private practice and becoming a professor at the University of Zurich in 1954. In 1971, together with a group of colleagues, he established the Daseinsanalytic Institute for Psychotherapy and Psychosomatics in Zurich. Not surprisingly, Boss's life and career were strongly influenced by prominent Swiss psychiatrists like Bleuler, Jung, and Binswanger. Like his mentors, Boss wrote extensively on a series of the topics, including dreams, perversions, and addictions, psychosomatic medicine, and the existential foundations of medicine. His best known works are *Psychoanalysis and Daseinsanalysis* (1963) and *Existential Foundations of Medicine and Psychology* (1979). Boss died in 1990.

Boss's intellectual and professional development went through a number of stages. A generation younger than Binswanger, Boss began his career as a traditional psychoanalyst. He started analysis with Freud, which he completed with Karen Horney in Berlin (Richardson 2003). During his psychoanalytic training, he was also exposed to the teaching and supervision of Theodor Reik, Hanns Sachs, Otto Fenichel, Kurt Goldstein, Ernst Jones, and others. After returning to Switzerland in 1938 from London, where he had been working with Jones, Boss began working with Jung. For ten years he attended a biweekly seminar with Jung and increasingly practiced in a Jungian manner. The fact that he gravitated toward Jung after a lengthy period of Freudian training is intriguing, since relations between Freudian and Jungians were never more fraught with bitterness and mistrust than they were immediately before and after the war.

Evidently, Boss was attracted to Jung's work because Jung categorically rejected the Cartesian mind-body dualism that beset Freudian metapsychology and so much of academic (experimental) psychology at the time. However, in due course, Boss became as disenchanted with Jung as he was with Freud, and gravitated toward Binswanger, who introduced him to Heidegger's writings. After the war, in 1946, Boss contacted Heidegger, and in his initial correspondence he commended Heidegger for capturing the essence of a therapeutic posture in the distinction between different modes of care or solicitude in *Being and Time,* these being "einspringende Führsorge" (interventionist, or leaping in) and "vorspringende Führsorge" (anticipatory, or leaping ahead) (see Frie 1997). The former, said Heidegger, is active and intrusive. Like medical treatment, it makes a deliberate project out of changing the patient in certain specific ways, in conformity with a preconceived concept of health. The latter, by contrast, respects the dignity and uniqueness of the person and allows them to unfold according to their own needs and values. It "lets Being be," as Heidegger said, and enables the person to sort themselves out and bring their latent potential for being to fruition. In short, it affords them the freedom of self-determination rather than trying to determine who or what they *should* be like.

For Heidegger, the experience of being-in-the-world implies an openness to being. Following Heidegger, Boss viewed the human being as a "shepherd of Being" who brings all things into light through his or her relationship to them. Boss conceived of mental health in similar terms: a positive and individual attunement to the openness of being-in-the-world was crucial to well-being. The condition of the healthy human being was characterized as the freedom to pursue all possibilities of relating to the world. These possibilities disclose themselves to the individual through the openness of his or her world. Psychopathology, in contrast, was seen as the shrinking of the possibilities of being-in-the-world. Illness is the privation of health (Boss 1971).

While Boss adopted Binswanger's term "Daseinsanalysis" to describe his Heideggerian approach to therapy, his turn toward Heidegger did not imply a complete turning away from Freud. After all, Boss made use of the analytic couch, arguing that having the patient recline, facing *away* from the analyst, promotes bodily relaxation, and this in turn promotes a willingness to relax self-censorship. By contrast, he suggests, "The conventional arrangement in which physician and patient sit facing opposite each other corresponds . . . to the traditional conception of two subjects, separate and standing opposite each other" (1963, 62–63). In addition to using the couch, Boss paid very close attention to dreams and psychosomatic disturbances. In short, he said that Freud's "technique" had merit, and often carried on as if Daseinsanalysis were really a revisionist Freudian school, rather than a radically different approach. In the introduction to part 2 of *Psychoanalysis and Daseinsanalysis*. He says, for example, "the criticism to which Daseinsanalysis subjects the basic concepts of psychoanalytic theory . . . is *positive*. The insights of analysis of Dasein will restore the original meaning and content of Freud's actual, immediate, concrete and most brilliant observations" (1963, 59). In the opening passages of chapter 4, entitled "The Intrinsic Harmony of Psychoanalytic Therapy and Daseinsanalysis," Boss states:

> we had best recall first Freud's fundamental therapeutic rule, which stands above all other rules in psychoanalytic theory; the patient must be absolutely honest and truthful with himself and the analyst. He is obliged to confess everything, whatever may pass through his mind or through his heart, and this without any exception. If this rule is followed, it means that all those possibilities of awareness, all feeling, thinking, imagining, dreaming and acting relationships with the world which either had been fought against until then, or had not been discovered up until then, are now accepted, realized freely, and appropriated with

responsibility as constituting one's own existence. . . . In other words, all of Freud's practical advice aims at enabling the patient to unveil himself and to unfold into his utmost openness. (1963, 60)

At the same time, Boss rejected Freud's theories of the primacy of instinct, of unconscious censorship and symbolization, of transference, and so on because "Daseinsanalysis . . . enables the practitioner to dispense with the tedious intellectual acrobatics required by psychoanalytic theory. He is free to discard the psychoanalytic libido theory as well as the labored psychoanalytic interpretations of symbols, both of them obstacles to an immediate understanding between physician and patient" (1963, 234).

To discern precisely what Boss wanted to keep and to discard in classical psychoanalysis, we must pay closer attention to Boss's actual words. He spoke of the convergence of psychoanalytic *therapy* and Daseinsanalysis, not between psychoanalytic *theory* and his own Heideggerian approach. In Boss's mind, Freudian "technique" was basically sound, though the metapsychology was radically misconceived. Boss's attempt to drive a wedge between analytic theory and therapy prefigures the ideas of psychoanalyst George Klein and his followers, who embraced what they called Freud's "clinical theory," which is based on careful naturalistic observation, while rejecting the "metapsychology," which invokes (or invents) all manner of abstract, hypothetical entities and processes that are remote from experience to account for phenomena, fostering a kind of hermeneutic incontinence, turning treatment into an arid, intellectualistic exercise. In this sense, Boss was ahead of his time.

However, Boss's efforts to extricate the (useful) technique from the (useless) theory in which it was imbricated obscured the important fact that Freud saw analytic technique rather differently than Boss did. While Boss eschewed the medical metaphor in correspondence with Heidegger, Freud had long since likened psychoanalytic interpretation to a surgical procedure, and the analyst to a skillful surgeon. Indeed, many learned papers are devoted to defending and embellishing on this dubious analogy, which Freud took very seriously (Stepansky 2001).

Unfortunately, it is impossible to square Boss's invocation of Heidegger's *vorspringende Führsorge* as the appropriate clinical posture with Freud's use of the surgical analogy, which places so much emphasis on the analyst's agency. Since Freud and Boss depicted the role of the therapist so differently, we are left to ponder whether Boss was simply wrong about the convergences between psychoanalysis and Daseinsanalysis, or whether the surgical analogy is really an inappropriate metaphor that does not convey what Freud was really up to.

While Boss was keen to conserve what is valid in psychoanalytic psychotherapy, and sometimes strikingly traditional in his prescriptions, he also resembles Jaspers in alerting his readers to the cultishness and sectarianism that beset the psychoanalytic movement. He called it "psychoanalytis":

> This syndrome (by no means rare) leads its sufferers to ritualistic thinking and talking in psychoanalytic terms and symbols. Circles and sects are formed of similarly afflicted persons. While many such adherents may lose the old symptoms, the neurotic nature of their new conduct is easy to detect. Instead of staying close to the immediately observable appearances of the world, they disregard them and speculate about what is "behind" them, unaware that their observations do not support their deductions. Instead of dwelling in openness toward the things and people they encounter, they "interpret" these same phenomena, human and material. Generally, such people cling rigidly to their theoretical convictions . . . [because] they have failed to arrive at an open and immediate world relation. Their fear of being contaminated by other ideas betrays their neurotically restricted mode of living, where genuine freedom and openness is always experienced as a threat. (1963, 236)

Boss's warnings were well warranted by the facts (see, for example, Kirsner 2000). His strictures against the dogmatism and rigidity of orthodox Freudianism (and its derivative offshoots) were major factors in the success of the Daseinsanalysis Institute in Zurich. However, Boss and his followers, who prided themselves on being "real" Heideggerians, disparaged and dismissed Binswanger's earlier version of Daseinsanalysis in ways that are strikingly similar to the sectarianism they deplored among the Freudian faithful (Boss 1957). After all, much as they differed on some points, the areas of convergence between Binswanger and Boss are as broad and as basic to understanding what psychotherapists are up to as one could possibly imagine.

First, remember that by contrast with Freud, who stressed the authority of the "expert" and the passivity of the patient, Buber, Binswanger, and Boss all agree that the psychotherapeutic relationship is essentially a *collaborative* one, although it begins as an *unequal* collaboration in which the therapist must first provide an environment in which the patient can begin to air their concerns and perplexities, and in the process be heard or seen in a way that they are not accustomed to being heard or seen in other relationships or situations.

Second, they both eschewed "interpretation," if by interpretation we mean a rhetorical strategy calculated to persuade patients that their present difficulties are caused primarily by past experiences, or their inability to recall and reckon with the impact of their past. The recollection of things past plays an important role in Daseinsanalysis, but only as a reflection of or prelude to the patient owning, accepting, or rejecting certain intrinsic possibilities of experience or action in the present.

Third, Freud and his followers interpreted adult psychopathology in terms of regression or fixation to earlier developmental stages. Indeed, for Freudians, human ontology is rooted in ontogeny, or the sequence of developmental stages that unfold from birth to maturity. Binswanger and Boss both eschewed the Freudian strategy of interpreting psychopathology as a reversion to an earlier psychosexual stage. Instead, they construed it as the expression of an existential impasse, as a way of distorting and constricting the expression of basic possibilities for deeper human relatedness.

Fourth, and finally, both Binswanger and Boss recognize that the goal of treatment is more than mere symptom alleviation, or even self-knowledge for its own sake. The goal of treatment, in their estimation, is to restore the patient's capacity to relate to others in a fully human way — in what Binswanger describes as the "dual mode," Buber's I and Thou, though Boss generally avoids this phrase out of respect for his philosophical mentor.

Recognition and the Limits of Reciprocity
Sartre, Lacan, and Laing

JEAN-PAUL SARTRE

Jean-Paul Sartre was born in Paris in 1905. His father, a naval officer, died when he was a few months old, and he grew up in the home of his maternal grandfather, Carl Schweitzer, a professor of German at the Sorbonne. Carl Schweitzer was a native German speaker from the Alsace region who had shifted his personal loyalties to France. But his love of France was seldom reciprocated. Despite his lifelong efforts to assimilate in Parisian circles, Carl Schweitzer was snubbed as a perpetual outsider. The grandfather's outsider status rubbed off on his studious, self-centered grandson, who retreated into books and fantasies. And in later life, the protagonists of Sartre's novels, though French speaking, had mostly German names, while Sartre's fame as a philosopher derived from his ability to interpret and synthesize German thinkers like Hegel, Husserl, Heidegger, and Freud into a distinctively French idiom.

After his secondary school education, Sartre attended the École Normale Superieure, where he met his future companion, Simone de Beauvoir, and many other people destined to become famous in their own right: Jean Hippolyte, Raymond Aron, Maurice Merleau-Ponty, Simone Weil, Emmanuel Mounier, and Claude Lévi-Strauss. Though he taught in Le Havre, Leon, and Paris after graduating from the École Normale in 1928, his studies continued apace. In 1933, Sartre studied phenomenology in Berlin, where he read Husserl, Scheler, Heidegger,

Jaspers, and Freud for one year. Sartre's first article, "The Transcendence of the Ego," published in 1936, attempted a rigorous synthesis of Husserl and Hegel, and was followed by a book called *L'imagination* — his first foray into phenomenological psychology. In 1938, Sartre published his first novel, *Nausea,* which brought him to world attention. In 1939, he published *Equisse d'une theorie des emotions,* and was drafted into the French army. In 1940, he became a prisoner of war and was released in 1941. His first play, "The Flies," was performed during the German occupation in 1943, the same year in which his magnum opus, *Being and Nothingness,* was published.

In 1945 Sartre founded an influential Parisian journal, *Les Temps Modernes,* with Merleau-Ponty, Aron, and de Beavoir. In 1946, Sartre published *L'Existentialism est une humanisme,* (which antagonized Heidegger deeply), and an intriguing analysis of French anti-Semitism entitled *Reflexions sur la questione Juive.* In 1947, he published an in-depth psychological portrait of the French poet Baudelaire, followed by another of novelist and playwright Jean Genet in 1952.

In 1948, Sartre helped to found an independent Socialist party in France, but this soon collapsed under the pressures of the cold war. Though never a member of the Communist Party, Sartre was critical of the American agenda in Europe and was often sympathetic to the Soviet perspective. Indeed, Sartre did not distance himself from the Soviets until they crushed the Hungarian insurrection in 1956. Now thoroughly disenchanted with Soviet Communism, Sartre still opposed American imperialism, and during the late fifties and early sixties was preoccupied with revising Marxist theory. Indeed, *Critique de la raison dialectique* and *Questions de methode,* both published in 1960, were attempts to articulate a kind of Marxist existentialism.

Long before they appeared in English translation, *Saint Genet, Critique de la raison dialectique,* and *Questions de methode* were summarized succinctly for English-speaking audiences by R. D. Laing and David Cooper in a book entitled *Reason and Violence: A Decade of Sartre's Philosophy* (1964). Sartre commended Laing and Cooper, saying theirs was "a very clear, very faithful account of my thought." Moreover, in a letter dated November 9, 1963, he said,

> Like you, I believe that one cannot understand psychological disturbances *from the outside,* on the basis of a positivistic determinism, or reconstruct them with a combination of concepts that remain outside the illness as lived and experienced. I also believe that one cannot study, let alone cure, a neurosis without a fundamental respect for the person of the patient, without a constant effort to grasp the basic situation and to relive it, without an attempt to rediscover the response of the person to that situation, and — like you, I think — I regard mental illness as the "way out" that the free organism, in its total unity, invents in order to live through an intolerable situation. (Laing and Cooper 1964, 6)

These words are instructive because they convey Sartre's attitude toward psychoanalysis and the frame of mind in which Sartre embarked on his last, most ambitious literary project. From 1960 to 1971, when blindness finally enveloped him, Sartre devoted most of his time to a projected four-volume study of Flaubert. Two volumes, totaling 2,130 pages, appeared in spring 1971. A third, massive volume appeared in 1972. He published little between then and his death in June 1980, but he was satisfied, and rightly so. The Flaubert trilogy was a masterpiece of social, historical, and psychological analysis. And it was also the longest "case history" ever written. His interpretation of Flaubert's life and work — like the earlier studies of Baudelaire and Jean Genet — was based on a deep and sympathetic immersion in his texts, supplemented by a thorough study of the social and historical circumstances that shaped Flaubert's personal and professional life. There was some precedent for this, of course. Freud's papers on great artists, including Michelangelo, Leonardo da Vinci, Goethe, Dostoyevsky, Edgar Alan Poe, Arthur Schnitzler, and others, applied psychoanalytic principles to the study of art and literature and eventually spawned the genre of historical writing we now call "psychobiography." In Freud's estimation, prodigiously gifted and insightful artists wrestle with deep inner conflicts that they "sublimate" in their work to avoid succumbing to mental disturbance — conflicts that can be elucidated after the fact if their artistic productions are interpreted "symptomatically." By this reckoning, the method, if not the task, of clinicians and biographers is essentially the same.

Sartre agreed. But when Freud attempted to unravel the artist's core conflicts, he emphasized the primacy of early childhood experience, the central role of Oedipal conflicts, or the incommensurability between the person's sexual needs and prevailing social pressures to repress them. By contrast, Sartre's artistic heroes were at odds with their environments regarding issues of class, ethnicity, and race, as much as sexuality and gender. They defied convention in a manner that, if somewhat self-injurious, also affirmed a vision of human freedom and possibility beyond prevailing cultural constraints. They refused to conform, to collude with the prevailing hypocrisy and "bad faith," or suffered somewhat when they tried to be "respectable." And while Sartre spoke plainly of their passions and privations, he did not presume to "diagnose" his subjects retrospectively, as examples of specific psychopathological syndromes, or to interpret his subjects through psychopathological lenses. And judging from his remarks to Laing and Cooper, Sartre felt psychotherapy should proceed in the same spirit as his literary biographies.

In contrast to Freud, Sartrean existential psychoanalysis did not privilege the past over the present, nor privilege sex and aggression as the only sources of inner conflict (Cannon 1991). And above all, for Sartre, especially the later Sartre, an existential analysis is always perforce a socioanalysis because the protagonist's inner conflicts (and his attempts to resolve them, whether through art, or by other means) can only be rendered intelligible in light of his historical "situation" and enveloping social context. This is because, from a phenomenological perspective, there is no independently existing psyche confronting an independently existing real world. Rather, following Husserl, Sartre argues that consciousness is intentional, which means that it always exists as a consciousness of something. Consciousness does not exist as interiority, at least in the first instance. The sense of interiority comes only when I reflect *back* on my experience. Sartre's phenomenological perspective disallows the notion of an unconscious realm inside the mind simply because consciousness has no "inside." This approach informs his critique of Freud's theory of repression.

In *Being and Nothingness,* Sartre argues that in order for repression and resistance to be possible, the person must be conscious of the impulses he or she wants to repress:

> How can we conceive of a knowledge which is ignorant of itself? . . .
> All knowing is consciousness of knowing. Thus the resistance of the patient
> implies on the level of the censor an awareness of the thing repressed
> as such, a comprehension of the end toward which the questions of the
> psychoanalyst are leading, and an act of synthetic connection by which
> it compares the *truth* of the repressed complex to the psychoanalytic
> hypothesis which aims at it. (Sartre 1956, 52)

Sartre insisted that resistance to the analyst's interpretation presupposes
that, on some level, we are aware of our disavowed impulses. Thus,
the unconscious censor is always conscious of that which it represses,
and if we remain unconscious of the "censor," that is a choice, a decision we make. Unconsciousness is intentional, too.

Sartre's rejection of the Freudian theory of repression does not imply
that he believed all experience was open to reflection. In order to explain
the nature of human experience, Sartre drew on the ideas of Johann
Gottlieb Fichte and the early German Romantic tradition and made
an important distinction between reflective and unreflected (or
prereflective) consciousness. Sartre argues that prereflective consciousness
is the condition of possibility of reflective consciousness. He cites
examples of the involvement in tasks to explain the nature of prereflective
consciousness: "When I run after a streetcar, when I look at the time,
when I am absorbed in contemplating a portrait, there is no I. There
is consciousness of *the streetcar-having-to-be-overtaken,* etc., and non-
positional consciousness of consciousness" (Sartre 1957, 49). Prereflective consciousness remains impersonal or prepersonal; there is
no I on the nonreflective level. For Sartre, the I emerges only with
reflective consciousness, though it does not refer to an underlying ego,
hidden in prereflective activity. I become aware of myself as an "I" when
I reflect on my activities, thoughts, and feelings.

In his later philosophy, Sartre referred to the experience of prereflective
consciousness as "lived experience," or *le vécu* — experience that can
never fully be known or conceptualized because the individual is per-
petually overwhelmed by what he or she is experiencing. Similarly, Sartre
said that a neurosis is a psychic fact that can neither be named nor fully
known. Experience is intentionally and consciously lived but not

known. Psychotherapy is predicated on the possibility of reflection, allowing me to comprehend the meaning of choices that have not yet been subject to reflection, and of choosing new possibilities that can reduce suffering or misery.

Sartre's account of prereflective experience prefigures recent developments in developmental psychology. In *The Interpersonal World of the Infant* (1985), Daniel Stern combines findings from infancy research, child development, and psychoanalysis to describe the birth of human subjectivity. Stern dismisses the Freudian theory of a symbiotic union in earliest infancy between mother and child, and therefore argues against Margaret Mahler's theory of developmental progression from normal autism to normal symbiosis and separation-individuation. Mahler sees human development in terms of the gradual separation of the child from its mother, and is concerned with the restructuring of the ego and id (Mahler, Pine, and Bergman 1975). Stern's perspective, by contrast, focuses on the emergence of the sense of self within an interpersonal developmental context. His account of the infant's sense of self illumines the psychological basis and developmental significance of Sartre's theory of prereflective self-consciousness.

In contrast to Mahler, Stern argues that infants begin to experience a sense of an emergent self from birth. In a manner akin to Sartre, Stern attributes to infants a "simple non-self-reflexive awareness" (Stern 1985, 7). Stern's thesis is that

> some senses of self do exist long prior to self-awareness and language. These include the senses of agency, of physical cohesion, of continuity of time, of having intentions in mind. . . . Self-reflection and language come to work upon these preverbal existential senses of the self and, in so doing, not only reveal their ongoing existence, but transform them into new experiences. (Stern 1985, 6)

When Stern speaks of "the self," he refers to an invariant pattern of awareness that constitutes a form of organization and arises through the infant's actions and mental processes. He refers to this organizing subjective experience as "the preverbal, existential counterpart of the objectifiable, self-reflective, verbalizable self" (Stern 1985, 7). The distinction Stern makes between a non-self-reflexive awareness and an objectifiable self-reflective self thus repeats — albeit in different form — the philosophical distinction between the prereflective and reflective consciousness.

These parallels are especially evident in Stern's discussion of the infant's early social development. Stern treats subjectivity as essentially pre-reflective and argues that the infant's development (through inter-action with the mother and others) hinges on this prereflective sense of self. Central to the development of a subjective self is the sharing of affective states, which is commonly referred to in the literature of developmental psychology as "mirroring." The word "mirroring" is used in clinical literature (Mahler, Pine, and Bergman 1975; Kohut 1977) to describe early interaction between the infant and its mother or father, in which the parent works within the same modality as the infant, imitating the infant's immediate behavior. Around the age of nine months, mirroring gives way to a more complex "affective attune-ment" (Stern 1985, 140–42), which forms the basis for the sharing of affect between the infant and mother. Stern actually prefers the notion of affective attunement to mirroring since it avoids the dilemmas of the reflection model of consciousness.

The problem, as Stern points out, is that "mirroring," which denotes empathic gestures conveying the "inner" sense of another's emotional state, "has the disadvantage of suggesting complete temporal syn-chrony" (Stern 1985, 144), and runs into the dilemma of "fidelity to the original." He elaborates the problem as follows: "'mirroring' implies that the mother is helping to create something within the infant that was only dimly or partially there until her reflection acted somehow to solidify its existence. This concept goes far beyond just participating in another's subjective experience. It involves changing the other by providing something the other did not have before" (Stern 1985, 144). The difficulties with this reflection model is that mirroring cannot be understood to create something that did not already exist before the act of reflection. On the contrary, the act of reflection is only possible as a result of a prereflective sense of self. Intersubjective relatedness elaborates but does not create this pri-mordial sense of self.

Not only is Stern's view on mirroring in accordance with Sartre's own perspective, he also reiterates the critique of self-presence. In contrast to Husserl, Sartre argues that the subject can never be fully present to itself. According to Sartre, it is the reflective act itself that brings the ego into being, and the act of reflection, or reflective consciousness, always presupposes prereflective consciousness. Not only is the ego external to consciousness, but also it is only present to consciousness in the reflexive act (Sartre 1957, 83). Yet the attempt to capture and analyze my own ego will be unsuccessful since it only fleetingly appears in acts of reflection.

Sartre's emphasis on the opacity of the ego stands in direct contrast to Husserl's notion of the "transcendental ego." For Husserl, the transcendental ego provides its own foundation, because it can fully relate to itself, taking the form of unmediated self-knowledge. Unfortunately, said Sartre, Husserl's account succumbs to the same solipsistic dilemmas that plagued Descartes's theory of mind. According to Sartre, "The ego never appears except when one is not looking at it. . . . The ego is by *nature* fugitive" (Sartre 1957, 88–89). Nor can the ego be discovered by looking inward; because the ego does not reside in consciousness, the act of introspection will find only isolated segments of the ego that cannot be reconstituted to form a whole. Sartre explains, "As soon as I turn my gaze toward it [the ego] and try to reach it . . . it vanishes. This is because in trying to apprehend the ego for itself and as a direct object of my consciousness, I fall back onto the unreflected level, and the ego disappears along with the reflective act" (Sartre 1957, 88–89).

Much of Sartre's philosophy constitutes a defense of the irreducibility of individual self-consciousness. Not surprisingly, perhaps, Sartre concludes that subjects are fundamentally divided from one another in their being. Sartre says so explicitly in his analysis of "the look." The humanness of the other becomes evident through the look that he or she directs at me. The look refers to the situation of my "being-seen-by-another." Sartre alleges that I exist as an object for the other whenever I am looked at. He explains the nature of being looked at in terms of the experience of shame, which is provoked by the presence of another person.

Sartre cites the example of peeping through a keyhole as evidence of shame. When performing the act, I am a subject that is freely engaged. However, if I should become aware that I am being observed as I am peeping through the keyhole, then I immediately become ashamed. The other's observation of me causes me to become an object of his or her gaze. Sartre maintains that when the other perceives me as an object, I become defined by my act of peeping. By identifying myself through shame with the other person's image of me, I acquire solid features, but I also experience an alienation from my original possibilities: "I am *no longer master of the situation*" (Sartre 1956, 265). The look of the other has the power to alienate me into an object for the other person.

As the object of the other's stare, I endure a sense of alienation and objectification, while the other emerges as a free and conscious being that I am unable to objectify. I discover the other as a subject through my experience of objectification. This experience is inflicted upon me by the other; it does not result from my actions. My consciousness of being seen by the other therefore also forms the starting point for my discovery of the other as subject.

In his discussion of the look, Sartre draws extensively on Hegel: the analysis of the look being a variation on Hegel's dialectic of self-consciousness, in which self-consciousness emerges out of desire and the possible satisfaction of desire. Following Hegel, Sartre asserts that my reduction to the status of an object in the other's look is not absolute. By refusing to identify with the other, I am able to integrate him or her into my world by depriving the other of his or her subjectivity. However, because the other is unwilling to relinquish his or her autonomy, conflict immediately ensues.

In Sartre's view, intersubjectivity, or being-for-others, is essentially a struggle to avoid being objectified by others. This is a crucial point. For Sartre, particularly in his early work, intersubjective relations are motivated by a single aim: to subjugate the other who has the power to make me into an object. Yet I can never succeed in this task. Neither I nor the other can exist both as a free look and a look enslaved. Because my intentions toward the other are similar to the other's intentions toward me, our relations are determined by conflict. In Sartre's words, "Conflict is the original meaning of being-for-others" (1956, 364).

While the parallels between Sartre and Hegel are considerable, there also are significant differences. For our purposes, the divergences are of greater relevance than the similarities. According to Hegel, the struggle is finally resolved in the intrinsic universality of reason, since the dialectical opposition moves toward synthesis. The individual struggle to satisfy desire and achieve recognition is overcome in the full mutual recognition of self-consciousness at a higher level of reason, in the "I that is a We and We that is I," which constitutes *Geist*. For Sartre, by contrast, the antipathy between self and other is primordial, and ultimately irreconcilable.

Although Sartre takes up the master-slave dialectic as the basis for his theory of the look, he presents it as a project that is doomed to failure. In Sartre's analysis of the look, slavery becomes a permanent and insurmountable human condition. While there is the perpetual changing of roles — the self and the other alternatively assume the position of master and slave — there can never be any mutual or reciprocal recognition. Sartre is following in the tradition of Thomas Hobbes, for whom the essence of human nature lies in its desire for mastery over itself and the other. Just as Hobbes presents intersubjectivity as a struggle for self-preservation against the "state of nature," Sartre concludes that intersubjective relations will always be predicated upon conflict as each consciousness attempts to establish its own absolute autonomy. This unresolvable struggle between consciousnesses is what leads Sartre to state in his play, *No Exit* (1944), "Hell is other people" (1955, 47).

The conflictual model of intersubjectivity also provides the basis for Sartre's analysis of love. By explaining love in terms of the look, love takes on the underlying structure of all human relationships; no matter how close it brings us together, it remains eternally fraught with conflict. Love, for Sartre, is always *the desire to be loved* — a desire that can never be fulfilled. The goal of love is based on the act of possession, as I attempt to preclude my own reduction to the status of a possession by absorbing the other as "mine."

Without accounting for the experience of reciprocity in relation, however, Sartre overlooks a key dimension of intersubjectivity. Buber and

Binswanger developed a theory of intersubjectivity in which the other exists, not as an object, but as an equal subject, if the encounter is characterized by immediacy, directness, and mutuality, and not by domination and dependency. This runs contrary to Sartre's ontology. For Sartre, the possibility of an I-Thou relationship is precluded by the dialectic of the look.

The consequences for the notion of love are profound. For Sartre, love is ultimately based on the principle of domination. Admittedly, our love for the other is usually determined by a desire to be loved in return. But desire, for Sartre, is never strictly sexual. It is, rather, a desire to possess the consciousness of the other. Sartre astutely observes how a love, motivated by selfish desire, can result in a cycle of domination and dependence. He refers to the appropriation of the other without letting oneself be appropriated in turn, as sadism. Conversely, the denial of one's subjectivity, and the refusal to be anything but an object for the other constitutes masochism. On Sartre's reading, love is characterized by the oscillation of these two basic attitudes, rendering the achievement of lasting equality a complete illusion. Sartre is unable to imagine a situation in which lovers relate as equals, without dependency or control.

In contrast to Sartre, Stern's work shows us the way in which interaction with others plays a key role in human development by enabling an emergent sense of self to unfold during infancy. Stern's model of the self acknowledges the facticity of individual subjectivity, but instead of taking individual autonomy as a goal, assumes that the individual exists within the context of continuing relationship to others. The issue then becomes not how we dissociate ourselves from others, but rather how we engage with the other in a relationship that sustains and enhances individual identity. This has also become a central issue in recent feminist psychoanalysis (Benjamin 1988) and will be discussed in the next chapter.

In sum, then, Sartre sheds light on the difficulties involved in the attempt to account for the self exclusively through an encounter with the other, but does not account adequately for the central role of human relationships for self-development. As R. D. Laing points out later, any account of self-consciousness must also account for the relational field in which the self exists.

Jacques Lacan

Jacques-Marie-Émile Lacan was born in Paris in 1901 and studied medicine and psychiatry at Sainte-Anne's Hospital and in the Clinic for Mental and Encephalic Diseases. In 1928, his training complete, he worked in the Special Infirmary Service under G. G. de Clérambault. In 1931, Lacan published his translation of Freud's "On Some Neurotic Mechanisms in Jealousy, Paranoia, and Homosexuality" in the *Revue Française de Psychanalyse*. The following year he published *Structure des psychoses paranoiaques,* his first foray into psychoanalytic psychiatry, and the next year he received his doctorate for his thesis, "De la psychose paranioque dans ses rapports avec la personalité." He sent a copy to Freud, who acknowledged the receipt of the manuscript, but declined to read or comment on it, and another to Binswanger, which bore a personal inscription suggesting a strong sense of kinship with the phenomenological psychiatry of that era. During 1933–1934, Lacan also attended Alexandre Kojève's lectures on Hegel's *Philosophy of Spirit,* which introduced him to the ideas of Hegel and Heidegger, whom he cited frequently in the early stages of his work.

In 1934, Lacan became a member of La Société Psychoanalytique de Paris (SPP) and began his five-year analysis with Rudolph Löwenstein. In 1936, Lacan published "Beyond the Reality Principle," and unveiled the first, unpublished version of his "mirror stage" at the fourteenth international congress of the International Psychoanalytic Association in Marienbad, becoming a full member of the SPP in 1938. During the war, Lacan published little and worked at Val-de-Grace military hospital in Paris. After a lengthy interruption, the SPP resumed its activities in 1946 and Lacan took charge of training analyses and supervisory controls. After the publication of his paper on the "mirror stage" in 1949, he played an increasingly important theoretical role as well.

Meanwhile, sharp disagreements over selection criteria and training procedures prompted him (and many sympathetic colleagues) to leave the SPP and found the Société Française de Psychanalyse (SFP) in 1953. Later that year, in September, Lacan gave his celebrated talk on "Function and Field of Speech in Psychoanalysis" in Rome and began his famous seminars at Sainte-Anne's Hospital under the banner of "the return to Freud." From 1953 to 1963, when he left Sainte-Anne's, Lacan wrote many of the texts found in his most famous book, *Ecrits*, published in 1966 (1977a).

Around 1961, the SFP members expressed a desire to be recognized by the International Psychoanalytic Association (IPA). However, the IPA was incensed over Lacan's notoriously brief therapeutic encounters, which frequently fell short of the standard "analytic hour" (typically lasting 50 minutes). Lacan argued that if the unconscious is "timeless," as Freud had said, it makes no sense to insist upon a standard length for sessions, and he insisted that his technique actually accelerated the analytic process. However, the next year the IPA delivered an ultimatum: Lacan could no longer function as a "training analyst." The majority voted in favor of the ban, and Lacan left the SFP shortly thereafter.

Undeterred, in 1964, Lacan moved his seminar to the École Normale Supérieure, where he met Jacques-Alain Miller, a student of Louis Althusser, an erstwhile Stalinist, and analysand of Lacan who helped to disseminate Lacan's increasingly structuralist vision of psychoanalysis among the French Left. Lacan also founded L'École Française de Psychoanalyse, which soon became L'École Freudienne de Paris (EFP), which he directed until 1980. Among other things taught at L'École Freudienne and Le Champ Freudienne were various topological models of unconscious mental processes, which Lacan first explored in the mid-1950s, and unveiled publicly in 1961–1962. During the seventies, Lacan expanded this initiative, offering lengthy meditations on "the Borromean knot" and various "mathemes" — formalized units representing complex structures and processes that are inaccessible to conscious introspection or, indeed, to anyone not initiated into Lacanian discourse.

In addition to wrestling with the mathemes during the 1970s, Lacan also lectured abroad and often dwelt on love, language, hysteria, and the relationships between men and women. Lacan claimed that despite the seemingly complementary nature of their desires, there is no real rapport between the sexes. In the unconscious, said Lacan, man knows nothing of woman, and woman knows nothing of man — an odd contention, when you consider Freud's insistence on our innate bisexuality.

In 1980, Lacan dissolved L'École Freudienne de Paris, which was wracked by schisms and dissensions, in which the chief protagonists all claimed to be "authentic" Lacanians. In a conference in Caracas in July of that year, Lacan told his astonished audience, "It is up to you to be Lacanians if you wish; I am a Freudian." Lacan died in Paris in 1981. Lacan's claim of unwavering fidelity to Freud is quite curious, considering that he abandoned Freud's cherished libido theories early on, and forbade his students from reading texts that Freud and his followers regarded as foundational, on the grounds that they were unrepresentative or actually misleading. Admittedly, Freud wrote some profoundly perceptive papers and parenthetical observations on language, and made frequent use of analogies from optics and physics, which Lacan emulated, exploited, and embellished. But by calling these innovations "Freudian," Lacan underrated and, to some extent, disavowed his own originality and difference from "the master."

In retrospect, Lacan's career can be divided into a number of stages. Initially, Lacan allied himself with Binswanger and phenomenological psychiatry, drawing freely on the ideas of Hegel, Heidegger, Kojève, and Sartre. Later, he turned first toward structuralism, drawing increasingly on the work of Lévi-Strauss, de Saussure, Jakobsen, and others and then to mathematics and mathemes. Lacan's avid interest in philosophy, literature, and language were evident throughout his career, but it is the shift from a predominantly phenomenological to a chiefly structuralist frame of reference that will concern us here. We will touch on those aspects of his work that are directly relevant to the conduct of psychotherapy from a human science perspective.

The initial phase of Lacan's work spanned from his inaugural presentation to the International Psychoanalytic Association in 1936, "The Mirror Stage," to the mid-1950s and his incorporation of structuralist principles. The early Lacan takes issue with a pervasive medical belief in the organic origins of mental illness, and explicitly allies his own research with that of Binswanger in the category of "works of phenomenological inspiration on mental states" (quoted in Dews 1987, 50). Like Binswanger, Lacan rejected Freud's biologically grounded theory of the ego and drew on the philosophies of Hegel and Heidegger to refashion the psychoanalytic theory of the ego. Lacan developed the relation between the ego and identity formation in terms of the specular mirror stage.

The notion of a mirror stage is absent from the Freudian account of early childhood, and prefigures Lacan's departure in 1953 from orthodox psychoanalysis. The mirror stage situates the ego before its entry into language. Lacan suggests that an infant first experiences a sense of bodily unity through the encounter with his or her own reflection in a mirror. The reflected image is what Lacan refers to as the I or ego (*moi*). The subject's self-recognition is, however, a misrecognition. The image of bodily unity perceived in the mirror stands in direct contrast to the infant's actual lack of control over his or her bodily functions. The discrepancy between the infant and imagined unity is never overcome. The formation of the ego through specular misrecognition anticipates a more profound splitting of the subject when it enters into the symbolic order.

Lacan's specular subject is constituted by a radical split that is somewhat reminiscent of early Sartre. For both thinkers, the ego is an imaginary construct. Like Sartre, Lacan rejects any notion of a unified subject, and undermines the Cartesian view of the ego as a locus of certainty and truth. He therefore takes issue with ego-psychology and Anglo-American psychoanalytic theory. Whereas these schools claimed to be following in Freud's footsteps, according to Lacan, Freud's formulation of unconscious mental processes profoundly challenged the primacy of the autonomous, self-determining subject. And though Freud posited a (potentially) integrated ego, whose goal is to master the unconscious id, Lacan took a more radical stand, arguing that the ego is *never* to be autonomous because it is eternally subordinated to the images with which it identified in its early development. From the beginning, the ego is subverted by its imaginary identifications, resulting in a profoundly divided self.

In reformulating the theory of the ego, Lacan, like Sartre, found an ally in Hegel, whose account of desire as transcending biological needs and drives lends itself — in the hands of Alexandre Kojève — to a careful discrimination among desires, demands, and needs. Following Kojève, Lacan distinguishes desire from needs and demands. Demands are answered by the satisfaction of biological needs. Yet, while needs can be satisfied and demands can be responded to, desire remains insatiable. The object of desire, according to Lacan, is the desire of the other. The search for satisfaction of desire through another self-consciousness underscores a fundamental lack at the heart of subjectivity. Desire refers to the awareness of lacking something other, upon which a sense of self depends. Thus, for Sartre, consciousness endures a desire for a totality that can never be fulfilled, while for Lacan, human existence is characterized by a perpetual lack: desire is a lack of being that can never be fulfilled.

The parallels between Lacan's and Sartre's notions of desire and otherness are extensive. Both thinkers present desire as the wish for totality, which can only be achieved through the other. Lacan and Sartre argue that the role of desire is particularly manifest in love. For Sartre, the lover not only wants to possess his or her beloved, but also wants to remain the object of desire. This is the impossible ideal of love: "For both partners in the relation it is not enough to be subjects of need, or objects of love . . . they must stand for the cause of desire" (Lacan 1977a, 287). Desire denotes the unconditional demand for love that can never be satisfied by any proof or object of love.

It is not surprising, then, that Sartre's analysis of "the look" provides the basis for Lacan's notion of "the gaze." He follows Sartre in asserting that the other is always caught in the subject's gaze. The thematic convergence of being-seen-by-the-other and being-for-others is appropriated by Lacan, who states that "from the moment this gaze exists, I am already something other, in that I feel myself becoming an object for the gaze of others. But in this position, which is a reciprocal one, others also know that I am an object who knows himself to be seen" (Lacan 1988a, 215). On this basis, the initial apprehension of the other is envisaged as the alienation of self, which forever subverts the possibility of genuine reciprocity. Self and other remain irrevocably at odds, precluding ultimate reconciliation, even in a Hegelian sense. Lacan's views are consistent with Hegel only to the extent that a sense of self is dependent upon the other. As Lacan asserts, "we must start off . . . with the subject's total acceptance by the other subject," and then "we will be obliged to admit an original intersubjectivity" (1988a, 217).

Thus, the Lacanian subject is social and intersubjective, but also doomed to (inner and interpersonal) conflict. Relations between the subject and other are never stable because the other is both (1) a necessary condition for the development of subjectivity, and (2) a reminder of the lack on which a sense of self is grounded. Following Sartre, for whom intimate relationships are inherently adversarial, Lacan recommended *Being and Nothingness* for its insights on love and intersubjective experience. In Lacan's own words, Sartre gives "a structuration to the phenomenology of the love relation which to me appears irrefutable" (Lacan 1988a, 216). Lacan also echoed Sartre by arguing that love constitutes a desire for an unobtainable unity, or oneness, with the other. He characterized love in terms of the desire to be loved, on the one hand, and the desire to dominate, on the other. The other must willingly relinquish his or her freedom in order to fulfill the desire to be loved. The impossibility of this goal implies that love will result in a situation of interpersonal domination and unfulfilled desire. The love relation, therefore, is incapable of satisfying the lack that is inscribed in the subject.

Lacan's early work reformulated Freud's theory of the ego, using concepts culled from continental philosophy. Lacan's "Rome Discourse" (1953; see Lacan 1977a) marks the apex of the existential-phenomenological influence on his work, followed by a dramatic shift toward structuralism and linguistics. His concern with the formation of the ego through imaginary identifications gave way to the elaboration of the deformations of subjectivity within the "symbolic order." The emphasis in this mature phase was on the ways in which human subjectivity is fractured and decentered by its dependence upon language.

Lacan's views on the relationship of the ego to speech and language are indebted to the structuralist anthropology of Claude Lévi-Strauss. Lacan adopted Lévi-Strauss's argument for the primacy of symbolic systems and argued that before the subject is born it already has a position within a kinship order, which he refers to as the symbolic order. When the subject acquires language, it is inserted into a predetermined position in the symbolic order. According to Lacan, the symbolic order is irreducible and "cannot be conceived of as constituted by man, but as constituting him" (Lacan 1977a, 68). The subject therefore takes on the reality of the symbolic order.

Lacan's approach to language derives from Saussure's concept of the linguistic sign. According to Saussure, the relationship between the signifier and signified is arbitrary because meaning is determined through difference from other meanings. Lacan accepts the arbitrary nature of the linguistic sign, but argues that there can be no direct relation between signifier and signified. In his view, the signifier is no longer dependent upon the signified because its content is determined by other signifiers. The location of the signifier within a system of a language endows it with the capacity for signification. The transition from language to meaning becomes dependent upon the "signifying chain." Meaning is implicit within the chain of signification that, as Lacan remarks, consists of "rings of a necklace that is a ring in another necklace made of rings" (1977a, 153). In Lacan's elaboration, "it is in the chain of the signifier that the meaning 'insists' but that none of its elements 'consists' in the signification of which it is at the moment capable" (1977a, 153). There is, as such, no straightforward movement from language to meaning.

For Lacan, the roots of human subjectivity are imbricated in the problem of the determination of meaning in language. The subject can appear in language only by making himself or herself represented through a signifier, to another signifier. In a manner reminiscent of the later Heidegger, Lacan writes, "The signifier now becomes a new dimension of the human condition in that it is not only man who speaks, but that in man and through man it speaks, that his nature is woven by effects in which is to be found the structure of language, of which he becomes the material" (1977a, 284). As an effect of the signifier, the subject must endure the semantic instability of language. The endless process of difference, which constitutes the signifying chain, is experienced by the subject as a radical dislocation. The subject's "entry" into the preexisting system of language — the symbolic order — exacerbates the process of splitting and the sense of lack first experienced when the subject encounters its specular image. "The subject, too," asserts Lacan, "if he can appear to be the slave of language is all the more so of a discourse in the universal movement in which his place is already inscribed at birth" (1977a, 148). Seen from this perspective, the subject is born into language, and it is through language that subjectivity is constituted.

According to Lacan, an emerging subject will learn the preexisting language — the symbolic order of articulated and interpreted signs — in order to express its physical needs in the form of demands. As such, the symbolic order presents a means for the satisfaction of desire. Yet, instead of satisfying desire, it separates the subject of desire from itself. Because the subject is dependent upon expressing itself through signifiers whose meanings have been endowed by others, the subject can never be certain whether the attention proffered is the recognition it desires, or merely an attempt to remedy physical need. Although the subject hopes to be able to satisfy its desire through the symbolic order, it is, in fact, the symbolic order that separates the subject of desire from itself.

The symbolic order is experienced by the subject as profoundly dislocative. In all intersubjective involvement, the subject searches for a confirming image or representation in the other person. Yet because language always "belongs" to another person, the *moi* identifies incorrectly with its reflection. The reflection of the *moi* appears autonomous, but is in fact the other of itself, which Lacan refers to as the *object petit a*. Identification with the Other results in a misapprehension of the *Je*, the true or unconscious subject. Descartes' famous dictum, "I think therefore I am" must be reformulated according to the eccentric position of the *moi* to the *Je*. In Lacan's formulation, "I think therefore I am," becomes "I think where I am not, therefore I am where I do not think," or more aphoristically, "I think of what I am where I do not think to think" (1977a, 166). The point is that the *moi* necessarily misapprehends the *Je* in the act of thinking.

The gap between the expression of self-identity in language and the subject's actual existence constitutes the otherness of language, which Lacan refers to as the subject of the unconscious. The unconscious subject, which is sought by the *moi,* is founded in the Other. Lacan also speaks of the *sujet de l'Autre.* Although Lacan's use of the Other is ambiguous, it generally designates the otherness of language, or the unconscious. The unconscious, for Lacan, is situated in the place of the other and is sought in every enunciation; it is a discourse that is structured like a language. The desire for recognition that motivates speech remains implicit or unconscious because the response of the Other determines the subject's situation.

The Other introduces an uncertainty into language that shapes the linguistic interactions between the subject and the other person. As Lacan puts it, "The subject is separated from the Others, the true Others, by the wall of language" (1988b, 244). The Other represents that place at which "the recognition of desire is bound up with the desire for recognition" (Lacan 1977a, 172). The point of completion for Hegel's dialectic of desire and self-consciousness is thereby moved into that unattainable realm of the Other. By introducing an elusiveness and unpredictability of meaning in language, the Other denies the subject's recognition of itself in the other, and causes desire to become insatiable. Language constitutes a wall, on one side of which are the subjects, who communicate indirectly through the echo of their speech upon it (1977a, 101). Lacan thus rejects the Hegelian idea of mutual recognition; the primacy of the Other over all subjectivity undermines the possibility of reciprocity in communication. In the symbolic order, language, interposed between subjects as the medium of intersubjectivity, is the absolute Other (Frie 1997).

According to Lacan, then, the subject searches for a confirming reflection of his or her self-identity in the other on both the imaginary and symbolic levels. His aim is to emphasize the illusory features of conscious self-identity. In the imaginary, the subject's identifications result in misrecognitions, and in the symbolic, self-coincidence through the other is rendered unobtainable by the otherness of language. For

Lacan, the subject is dislocated and decentered, though never entirely subverted — a fact that sets his work apart from most versions of post-structuralism.

For Lacan, the subject's reality is the symbolic order. As a psychoanalyst, he is primarily concerned with what can be articulated within this linguistic paradigm. He therefore attributes relatively little importance to a theory of affect, depriving such nonlinguistic phenomena of any power or meaning outside the realm of symbolic interaction. According to Lacan, the transference of affect is actually a transference of image, or an "imaginary transference." The emotional relationship in which the analysand redirects his or her affects and emotions of past experiences toward the analyst, or transference love, was construed as a relationship of identification. In his seminar, "Encore" (1972–1973), Lacan addressed the notion of the demand for love in the analytic session, arguing that it is a phenomenon that cannot be expressed in language. For Lacan, the analysand's affect becomes important to the course of analysis once the analysand is able to articulate the affect's meaning. Only thus is the movement from the imaginary to the symbolic achieved. The effectiveness of an analysis is dependent upon the primacy of the symbolic. As such, the function and structure of language must remain at the forefront of analytic experience.

Lacan asserts that communication in the context of intimate relationships is always subject to the otherness of language. A person can never be certain of the other's response to his or her demand for love: the meaning of the demand is not intrinsic, but is determined in part by the response of the other. The attention proffered is unable to fulfill the demand because we cannot know if we are loved for our own particularity, just as in the same way we can never know for certain what meaning the listener associates with our utterances. For Lacan, the meaning of a speaker's discourse is determined by who hears it, which has important consequences for the possibility of reciprocity in relation: "Speech is constituted by an *I* and a *you*. These are two counterparts. Speech transforms them, by giving them a certain appropriate relationship, but — and this is what I want to insist upon — a distance that's not symmetrical, a relationship that isn't reciprocal" (Lacan 1993, 274). The contrast with Buber's notion of an I-Thou relationship could not be more striking.

Like Sartre, who argues that the demand for love occurs only to fulfill an impossible desire for oneness, Lacan refers to love as the "phantasy of oneness." He formulates the problem as follows: "*We are as one*. Of course everybody knows that it has never happened for two to make one, but still, we are as one. That's what the idea of love starts out from . . . the problem then being how on earth there could be love for another" But whereas the early Lacan situates the idea of unity in the imaginary, his late texts assign the phantasy of oneness to the symbolic and the sexual relation. Lacan refers to love as narcissistic, insofar as it is a desire for an impossible unity. This myth of oneness acts as an obstacle to the sexual relation; it creates the *idea* of unity through which division is disavowed by both partners. In Lacan's words, "Love rarely comes true, as each of us knows, and it only lasts for a time. For what is love other than banging one's head against a wall, since there is no sexual relation?" (quoted in Mitchell and Rose 1982, 46). In effect, Lacan was saying that sexual intercourse, like symbolic interaction at the level of speech, seeks the impossible. Complementarity, in turn, is a phantasy because language invariably intervenes (Lacan 1988b, 244). Language constitutes the subject in relation to the other, radically dividing subjects themselves and one another.

When we compare Sartre and Lacan in light of the heuristic schemata introduced at the beginning of the volume, we arrive at some startling conclusions. Were they rationalists? Yes and no. Though the main thrust of his work is anti-Cartesian, in most respects there are some stubborn and deep-seated strains of Cartesianism in Sartre that dismayed Heidegger and prompted him to distance himself from his younger French contemporary. In *Being and Nothingness* (1941), for example, Sartre remarked that existential psychoanalysis rejects the hypothesis of the unconscious and makes the psychic act co-extensive with consciousness. But from a Freudian standpoint, equating "the psychic" with consciousness — as Brentano, Dilthey, and Husserl were also wont to do — is nothing less than a wholesale reversion to Cartesian thought, a summary dismissal of the whole Freudian project. Somewhat later, in "Existentialism," published in 1945, Sartre gave us an even stronger avowal of his Cartesian sympathies. Responding to his critics on the Left, he wrote,

> Subjectivity of the individual is indeed our point of departure, and this for strictly philosophic reasons. Not because we are bourgeois, but because we want a doctrine based on truth. . . . There can be no other truth to take off from than this: *I think, therefore I exist.* There we have the absolute truth of consciousness becoming aware of itself. Every theory which takes man out of the moment in which he becomes aware of himself is, at the very beginning, a theory that confounds truth, for outside the Cartesian cogito, all views are merely probable. (36)

Significantly, a page or so later, Sartre attempts to rid his Cartesianism point of departure of the danger of incipient solipsism by squaring it with Hegel's dialectic of mutual recognition:

> Descartes and Kant to the contrary, through the *I think* we reach our own self in the presence of others, and the others are just as real to us as our own self. Thus, the man who becomes aware of himself through the cogito perceives all others, and he perceives them as the condition of his own existence. He realizes that he can not be anything (in the sense that we say that someone is witty or nasty or jealous) unless others recognize it as such. In order to get any truth about myself, I must have contact with another person. The other is indispensable to my own existence, as well as to my knowledge about myself. (37–38)

Unlike Sartre, we see the Cartesian and Hegelian accounts of the origins of self-consciousness as alternative and incommensurable versions, and not as points on a continuum, which is how Sartre depicted them. Nevertheless, the fact that he tried to integrate them in this way is intriguing. Having taken the concept of the unconscious to heart in a way that Sartre did not, Lacan's rationalism is more sublimated and subdued, and less overtly Cartesian in character. But Lacan's latent rationalism shows indirectly in his emphasis on the need for austerity in the analytic setting and his tendency to consider strong expressions of affect only in terms of their linguistic expression. Despite these noteworthy differences, Sartre and Lacan converge strongly in their emphasis on the illusory nature of the ego. For Sartre, the ego is merely glimpsed — never *grasped* — and then only in action, after the fact, or in passing. And for Lacan especially, self-estrangement is primordial, irrevocable, and practically identical with the birth of subjectivity.

Much as they may matter to their respective followers, the differences between Sartre and the early Lacan on the nature of the ego are more a matter of emphasis than of deeply divergent orientations. The net result is the same: a perpetual state of internal disequilibrium, the futility of desire, and a ceaseless will to power in the interpersonal arena. Though both of them invoke the desire for recognition as one of the strongest motives for human conduct, there is no Hegelian *Aufhebung*, no ultimate reconciliation of needs or perspectives. Indeed, what Sartre and Lacan call love is nothing more than a combination of lust, dependency, and a naked will to power. On occasion, Lacan alludes to a fundamental difference between desire, which he calls an "imaginary passion," and what he terms "the active gift of love" that occurs in the symbolic register. Though never spelled out in detail, Lacan evidently believed that a form of love unburdened by desire, rooted in simple generosity toward the other person, identified with the Christian *agape*, remains an objective possibility. But unless we are mistaken, reciprocity of the I-Thou variety is neither sought nor offered here. With conflict inscribed so deeply in the human condition, and genuine love so fleeting or ineffectual, we can only describe Sartre and Lacan as profoundly *anti-utopian* thinkers.

Were they religious or irreligious, or something in between? Like Marx, Nietzsche, and Freud, Sartre was a militant atheist and could not conceive of existentialism or humanism in theistic form. Lacan was more ambiguous on this score. Elizabeth Roudinesco (and many French leftists) insist that Lacan was an atheist. But Lacan explicitly rejected Freud's antipathy to organized religion as exaggerated and ill advised, coining a third register, "the Real," as the realm of experience beyond language. In *The Four Fundamental Concepts of Psychoanalysis*, he declared himself a "Gnostic" or "Kabbalist," hinting at a deeply heterodox attitude toward religion that falls short of outright atheism.

Inconsistencies like these abound in his life and work (Roazen 2000b, chap. 8). No doubt they were often quite deliberate, indicating complex conflicts.

Were these philosophers modern or postmodern? It is difficult to sort them out neatly on either side of this binary classification. Whereas their similarities are quite impressive, their differences loom larger. Sartre's existentialist emphasis on individual self-authorship, the idea that we create ourselves through choice and decision, is a simply a modern twist on an old humanist trope that dates back to Aristotle and the Stoics. Despite his anti-Cartesian view of consciousness, Sartre never wavered in his rather one-sided emphasis that human agency is the central fact of existence. Indeed, he was severe and unrelenting in his implication that each and every human being is "doomed to freedom" and therefore entirely responsible for his or her actions and decisions. The self as agent — however conflicted, immersed in "bad faith" or self-deception — was central to all of his philosophical reflections. At the same time, Sartre insisted on the opacity of the ego and the "nothingness" at the heart of Being — arguments that prefigure the postmodern mentality (Frie 1997).

By contrast with Sartre's voluntarism and radical individualism, Lacan's structuralism and linguistics tend to undercut any notion of individual self-determination, rendering him more akin to postmodernism. By this account, individuals are born into a kinship system, into language, and into ready-made identities and roles that effectively determine who they are. This way of thinking issues in a kind of environmental or sociological determinism that relativizes the notion of individual agency and personal responsibility and is therefore antithetical to Sartre's "existential psychoanalysis." Admittedly, there are some instances where Lacan attributes a degree of agency to experience and behavior, such as when he speaks of "the active gift of love." But by Lacan's own reckoning, disinterested love is a rarity, and it is difficult to imagine such radically decentered, fragmented subjects as being capable of such proffering such a "gift of love" to others.

R. D. LAING

Ronald David Laing was born in Glasgow in 1927, the only child of David and Amelia Laing. He received a licentiate in music from the Royal Academy of Music at 16 — a rare distinction, even today. At school, he excelled in classics, and at 17 he enrolled in Glasgow University. At 18, Laing decided to specialize in medicine, though he spent as much time studying philosophy as he did studying medicine. Military service was mandatory in Scotland in the late 1940s, and so Laing underwent basic training in 1949 and spent his leisure hours reading Sartre's *Being and Nothingness.* Judging from his correspondence with Marcelle Vincent and the recollections of close friends, reading Sartre transformed his life. After a brief apprenticeship in neurosurgery at Killearn in 1950, Laing spent 1951 as an army psychiatrist whose task was to differentiate soldiers who were truly disturbed from malingerers. In 1952, now an army captain, Laing was placed in charge of the army hospital in Catterick, in Yorkshire. Soon thereafter, he left the army for the Royal Gartnavel Hospital and Southern General Hospital in Glasgow, In 1954, Laing came to the attention of Dr. J. D. Sutherland of Edinburgh, who was then the director of the Tavistock Clinic in London. With the help of Sutherland, his successor, John Bowlby, and Charles Rycroft, Laing came to London in 1956 so that he could train as a psychoanalyst.

During his analytic training Laing worked as the registrar of the Adult Services Section at the Tavistock Clinic and completed *The Divided Self,* a classic in existential psychiatry (1960). Meanwhile, in 1958, John Bowlby introduced Laing to Gregory Bateson's double bind theory of schizophrenia, which Laing incorporated into his second book, *Self and Others* (Laing 1961, chap. 7). Laing was intrigued with American research on the families of schizophrenics, and blended that approach with ideas culled from Husserl and Sartre in a study of 100 such families in East London between 1959 and 1963. In 1964, Laing and co-author Aaron Esterson published some of these cases in *Sanity, Madness and the Family* (Laing and Esterson, 1964; Laing 1967, chap. 5; Burston 2000, chap. 4). In 1965, Laing, Esterson, and David Cooper founded the Philadelphia Association, a charitable trust that was originally devoted to creating therapeutic communities that were free of the labeling and coercion found in most mental hospitals, and which has since become one of Britain's leading psychotherapy training institutes.

In 1966, Laing published *Interpersonal Perception: A Theory and a Method of Research* (with Phillipson and Lee), and in 1967, he published *The Politics of Experience,* which became a best seller. That same year, David Cooper published *Psychiatry and Anti-Psychiatry* (Cooper 1967), in which he coined the term "anti-psychiatry" and described Laing as an "anti-psychiatrist." Laing disliked the label, but, sadly, it stuck and is still widely used as a generic term to describe the disparate perspectives of Thomas Szasz, Laing, and Foucault. In 1970, Laing left for an 18–month interlude of meditation and study in India and Sri Lanka. The American edition of *The Politics of the Family* was published in his absence in 1971. In 1976, he published *The Facts of Life,* which contained some lengthy autobiographical fragments, followed by *The Voice of Experience* (1982). In 1983, internal conflicts and his own erratic behavior prompted Laing to resign as chair of the Philadelphia Association, and Laing commenced work on *Wisdom, Madness and Folly* (1985), an autobiographical sketch that chronicled his life from infancy to age 26, when he began to write *The Divided Self.* He died in 1989.

Summarizing Laing's work is tricky because, by his own admission, Laing was an antisystematic thinker. Like his adolescent heroes, Kierkegaard and Nietzsche, Laing was simply not interested in constructing a grand theoretical edifice (Burston 2000). And like Binswanger, Laing was not interested in effecting a rigorous adaptation of any single philosopher's perspective to the practice of psychotherapy. While indebted to Sartre, Laing also quoted freely from Hegel, Dilthey, Husserl, Scheler, Jaspers, Heidegger, Buber, and Tillich when it suited his purposes. Finally, Laing's reflections on a "science of persons," interpersonal phenomenology, and the practice of psychotherapy are scattered among numerous books and papers, rendering an overall appraisal difficult. Still, there is a lucid, intelligible core to his work, and in light of the Hegelian motifs running through Sartre and Lacan, the best place to begin is with the Hegelian dimension of Laing's ideas.

Laing's concept of personal identity hinges on a dialectical distinction between being "for myself" and "for others," and an exquisitely detailed description of the nuances of reflective self-consciousness that shows his Hegelian underpinnings clearly. In *Interpersonal Perception*, for example, he wrote that

> Self identity (my view of myself) and meta-identity (my view of your view of me) are theoretical constructs, not concrete realities. *In concreto,* rather than in abstracto, self-identity ("I" looking at "me") is constituted not only by our looking at ourselves, but also by our looking at others looking at us and our reconstitution and alteration of these views of others about us. At this more complex, more concrete level, self-identity is a synthesis of my looking at me with my view of others' views of me. These views of others of me need not be passively accepted, but they cannot be ignored in my development of a sense of who I am. (Laing, Phillipson and Lee 1966, 5)

Laing is describing an *adult* sense of personal identity in which one's being "for oneself" and "being for another" are always inextricably intertwined. But being a psychoanalyst, Laing was not content to stop there, and he sought to discover how a prototypical adult self-consciousness (and its accompanying modes of authenticity and inauthenticity) evolve from infancy onward. Chapter 7 of *The Divided Self* is devoted to the theme of self-consciousness and stipulates that from the very outset "self" and "other" are reciprocally constituted. To make his case, Laing quoted at length from *Beyond the Pleasure Principle* (Freud 1920), citing Freud's analysis of the *fort-da* game played by his nephew to assuage anxiety experienced in his mother's absence. According to Laing, the mother's presence is not just vital for the satisfaction of instinctual needs, as Freud insisted, but for ratifying and affirming the very being of the child — to bestow a sense of "being there" (and being valued) by her words and gestures:

> It seems that loss of the mother, at a certain stage, threatens the individual with loss of his self. The mother, however, is not simply a *thing* which the child can see, but a person who sees the child. Therefore, we suggest that a necessary component in the development of the self is the experience of oneself under the loving eye of the mother. . . . But being seen is simply one of innumerable ways in which the infant's total

being is given attention. He is attended to, by being noticed, rocked, cuddled, thrown in the air, bathed: his body is handled to an extent that it never will be again. Some mothers can recognize and respond to the child's "mental" processes but cannot responsively accept its concrete bodily actuality and vice versa. It may be that a failure on the mother's part to one or other aspects of the infant's being will have important consequences. (Laing 1960, 116)

Though he did not say so here, Laing's emphasis on the primacy of preverbal and nonverbal forms of interpersonal rapport in the onto-genetic sequence is characteristic of his whole approach to therapy, and it stands in dramatic contrast to Lacan's rationalistic (and faintly contemptuous) dismissal of emotional experience or expression that is not verbalized. As an army psychiatrist, and later in private practice, Laing spent many hours in silent communion with mute and catatonic patients. He often said that, even with less disturbed patients, many of the important moments in therapy pass in perfect silence or simply defy our attempts to express them in language. Like Lacan, however, Laing was very interested in "mirroring" and self-reflection as constitutive elements in the formation of the self. Indeed, while pondering the implications of Freud's nephew's mirror play (which Freud described in a footnote), Laing argued that the little boy's evident satisfaction at making himself "disappear" and "reappear" presages an identification with the standpoint of the external observer. Self-observation, Laing suggests, crystallizes around a phantasied identification with "the person by whom one is seen," at least in the first instance.

In any case, by Laing's account, the "existential birth" of the subject, or the emergence of self-consciousness, begins at about two to three months of age. As time passes, the growing child develops a deeper, more complex identity in conjunction with relations with significant others. But the earliest identification with the (m)other lays the basis for subsequent self-reflection and is crucial for future development. If the infant's mother is unaware, indifferent, or actually hostile to the infant's bodily and affective expressions, the child's subsequent self-appraisals may be withering as well. Indeed, an inauthentic mode of relatedness to others ensues when the mother affirms the infant's behavior if, and only if, it conforms to the (m)other's expectations of what a "good" child is — where "goodness" is defined in terms of compliance with someone else's needs or standards rather than as the self-willed expression of an intrinsic virtue.

An excess of being "good" to secure approval and avoid punishment sets the stage, developmentally, for what Ronald Fairbairn, Donald Winnicott, Harry Guntrip, and Laing call a "false self." As the child becomes more inauthentic in his or her dealings with others, the "false self" begins to overshadow and oppress the "true self," which is experienced increasingly as either invisible to, menaced by, or somehow impinged upon by the reifying gaze of others. For like Lacan, Laing incorporated Sartre's notion of "the gaze" into his work. However, he did not treat it as integral to the human condition or the structure of infancy per se. On the contrary, he treated the experience of being objectified in the other's gaze as a symptom of severe interpersonal estrangement called "ontological insecurity." Ontological insecurity entails anxieties and guilt feelings that differ *qualitatively* from the anxiety and guilt experienced by those who enjoy the more prevalent (statistically normal) orientation to reality, called "ontological security." Ontologically secure people have a false self, too, but when circumstances permit, they are able to shed their masks and risk authentic self-disclosure because they have a strong and stable sense of personal identity. They do not fear the scrutiny of others, and characteristically suffer conflicts over the pursuit of pleasure and security or "instinctual satisfactions," as Freud described them. In other words, an ontologically secure person's guilt and anxiety revolves around doing (or not doing) certain things with or to others, having (or not having) certain kinds of intimacy, access, prestige, and so on.

By contrast, ontologically insecure (or "schizoid") people seldom relinquish their false selves for fear of being even more damaged than they are already. Their conflicts are fraught with anxiety and guilt, not about doing or having this or that, but about *being* and nonbeing. They are plagued by fears of inner emptiness, existential annihilation or engulfment (rather than bodily damage or death), fears of being found out, guilt about self-betrayal, chronic dishonesty and pretense, even guilt for just being there in the first place. These people may seek (and find) "instinctual satisfaction" in pseudorelationships where their libido is engaged but their real self is not, resulting in "inner" and interpersonal conflicts regarding sincerity and self-representation that are not adequately addressed from the Freudian perspective.

Laing provides several illuminating examples of these sorts of conflicts, but the most tragic appears in chapter 9 of *The Divided Self*. There we find an anonymous vignette about an apparently normal man in his fifties who, for sake of convenience, we will call Edmund. One summer afternoon, while picnicking with his wife and children, Edmund suddenly stripped and waded into a nearby river, dousing himself repeatedly. When asked what on earth he was doing, he replied that he was baptizing himself for his sins. When asked *what* sins he was atoning for, Edmund declared that he had never really loved his wife and children. Moreover, he refused to come out of the river until he was "cleansed," and was dragged away by the police, who hospitalized him immediately thereafter (Laing 1960, 148).

Admittedly, Edmund was behaving in an odd, tactless, and obstinate manner. But even if his symbolic gestures were silly, desperate, and histrionic, his claim that he never really loved his wife and children, far from being delusional, might actually have been true. Laing said that in such a case, the abrupt repudiation of a hitherto successful "false self" prompts the emergence of psychotic behavior, but that crises like these need not be catastrophic. With the help of a skillful psychotherapist, Edmund's "midlife crisis" might present an unexpected opportunity to begin anew and create a more authentic and integrated existence. Laing expressed this idea in the pithy and often cited statement: "Madness need not be all breakdown. It can also be a *breakthrough*."

Laing's purpose in writing *The Divided Self* was to make the process of going mad intelligible to ordinary people. Throughout this book, he echoed Sartre's insistence that one cannot understand psychological disturbances "*from the outside,* on the basis of a positivistic determinism, or . . . with a combination of concepts that remain outside the illness as lived and experienced," and that one "cannot study, let alone cure, a neurosis without a fundamental respect for the person of the patient, without a constant effort to grasp the basic situation and to relive it" (Laing and Cooper 1964, 6).

Laing was critical of Freud's attempt to root psychoanalysis in the natural sciences, since this way of framing the patient's utterances and experiences often robbed them of their personal meaning, their agency and their social intelligibility. Instead of explanation in natural scientific terms, Laing advocated a "science of persons" based on the rigorous application of the *Verstehende* approach pioneered by Dilthey — one that seeks to *understand* others rather than to generate models and hypotheses that will enable us to predict and control their behavior. To understand others empathically is to see their behavior as an expression of their experience of the world, and of their intentions toward it, rather than as a concatenation of mechanical or organic processes governed by natural law. Despite Freud's recommendations about "neutrality," being a blank screen, and so on, the kind of objectivity sought by the natural sciences is simply out of place here because in the absence of empathy, says Laing, real understanding of the other person *as a person* eludes us, even if we carefully enumerate all the "signs" of their disorder according to prevailing diagnostic criteria. As a result, says Laing, it is possible to know

> just about everything that can be known about the psychopathology of schizophrenia or of schizophrenia as a disease without being able to understand a single schizophrenic. Such data are all ways of *not* understanding him. To look and to listen to a patient and see "signs" of schizophrenia (as a "disease"), and to look and to listen to him simply as a human being are to see and to hear in as radically different ways. (1960, 33)

Nevertheless, in the final analysis, Laing's critique of Freud is not as stark or uncompromising as Sartre's. In *The Politics of Experience,* for example, he notes that unconscious mental processes like repression, projection, denial, or splitting are indeed intentional, as Sartre said, but that

> the person appears to be unaware that he is doing this to himself. Even when a person develops sufficient insight to see that "splitting" is going on, he usually experiences this splitting as . . . an impersonal process . . . which . . . he can observe but cannot control or stop.
>
> There is thus some phenomenological validity referring to such "defenses" by the term "mechanism."

However, Laing continues, "As he becomes de-alienated [the patient] is able first of all to become aware of them . . . and then to take the second, even more crucial step of progressively realizing that these are things that he does or has done to himself. Process becomes converted back to praxis, and the patient becomes an agent" (Laing 1967, 34–35). In other words, Laing says, "defense mechanisms are actions taken by the person on his own experience. On top of this he has dissociated himself from his own action. The end product of this twofold violence is a person who no longer experiences himself fully as a person, but as a part of a person, invaded by destructive psychopathological 'mechanisms.'"

Laing did not construe the various mechanisms described by Freud and his followers as defenses against instincts as such, but as ways of avoiding a lucid awareness and ownership of one's own choices, attitudes, and desires. In framing the issue this way, Laing anticipated American psychoanalyst Roy Schafer (1976), whose "action language" approach to psychoanalysis could also be described as a technique for turning process into praxis. But Laing did not stop here. While classical psychoanalysis does a good job of enumerating and describing the various "intrapsychic" processes that estrange us from our own experience, said Laing, it fails to address what he termed *interpersonal defenses,* where people do not disavow their own agency or experience, but act destructively on the experience of others through collusion, injunctions, and attributions, and processes of invalidation, mystification, and so on. Psychiatry and psychoanalysis lack a vocabulary to describe these destructive forms of interpersonal communication, which speaks volumes about their respective biases. In fact, Laing said, "intrapsychic processes" of the kind Freud described only occur in social fields fraught with these kinds of interpersonal distortions, which prescribe and proscribe certain kinds of thoughts, feelings, or experiences as invalid and estrange us from ourselves and each other (Burston 1996b, chap. 7). So for Laing, as well as for Sartre, a psychoanalysis automatically entails a socioanalysis as well.

In addition to being critical of Freud, Laing was conciliatory toward Jung, in some respects. Like Jung — and like Winnicott, incidentally —

Laing did not equate the ego with the self, and he sometimes saw the former as the adversary of the latter (Burston 2000). Like Jung, Laing rejected Freud's rationalistic appraisal of phantasy as incipiently infantile or pathological. Recall that for Freud phantasy (or "primary process thought") is always our first way of being-in-the-world, and to a great extent remains so beneath the threshold of consciousness. But by Freud's reckoning, phantasy is rooted in an inability or refusal address or acknowledge unpleasant truths, whether these truths represent states of affairs that exist in "external reality," or within ourselves. So the primacy of "primary process thought," though doubtless a given, is something to be struggled with and overcome as much as possible in the interest of strengthening the ego. For Jung, by contrast, phantasy is not just a distortion or an obstacle to apprehending the truth. Very often it expresses unpalatable truths of which the conscious ego is quite ignorant. As Laing says in *The Politics of Experience,*

> [Phantasy] has its own validity, its own rationality. Infantile phantasy may become a closed enclave, a dissociated undeveloped "unconscious," but this need not be so. This eventually is another form of alienation. Phantasy as encountered in many people today is split off from what the person regards as his mature, sane, rational adult experience. We do not then see phantasy in its true function but experienced merely an intrusive, sabotaging infantile nuisance. (Laing 1967, 27)

Nowhere is Laing's debt to Jung more apparent than in his ideas about psychosis. Freud and his followers regarded madness in purely privative terms, as the loss of reason, the loss of ego boundaries, or ego functions; or of adaptation, relatedness, the capacity to form a transference, and so on. By contrast with Freud, Jung regarded madness as a tragic misfortune, a shattering blow, but one with potentially redeeming consequences.

According to Freud, psychotics retreat into a world of phantasy because they despair of sustaining relationships with others, which have become too frustrating or fraught with conflict and uncertainty to be a secure source of gratification or love. Lacking tangible incentives to stay related, said Freud, psychotics withdraw their libidinal cathexes from external "objects" and reinvest their free-floating libido in their own egos — a process Freud called "introversion," before coining the term "secondary narcissism" to denote this redeployment of psychic energy (Freud 1914). Jung agreed with Freud about the psychotic patient's retreat from the "external" world, but added that the phantasies of cosmic death and rebirth that many psychotics cherish represent a stubborn attempt to make a new beginning (Hogenson 1983). Borrowing from the New Testament, Jung called this search for a self-cure *metanoia*, which is translated variously as "repentance" or turning around, and which signifies a radical and irreversible change in perspective. Though Laing did not adopt the term "metanoia" until 1963, his affinities with Jung become even more apparent when he decries our collective alienation from "inner space" in *The Politics of Experience*. The process of metanoia, as Jung understood it, involves the death or eclipse of the ego as a prelude to the rebirth of the self — an attempt to restore balance and wholeness in a mind that is radically estranged from its own psychic interior. In a very similar vein, Laing's once famous epigram from *The Bird of Paradise* ran as follows: "If I could turn you on, if I could drive you out of your wretched mind, if I could tell you, I would let you know." This quote implies that absent the requisite return or recovery of a sense of "inner space," true sanity eludes us forever.

Laing's affinities with Jung contributed to his sharp and sweeping dismissal of ego psychology, and to any approach to psychotherapy that construes the goal of therapy as the strengthening of the ego or as "normalization." Far from being clear, said Laing, terms like "sanity" and "madness" are profoundly ambiguous in our time. People deemed eminently sane or successful by the majority of their peers often pose a much greater menace to the safety and stability of the world than their overtly psychotic counterparts. Why? Because in our present state of collective alienation, normality is really a form of pseudosanity, marked by complicity in "social phantasy systems" and adaptation to pervasive "pseudorealities." To those who share our particular mythology or ideology, our actions and attitudes appear "normal." But considered from the standpoint of outsiders, the same actions and attitudes may seem completely deranged.

While the vast majority of his contemporaries thought of "normality" and "mental health" as equivalent or interchangeable terms, Laing saw normality as a kind of deficiency disease that robs us of authenticity, compassion, and the ability to think critically about our enveloping social contexts. It also robs us of the yearning for transcendence and the ability to love and to connect with others authentically, except in rare or exceptional circumstances. Moreover, Laing did not embrace the rationalist Freudian view of love as a quasi-delusional state that obstructs or distorts our grasp of reality, but like Scheler and Buber, he saw it as an intimate experiential way of knowing others and the world more deeply. And though he eschewed the "anti-psychiatry" label thrust on him by his erstwhile collaborator, David Cooper, to the end of his life, Laing chastised psychiatry (and other mental health professions) for promoting conformity rather than genuine mental health, and for an essentially loveless stance toward those in their care.

In terms of our heuristic schemata, Laing was an irrationalist with somewhat utopian leanings, though he was also demonstrably inconsistent in his political orientation and ideas. During the sixties, Laing was the darling of the British Left, but after a period of deep disenchantment with left-wing politics, he started drifting toward a more liberal humanism during the late sixties and early seventies. By the late seventies and early eighties, Laing's political position was moving toward conservatism, basically the reverse of Sartre's, whose radicalism deepened, rather than diminished, with each passing decade.

Laing was also inconsistent in his attitudes toward religion, posing as a militant atheist in early life, but wavering between heartfelt professions of faith and an anguished, reluctant agnosticism in later life. Like Sartre and Lacan, though for different reasons, Laing was also difficult to classify along the modern-postmodern axis. Borrowing from Hegel, Laing always insisted that one's sense of selfhood and identity is constructed intersubjectively, and that the ego is a largely an imaginary construct — a creature of expediency embedded in social phantasy systems. And though he never minimized the horror and confusion that accompanies acute psychological distress, as critics claimed, Laing often treated psychiatric diagnoses as little more than social constructions invoked to legitimate our patients' involuntary hospitalization and treatment. In Laing's estimation, psychiatric diagnoses give us little or no leverage, therapeutically speaking, because from the standpoint of genuine insight, diagnoses are ways of *not* understanding patients, if by "understanding" we mean the apprehending of utterances, attitudes, and behavior humanly, rather than as symptoms of an underlying brain disease.

In many ways, Laing's varied, perceptive, and sometimes contradictory reflections on the politics of diagnosis and the uses and abuses of psychiatric authority parallel and presage the ideas of Michel Foucault, whose book *Madness and Civilization* first appeared in English translation in 1961 in a series entitled "Studies in Existentialism and Phenomenology" that Laing edited for Tavistock Press (Burston 1996b, 177). Indeed, Laing admired Foucault, and to the very end insisted that his later work was phenomenological, despite the fact that Foucault had long since renounced any ties with phenomenology. This is the postmodern dimension of Laing, which was also by far the more disturbing and controversial for most of his readers — whether inside or outside of the mental health professions. But these postmodern gestures must be balanced against many modernist tropes, including his typically humanist emphasis on the fundamental unity of the human species, the need to experience and express solidarity with the mad, psychotherapy as a collaborative search for truth, and the ineluctable role of human agency in understanding human behavior (Burston 2000).

Psychoanalysis and Intersubjectivity
Sullivan, Fromm, Merleau-Ponty, Benjamin, and Stolorow

Our travels thus far have brought us from the early seventeenth to the mid twentieth century, covering what is commonly known as the "modern era." The themes, thinkers, and clinicians whose work we explored were all rooted in European soil. And with the exception of Freud, a neurologist by training, those who were not philosophers were invariably psychiatrists and psychoanalysts. Not a single psychologist has come to our attention. Until now, our approach has been comparative and historical, situating thinkers in our fourfold heuristic, and whenever possible, chronological sequence. In the last two chapters, as we approach the "postmodern" era and the ideas of many living thinkers whose work is still unfolding, we will adopt a more issue-oriented and thematic approach, to consider the impact of continental thought on North American psychology and psychoanalysis.

Several cultural and historical trends contribute to this new climate of discussion. First, note the near disappearance of psychoanalytic psychiatry in North America in the final quarter of the twentieth century. Since the 1980s, the shift to a more biologically oriented approach in psychiatry, coupled with advances in medications and cultural and economic pressures to medicate patients has meant that relatively few analytically oriented psychiatrists are still in practice today. The pervasive bureaucratization of mental health has similarly encroached on the practice of psychoanalysis. Second, existential psychiatry, a once powerful and protean force, has become a marginal voice in the mental health field since the mid-1970s, at least in North America. With rare exceptions like Irving Yalom, who still commands a wide and attentive audience outside of psychiatry, few psychiatrists identify themselves with the existential-phenomenological tradition. The concurrent declines of psychoanalytic and existential psychiatry have a common cause — the resurgence of neo-Kräpelinian, biologically based psychiatry, which mandates drug-based approaches to treatment and discourages so-called "talk therapy." As a result of this trend, newly minted psychiatrists in North America often have little training in psychotherapy.

Psychiatry has slowly ceded the practice of psychoanalysis and psychotherapy to psychologists, social workers, and counselors, and in the process continental philosophy has had an increasing impact on psychology and social work in the last three decades. Nowhere has the impact of continental philosophy on psychological theory and practice been more obvious than in the discussion of intersubjectivity, defined most broadly as the relationship between self and other. In this chapter we will be concerned with the ways in which the metatheoretical notion of intersubjectivity has been understood philosophically and applied clinically by Harry Stack Sullivan, Erich Fromm, Maurice Merleau-Ponty, Jessica Benjamin, and Robert Stolorow and his colleagues. Of this group of clinicians, Merleau-Ponty is the only philosopher, though his writing and seminars as a professor of child psychology and pedagogy at the Sorbonne directly address clinical concerns. Indeed, Sullivan, Fromm, Benjamin, and Stolorow all identify themselves as psychoanalysts, which requires some explanation, as throughout our discussion we have chiefly employed the term "psychotherapy."

As a result of revisionist forms of psychoanalysis, particularly interpersonal, relational, and intersubjective approaches, traditional distinctions between psychoanalysis and psychotherapy have given way to the possibility of integrating clinical theories and techniques. This dispersion points toward a broadening of psychoanalysis. It suggests that psychoanalysis is not a monolithic Freudian entity and cannot be owned or appropriated by an exclusive set of ideas and beliefs. All too often psychoanalysts are lumped together by their critics under the rubric of classical Freudianism. In fact, contemporary psychoanalysis has moved well beyond Freud so that revisionist forms of psychoanalysis have much in common with contemporary existential and humanistic psychotherapy. Not surprisingly, perhaps, the influence of continental philosophy is equally evident in the work of James Bugenthal, Tom Greening, Mike Arons, Ilene Serlin, Kirk Schneider, and others, who seek to fuse (European) existential psychotherapy with (American) humanistic psychology. And despite Jung's sometimes disparaging remarks about Hegel and Heidegger, since the 1980s Jungian analytic psychology has taking continental thought to heart, as evidenced in the publications of James Hillman, Robert Romanyshyn, Stan Marlan, Roger Brooke, and others.

Thus, although there has been a profound decline in the influence of continental philosophy in psychiatry, in other mental health professions the impact of continental thinking is both deeper and more diffuse, intermingling with other indigenous influences, including systems theory, feminism, pragmatism, constructivism, and so on. And at the risk of belaboring the obvious, continental philosophy has itself changed dramatically since the late 1960s. In the following chapter, we examine these changes and the impact of poststructuralism, deconstructionism, and postmodernism in the clinical domain.

HARRY STACK SULLIVAN

Probably no American psychiatrist had a greater impact on contemporary approaches to intersubjectivity than Harry Stack Sullivan. Sullivan (1892–1949) was born in a rural farming community in New York State and received his medical degree from the Chicago School of Medicine and Surgery in 1917. Sullivan began his psychiatric career at St. Elizabeth's Hospital in Washington, D.C., where he trained with Adolph Meyer and William Alanson White, two prominent American psychiatrists. While training with White, Sullivan first learned about psychoanalytic method and modified its technique for the treatment of schizophrenic and bipolar (manic-depressive) patients. Meanwhile, Sullivan initiated a fruitful collaboration between psychiatry and the social sciences in the 1920s. For example, Sullivan made a close study of sociologist George Herbert Mead, whose concepts of mind, self, and society were strongly influenced by Hegel and were subsequently incorporated into Sullivan's theory of personality. Sullivan was also influenced by anthropologists and linguists like Edward Sapir, Franz Boaz, Ruth Benedict, many of whom were members of his salon, known as the Zodiac Club.

During the 1930s and 1940s, Sullivan worked with Frieda Fromm-Reichmann at Chestnut Lodge Hospital, and founded the Washington School of Psychiatry. Sullivan's work with Fromm-Reichmann, her former husband, Erich Fromm, and Clara Thompson led to the founding of the William Alanson White Institute in 1946, named in remembrance of Sullivan's teacher. Although Sullivan only published two books when he died in 1949, the posthumous publication of his lectures helped to solidify his standing and to extend his influence.

To appreciate Sullivan's ideas, it is important to remember that classical psychoanalysis was the dominant therapeutic technique used by psychiatrists at the time. Classical psychoanalysis prescribed a relationship between the analyst and the patient based on the twin pillars of objectivity and neutrality. According to the classical account, the analyst observes and identifies the patient's mental processes working in a detached and objective manner. A crucial aspect of this process rests on the analyst's ability to bracket out distorting prejudices and thereby maintain a neutral stance, offering up a blank screen, thus avoiding interference in the intrapsychic life of the patient and allowing transference to unfold spontaneously.

Among the first to reject this model for practice in the United States, Sullivan pioneered the psychotherapeutic treatment of schizophrenia and authored *The Interpersonal Theory of Psychiatry,* which in turn spawned the interpersonal approach to psychoanalysis. Sullivan's approach has much in common with that of Binswanger, though the two were apparently unfamiliar with each other's work. The considerable parallels between them provide a useful way to understand Sullivan's interpersonal theory and demonstrate its considerable, if unacknowledged, links to the existential-phenomenological tradition.

Sullivan's and Binswanger's theoretical and clinical perspectives originated in different cultural and intellectual milieus, yet their positions are close in many ways. Both of them rejected the determinism of Freud's philosophy of mind and all but dismissed the causality of Freud's drive theory and concept of the unconscious. In the process, each sought to develop theories that were more true to their patients' lived experiences, and created new vocabularies to describe their patients' modes of relatedness to themselves and the world.

In contrast to Freud, who argued that psychoanalysis was appropriate only for neurotic patients, Sullivan and Binswanger worked extensively with patients in the psychotic, schizophrenic, and manic-depressive (bipolar) spectrums. As a result, they developed an interpersonal style of interaction, more appropriate for communicating with and ultimately helping their patients. Sullivan's technique was also much influenced by the work of Clara Thompson's first analyst, Sándor Ferenczi, whose use of "active technique" and of "mutual analysis" antagonized Freud. By fostering a climate of equality and reciprocity between therapist and patient, Ferenczi's "mutual analysis" eschewed the traditional authoritarian psychiatric relationship. Today, Ferenczi's work ranks alongside Sullivan's as a major component in contemporary interpersonal and relational psychoanalysis.

Like Binswanger, Sullivan challenged Freud's structural model of the mind and relegated biological drives or instincts to a much more limited role, emphasizing the importance of interpersonal connectedness. Sullivan states, "Everything that can be found in the human mind has been put there by interpersonal relations, excepting only the capabilities to receive and elaborate the relevant experiences. This statement is intended to be the antithesis of any document of human instincts" (1950, 302).

Though opposed to the causal model or "psychic determinism" in Freud's conception of unconscious drives, Binswanger and Sullivan nevertheless acknowledged the role that unconscious processes play in human behavior. The way in which they conceived of the unconscious, however, was radically different from Freud. According to Binswanger (1955), although the unconscious may refer to a part of the human mind, it does not exist as a "world" of its own, nor does it relate to itself through a world. Similarly, as Sullivan states, "The unconscious . . . is quite clearly that which cannot be experienced directly, which fills all the gaps in mental life" (Sullivan 1950, 204). Not surprisingly, perhaps, given his opposition to Freud, Binswanger's view of the unconscious was less elaborate than Sullivan's. Conversely, Binswanger paid greater heed to dreams and their relevance in treatment than did Sullivan. Rather than interpret dreams from the perspective of Freudian metapsychology, Binswanger (1993b) described dreams in terms of the dreamer's world designs, not as psychic processes.

Much of what Binswanger said about the unconscious can be understood along the lines of Sullivan's (1953) notion of "unformulated experience." Both paid close attention to the notion of "implicit experience," which has become a topic of wider investigation (Damasio 1999; Frie 1999c). For Sullivan, the unconscious refers to experience that has yet to be articulated, elaborated, and fully understood. He suggests that when experiences are too fraught with anxiety, they are not readily assimilated in language: "One has information about one's experience only to the extent that one has tended to communicate it to another or thought about it in the manner of communicative speech. Much of what is ordinarily said to be repressed is merely unformulated" (1953a, 185). Sullivan elaborated the defensive use of unformulated experience in a much clearer sense than Binswanger. Unlike repression, in which an experience is defensively thrust out of awareness by an unconscious "censorship," Sullivan suggested that certain experiences are never present to consciousness to begin with, and remain eternally "unformulated," that is, divorced from linguistic representation (Stern 1997). Like Sartre, and for similar reasons, Sullivan dismissed the existence of repression and censorship, referring instead to "selective inattention," an intentional refusal to acknowledge one's motives for not experiencing and/or for doing certain things. By his account, whatever goes on at an "intrapsychic" level reflects ongoing processes in a fluid interpersonal field. Indeed, Sullivan was adamantly opposed to any notion of "interiority" and the idea of a core, nuclear self that exists apart from relationships.

According to Sullivan (1953a, 1953b), whose writings on technique are more extensive than Binswanger's, psychoanalyst and patient attempt to achieve "consensual validation" of the patient's experience of relating to others and the world. Consensual validation signals the arrival of the patient at a "syntaxic," or interpersonally verifiable view of reality. The goal for the interpersonal psychoanalyst is to identify and elaborate the patient's "parataxic" mode of relating: the arbitrary, private, and frequently distorted mode of interpersonal experience.

For Sullivan and Binswanger, the aim of psychoanalysis is not to make the unconscious conscious in the traditional Freudian sense, but to free patients from distorted modes of relating to others and the world around them. From this perspective, both concentrate on the way in which the person structures reality, not on building structure *within* the person. Sullivan's and Binswanger's interest in the social context of human existence led them to develop new and innovative ways of conceptualizing mental health and human development. For Binswanger, Husserl, Heidegger, and Buber were central. For Sullivan, the sociology of George Herbert Mead and the philosophy of John Dewey helped to frame the interpersonal perspective. Although the continental and pragmatist approaches to philosophy differ in many ways, their opposition to the Cartesian notion of the isolated mind, and their attempts to find news ways of conceptualizing human experience and interaction, are often very similar.

Drawing on Mead, Sullivan argued that the self is always relationally generated and maintained. In "The Illusion of Personal Individuality," Sullivan maintains that the contents of consciousness are socially derived and give rise to an illusory sense of self. Sullivan defined the human being as the sum total of his or her relations with others, and posited the existence of "multiple selves." He recommended that clinicians give up the attempt to define a unique individual self and try to grasp what is going on at any particular time in the interpersonal field.

Sullivan's dismissal of the unique individual constitutes an extreme position in interpersonal thinking and has engendered much criticism and debate (compare Wolstein 1971; Greenberg and Mitchell 1983; Stern 1997; Frie 2003; Fiscalini 2004), yet it also has had direct and significant implications for the formulation of individual subjectivity. Indeed, although the notion of the person as subject is undeniably central to the clinical work of psychoanalysis, the concept of subjectivity remains much debated in psychoanalytic discourse. Sullivan, like Freud before him, sees individual subjectivity as fully controlled by the causal determinism of mental phenomena. As a result, there is little space for individual action, or for the conceptualization of agency and will. In Sullivan's words, which have an unmistakable ring of finality, "I know of no evidence of a force or power that may be called a *will*, in contradistinction to the vector addition of integrating tendencies" (1953a, 191). Yet a theory of agency and will is important for psychoanalysis and psychotherapy, and like the notion of individual subjectivity, its valence is often taken for granted. Perhaps this points to the inevitable distinction between the formulation of theory and actual clinical practice, which we will discuss in the following chapter.

Erich Fromm

While Sullivan develops an interpersonal approach to the theme of intersubjectivity, Erich Fromm's work emphasizes the fundamental role of culture and society in understanding human interaction. Fromm was born in Frankfurt in 1900. His mother and father were descended from illustrious rabbinic families, and in 1920, he studied at a Jewish adult education center in Frankfurt, the Freies Jüdisches Lehrhaus, directed by Martin Buber and Franz Rosenzweig. In 1922, Fromm completed a doctorate in sociology under Alfred Weber in Heidelberg, and after a brief stint as a newspaper editor, he decided to become a psychoanalyst, studying one year with Wilhelm Witenberg in Munich in 1924, another with Karl Landauer in Frankfurt, finishing up with a year under Hanns Sachs and another under Theodor Reik in Berlin (Burston 1991).

In 1927, Fromm was appointed director of the section on social psychology at the Frankfurt Institute of Social Research by Max Horkheimer, publishing numerous papers on psychoanalysis and social theory in their house organ, *Zeitschrift für Sozialforschung*. As the situation in Europe deteriorated, Fromm fled the Nazi menace, and on arrival in the United States in 1933, he joined Sullivan's salon, the Zodiac Club, rubbing shoulders with leading American psychiatrists, anthropologists, and linguists. In 1938, Fromm left the Frankfurt school — which had relocated to Columbia University — and began a book on the psychology of fascism called *Escape from Freedom* (1941). This book was followed by *Man for Himself* (1947), *The Forgotten Language* (1951), *The Sane Society* (1955), *The Art of Loving* (1956), *Sigmund Freud's Mission* (1959), *Zen Buddhism and Psychoanalysis* (1960), *Beyond the Chains of Illusion* (1961), and many others.

While Fromm gained a wide and admiring audience outside psychoanalytic circles, his early and outspoken critique of Freud's patriarchal and bourgeois bias (see, for example, Fromm 1959) alienated the Freudian establishment. As a result, the New York Psychoanalytic Institute suspended him from supervising students in 1944, and in 1945 he was formally suspended from the American Psychoanalytic Association. Undeterred, Fromm joined Clara Thompson, Harry Stack Sullivan, and ex-wife Frieda Fromm-Reichman, among others, to found the William Alanson White Institute, where he was clinical director from 1946 to 1950, when he moved to Mexico. The International Psychoanalytic Association did not approve of Fromm's ideas or activities in Mexico, and dropped him as member in 1954. Though active in the anti-Vietnam war movement, the environmental movement, the McGovern presidential campaign, and various other causes during the fifties and sixties, Fromm lived and worked for most of the year in Mexico until 1976, when he suffered a heart attack. Upon recovering he retired to Locarno, Switzerland, where he died in 1980.

Fromm's approach to intersubjectivity was predicated on the idea that each and every human being is confronted with the task of overcoming "existential aloneness." Efforts to transcend existential aloneness take place in cultural and social contexts that shape or deform our subjectivity and may constitute a severe impediment to achieving lasting intimacy with another human being. To get a grasp of what is at stake here, we will begin with Fromm's analysis of sadomasochism in *Escape From Freedom* (1941) and *The Art of Loving* (1956). Like Wilhelm Reich, whom Fromm briefly admired (Burston 1991, chap. 2), Fromm said that sadistic and masochistic attitudes are integral to the fascist mentality, or what they jointly referred to as "the authoritarian character." Fromm's analysis of Hitler's speeches (and fascist propaganda generally) vindicated Freud and Reich's contention that sadism and masochism are intimately conjoined in the unconscious. But although he drew extensively on Freud and Reich here, *Escape from Freedom* also marked a dramatic departure from "the master." Freud had explained characterological strivings for dominance or submission as the sublimated derivatives of a sexual orientation in which the individual must administer and/or suffer pain in order to achieve arousal and satisfaction. By Freud's account, perverse sexual desire *precedes* the character trait and accompanies it eternally in the unconscious, even in the absence of overtly "kinky" sexual practices. Wilhelm Reich agreed.

By contrast, Fromm argued that sadism and masochism, dominance and submission, are not sexual phenomena in the first instance, but constitute inadequate "answers" to the fundamental problem of human existence, namely our "existential aloneness" and the consequent need for relatedness to others. As such, the dominant and submissive attitudes are really defenses against psychosis — a fear of total aloneness, of being (or becoming) mad — which only become sexualized secondarily, after the fact. As character traits, said Fromm, sadism and masochism are manifestations of what he called the *symbiotic solution* to the problem of human existence, which permits sordid intimacies of one sort and another, but lacks and discourages the cultivation of real respect or reciprocity, which are preconditions for genuine love.

Another common solution to the problem of existential aloneness is the "orgiastic solution," in which the individual loses his or her sense of separateness through a powerful sense of fusion with the tribe or the cosmos at large. Orgiastic experiences are facilitated by the use of drugs, alcohol, and group rites like dancing, chanting, and drumming.

Like Nietzsche's Dionysian orientation, they permit a deep and gratifying sense of immersion in nature, a loss of ego boundaries. But however convulsive or compelling are the experiences afforded by orgiastic
rites and practices, the relief from loneliness is transient; when the ecstasy
wears off, the person is even lonelier than before.

A third solution to the problem of existential aloneness that is less
convulsive and episodic than the orgiastic approach is what Fromm called
"automaton conformity," which entails a pervasive (but semideliberate)
numbing of our humanistic conscience and our critical faculties — a
state of frictionless adaptation to one's surroundings. The lack of individuation, and hence of clarity, conviction, and sincerity of emotional
expression that results renders genuine intimacy impossible under such
circumstances. Relationships based on conformist attitudes lack the transgressive and explosive quality of sadomasochistic liaisons. They are not
based on power plays and florid fantasies, but on quiet collusion,
mutual convenience, and shared complacency. Such relationships may
be relatively stable, but they lack genuine passion and offer an escape
from loneliness that leaves the person somewhat brittle and emotionally unfulfilled, rather than challenged and nourished from immersion
in deeply shared experience. The only dignified and durable answer to
the problem of existential aloneness, said Fromm, is love, a form of
union based on openness, generosity of spirit, and the reciprocal recognition and enhancement of individual differences.

Though Fromm seldom cited existential or phenomenological theorists while discussing the dynamics of human relationships, his approach
to sado-masochism put him in the same universe of discourse. Like
Binswanger, for example, Fromm rejected Freud's mechanistic model
of the mind (*homo natura*), and like Heidegger and Sartre, Fromm
took human existence to be a "problem" with no predetermined solution. Though we lack the space to explicate this fully, Fromm's "conformist solution" is strikingly convergent with Heidegger's account of
inauthenticity and the They-self, and with Sartre's notion of "bad
faith." Moreover, like Sartre, though for different reasons, Fromm
acknowledged that sadism and masochism are not symptoms of fixation
to an "infantile" libidinal orientation, but permanent possibilities for
human relatedness. And like Scheler, Buber, and Binswanger, Fromm

rejected Freud's characterization of love as "the normal prototype for the psychoses." By his reckoning, love is a result of maturity, vitality, and strength, rather than of a (real or perceived) lack. Following Spinoza, Fromm distinguished between rational and irrational passions — or passions that deepen and enhance our grasp of reality and those that are detrimental to the growth of reason. Fromm considered love a rational passion, and as the only satisfactory solution to the problem of human existence, the only way of overcoming aloneness that preserves and enhances our dignity and love of life (1956). Indeed, Fromm maintained that while the passions that drive sadomasochism, abject (or aggressive) conformity, and orgiastic practices all erode our capacity to think critically, a truly loving disposition and a *truth-loving* disposition generally go hand-in-hand.

Though he rejected Freud's views on love, Fromm commended Freud for emphasizing the *disillusioning function* of the analytic dialogue, arguing that unless or until a person relinquishes his most cherished illusions, he cannot experience the truth or become truly free (Fromm 1962). Fromm believed that the candid self-scrutiny fostered by analytic inquiry promotes a gradual process of decentration — in Jean Piaget's sense — that enables the individual to be more "objective" about himself or herself, but without nullifying or denying his or her own subjectivity or somehow capitulating to the subjectivity of another. Acquiring greater objectivity, in Fromm's sense, entails a deepening and strengthening of subjectivity rather than its overcoming or erasure because truth is always apprehended from the standpoint of a thinking, feeling, experiencing human subject who is engaged in passionate striving.

Fromm was also aware that subjectivity is embedded in cultural and social worlds that shape and distort individual awareness. Fromm said that many distortions of this sort are purely ideological, which justifies oppression and exploitation by emphasizing the "natural" or divinely ordained "superiority" of one language, class, gender, nation, or faith over another. But in addition to class- and caste-based perspectives on reality, said Fromm, individual awareness is profoundly shaped by subtle "social filters" that hinge on the language, grammar, and logic that a given society characteristically relies upon. Echoing Scheler's earlier reflections on the role of language in shaping inner perception or self-knowledge, Fromm pointed out that some languages fail to distinguish between jealousy and envy, or between guilt and shame, or between genuine humility and abject self-abasement. Lacking words to describe these emotions, it difficult for anyone to grasp their nuances, much less their motives or consequences. They remain on the level of what Sullivan called "unformulated experience." And similarly, in Western cultures where the linear logic of Aristotle's law of noncontradiction — *A* cannot be *A* and non-*A*, simultaneously — prevails, efforts to achieve clarity and consistency may encourage dichotomous thinking and obscure the complexity of human emotions — that one can love and hate, admire and revile the same person.

One way to approach Fromm's "social filters" is to contrast them with an idea that enjoys greater currency. Like the Freudian superego, social filters perform a kind of routine censorship over domains of thought and feeling, hindering the entrance of certain things into consciousness, the difference being that these social filters are not merely "intrapsychic" systems or processes, but are diffusely distributed through society at large. Moreover, they sustain a cultural status quo, rather than an individual's neurotic equilibrium. Finally, unlike the Freudian superego, social filters do not punish those whose experiences are deemed odd, transgressive, or invalid by the cultural mainstream. Society itself takes care of that. People who lack conventional social filters are apt to experience the world rather differently than their peers, and the resulting inner and interpersonal conflict, if it is deep or acute enough, may imperil their sanity or put them at risk for some form of punishment or excommunication. Fromm said that one task of analysis should be to enable analysands to shed ideological illusions and social filters that prevent them from being fully human and embrace a more grounded, ethically centered, nonconformist stance, to "live soundly against the stream."

Freud's studies on "the pathology of civilized communities" focused on how civilization breeds inner and interpersonal conflict by obligating individuals to renounce instinctual satisfactions that are deemed incompatible with social harmony. By contrast, Fromm's social psychology focused less on neurotic conflict than on statistically *normal* character traits that enhance, rather than hinder, the average person's adaptation to society, and which tend to diminish inner and interpersonal conflict; Fromm called them "socially patterned defects" (Burston 1991). For example, in an authoritarian society, sadistic or masochistic character traits are not experienced as "deviant," but are harnessed in the service of the prevailing cultural agenda. Rather than being a source of lively distress, these traits are "ego-syntonic" and culturally congruent at the same time, and apt to elicit significant rewards for "good behavior."

Unfortunately, socially patterned defects also diminish our capacity to think critically, to experience and express solidarity with out-group members, and to develop and maintain loving, intimate relationships with others. They pass for health, but are really a kind of conformist-based "pseudosanity." A "sane society," by Fromm's reckoning, would dispense with these tepid compromises and promote individual development and self-expression within the context of a vibrant communal life. Here, then, we have an approach to intersubjectivity that takes the role of society and culture more fully into account. Though he did not often cite him by name, Fromm clearly sided with dialogical approach of Martin Buber and explicitly disavowed Freud's pessimistic belief that instinct and culture, or the interests of the individual and of society at large, are necessarily at odds with each another. Indeed, anticipating the post-Enlightenment approach of Jürgen Habermas, who stressed the positive role of intersubjectivity in accounting for individual interests, Fromm argued that the real interests of individuals and society at large are more convergent than otherwise.

MAURICE MERLEAU-PONTY

Unlike Sullivan and Fromm, Maurice Merleau-Ponty (1908–1961) was not a clinician per se. And though he read Freud's work with unusual perspicacity, his contributions to contemporary notions of intersubjectivity are not rooted primarily in clinical work, but in the postwar movement of existential phenomenology. Merleau-Ponty was born in Rochefort-sur-Mer in 1908. When he was still a child, Merleau-Ponty's father died, and he and his sister were subsequently raised by their mother in Paris. Although raised a Catholic, he ceased to practice as an adult, but despite his Marxist sympathies, he was buried with the solemn rites of the Catholic Church.

Merleau-Ponty was educated at the Lycée Louis-le-Grand and went on to the École Normale Supérieure, graduating in 1930. As a student he was drawn toward the works of the German phenomenologists, having attended Husserl's 1929 lectures in Paris (the "Cartesian Meditations") and studied Heidegger's writings. In the ensuing decade he taught at *lycées* in Beauvais and Chartres and, after 1935, as a junior member of the faculty at the École Normale. Following the start of World War II, he entered the army and served as a lieutenant in the infantry. With the collapse of France, Merleau-Ponty was demobilized and returned to teaching. During the Nazi occupation he was active in the resistance. When the liberation came, he joined the faculty of the University of Lyons and became coeditor (with Sartre) of the new journal *Les Temps Modernes.* In 1950 Merleau-Ponty was invited to the Sorbonne to become professor of child psychology and pedagogy. He held the chair for two years and was then elected to the Collège de France to the chair of philosophy (formerly occupied by Henri Bergson), which he retained it until his early death in 1961.

Merleau-Ponty's first book, *The Structure of Behavior,* was published in 1942. Merleau-Ponty discussed the work of Gestalt psychology and developed an important critique of behaviorism. This was followed by *The Phenomenology of Perception* (1945), which bridged the phenomenological perspectives of Husserl and Heidegger and provided a new approach to understanding the nature of embodiment. Merleau-Ponty's interest in psychology was evident in his use of Binswanger's case studies to explain the role of perception in human psychology. Indeed, all of Merleau-Ponty's work demonstrates familiarity with the scientific research of his time and with the history of philosophy.

Like other French existentialists, Merleau-Ponty was concerned with challenges of contemporary politics as well as with issues of art, literature, and film. He wrote actively in newspapers and journals, and his essays on Marxist theory were published in two collections: *Humanism and Terror* (1947) and *The Adventures of the Dialectic* (1955). The latter work contains a powerful critique of orthodox Marxism and the French Communist Party, which led to an open break with Sartre and to Merleau-Ponty's resignation from the editorship of *Les Temps Modernes*. Merleau-Ponty's writings on art and painting were published as the collections *Sense and NonSense* (1948) and *Signs* (1960). At the age of 53, Merleau-Ponty died suddenly of a coronary thrombosis while working on what would become his last book, *The Visible and the Invisible*, which examines the complex relationship between phenomenology and ontology.

Merleau-Ponty's work is crucial to understanding intersubjectivity from the standpoint of bodily experience. He followed Heidegger to the extent that he sought to demonstrate ways in which we are always situated in the world. But Merleau-Ponty moved well beyond Heidegger in developing the notion of embodiment. He argued that the mind can only be understood in terms of the body: "The perceiving mind is an incarnated body" (Merleau-Ponty 1964, 3). His specific goal was to collapse once and for all the Cartesian duality of mind and body by arguing that the human subject essentially *is* a body. To this end, Merleau-Ponty (1945) introduced the notion of the "body-subject," which drew on Binswanger's earlier (1935) exploration of the same theme. For both thinkers the mind can only be understood in terms of its body and its world. As Merleau-Ponty notes: "For us the body is much more than an instrument or a means; it is our expression in the world, the visible form of our intentions" (1964, 5).

In order to elaborate Merleau-Ponty's theory of embodiment, we will examine three key concepts that span the length of his career: the body-subject, reversibility, and flesh. Each of these concepts is complex and must be understood in the larger context of Merleau-Ponty's phenomenological project. His objective in *The Phenomenology of Perception* (1945) was to study the process of perception in order to overcome the Cartesian duality between mind and body, subject and object. It is by virtue of our embodiment, according to Merleau-Ponty, that we perceive things around us. We can never experience things independently of our bodily existence in the world. Space is always experienced in relation to our bodies as situated in the world, and the same is true of time. As embodied beings, we can never be in two places at once. For Merleau-Ponty, therefore, our bodies are a dimension of our very existence.

Merleau-Ponty uses the example of a "phantom limb," in which someone has lost an arm but continues to feel it, to explain the nature of the body-subject. He asserts that the phenomenon of the phantom limb can only be understood from the point of view of a subject for whom the body is indelibly linked to consciousness, to the extent that it forms the very basis for existing within the world. In other words, the subject who experiences the phantom limb is not consciousness that is in some way only attached to a body. On the contrary, consciousness must be understood to be fundamentally embodied. To feel an arm that one no longer has is "to remain open to all those actions of which the arm alone is capable; it is to keep the practical field that one had before being mutilated" (Merleau-Ponty 1989, 81). The phantom limb points to the learned bodily schema by which we interact with the world.

For Merleau-Ponty, the lived body is not an object for a subject, but the way in which the subject exists in the world. The perceiving subject is always a worldly, embodied subject. The lived body is not, as Descartes would have us believe, an object in and of itself. Rather, it is the way the subject is present in the world and aware of it. Indeed, the phantom limb points to the existence of a subject intimately bound up with the world through the intentionality of the body.

It is important to note that the perceptual consciousness described by Merleau-Ponty does not constitute an interiority. It is a bodily presence in the world — precisely the means through which conscious awareness of the world is achieved. To be sure, the body has a meaning-bestowing function and in this sense bears a resemblance to Husserl's transcendental ego. But the body does not function as a transcendental ego, as it does for Husserl. It is not an agency underlying the organization of experience, nor is it the foundation of an a priori (transcendental) constitution. Moreover, the body does not seek to synthesize the world. Rather, it seeks understanding from the bodies with which it interacts. In other words, the body-subject does not constitute the world as horizon of possible experience, but interprets and seeks to understand the world.

This brings us to the notion of *reversibility*. According to Merleau-Ponty, the body is a phenomenon situated among other phenomena within the world. Merleau-Ponty argues that my body and yours are not the private, mutually exclusive, solipsistic domains of Cartesian philosophy. Rather, there is a relation of reversibility between the perceiver and the perceived, between the body as sensing and the body as sensed, between my body and yours.

The notion of reversibility is introduced in his late, unfinished work, *The Visible and the Invisible* (1968). It is prefigured by the notion of "double sensation," of touching and being touched, which is discussed in *The Phenomenology of Perception*. Merleau-Ponty uses an everyday example in which I am in the process of touching an object with my right hand, when suddenly my hands cross and I touch my right hand with my left. My right hand, which was touching an object, now becomes touched. At that moment it ceases to be a "sensing" subject and becomes a "sensed" object. The body reflects, or turns back on itself, and reveals itself as both subject and object. It is, in essence, a two-sided being: subject and object at the same time. The objective of this example of double sensation is to demonstrate the natural reflexivity of the body. In this situation, the body is neither completely a subject nor completely an object. It is, rather, a reversible circularity in which the subject/object distinction is fundamentally blurred.

Merleau-Ponty extends this analysis to the relation of the body and the world. The perception of the body is at the same time the perception of the world: "The lived body is in the world as the heart is in the organism; it keeps the visible spectacle constantly alive, it breathes life into it and sustains it inwardly, and with it forms a system" (Merleau-Ponty 1989, 205). Body and world coexist in a dialectical relationship.

In *The Visible and the Invisible*, Merleau-Ponty elaborates the meaning of reversibility. To do so, he returns to his earlier example of "touching." He provides an example in which interrogator and the interrogated are so close to each other as to be able to touch one another. Merleau-Ponty begins by pointing out that my hand would not be able to sense anything were it not for the fact that it can sense. Therefore, when my hand is able to touch, it is because it is both "tangible" and because what is touched can be sensed from the inside. Merleau-Ponty develops a similar argument in regard to vision. Accordingly, I can see precisely because I myself am visible: "he who sees cannot possess the visible unless he is possessed by it, unless he is of it" (Merleau-Ponty 1968, 135). From the same perspective, the body by which I am in the world is itself a part of the world. The lived body and perceived world are correlatives. The point is that the body belongs to the order of both the object and the subject. And it is precisely for this reason that Merleau-Ponty chooses to refer to the body as "the flesh."

In Merleau-Ponty's later work, then, a revision has taken place. Perception is called "vision," and the body itself is referred to as "the flesh." The body is no longer just an object of perception, but flesh, a philosophy of "brute being" and the basis of Merleau-Ponty's ontology. Flesh is the formative medium of object and subject. As Merleau-Ponty states, "We must not think the flesh as starting out from substances, from body and spirit — for then it would be the union of contradictories — but we must think it . . . as an element, as the concrete emblem of a general manner of being" (Merleau-Ponty 1968, 147).

In *The Visible and the Invisible,* the act of perception is presented as touching, seeing, and feeling itself. There is no representation at the level of perception. There is only flesh that is in touch with itself. Perception, from this perspective, is a worldly event, not something that occurs privately, since flesh undercuts and precedes the division of subject and object. This has implications for the problem of solipsism as well. According to Merleau-Ponty, the other's world is my world because the two views are reversible. My right hand, being touched by my left, can reverse the roles and touch my left hand back. Similarly, my body, being seen by another person, can reverse roles and take up the other's perspective on itself. The commonality between the other and myself is grounded in the flesh that we both visibly are, not in the transcendental consciousness I have of that person.

It is through one's own body that one is able to begin to understand the world. Merleau-Ponty argues that we must learn to think of the relation of the body to the world as the relation of flesh to flesh, according to the model of one hand touching another. In other words, flesh refers to the body's capacity of being able to fold in upon itself, its simultaneous orientation to inner and outer. This folding in on itself is decentered because it takes place at a level prior to the emergence of conscious, I-centered personal reflection. It is being that is prepersonal, prior to subject-object differentiation. Thus, subject and object are inherently open to each other because they are constituted in the flesh.

The radicality of Merleau-Ponty's notion of the flesh exists precisely in his attempt to reconceptualize materialism. The separation of mind and body, subject and object is replaced by the interchangeability and shared participation of touching and tangible, toucher and touched, seer and seen. In Merleau-Ponty's account, lived human experience is a seamless web. Merleau-Ponty's account of the flesh demands that we pay attention to the connectedness and immersion of the body in the world. But how does this fundamental shift in the way we conceptualize the body translate into theory and practice in psychotherapy? One answer can be found in the way we think about cognition or understanding. Merleau-Ponty's basic insight that "the perceiving mind is an incarnated body" suggests that our bodies continually provide us with a sense of the situations and contexts in which we exist and interact. This bodily, or felt, sense is not a product of reflective thought. Rather, our bodily sense is prereflective and helps us to orient ourselves and know what we are doing. This "bodily sensing" is neither external observation nor subjective and internal, but a form of interaction. Speaking, in turn, can be said to "carry forward" (Gendlin 1992) our bodily interaction with our environment.

JESSICA BENJAMIN

Thus far we have examined the ways in which Sullivan, Fromm, and Meleau-Ponty elaborate interpersonal, cultural, and embodied perspectives on intersubjectivity. In contrast, Jessica Benjamin's work is concerned chiefly with the developmental and feminist facets of intersubjectivity. As a psychoanalyst, Benjamin's work is commonly described as "relational" and is closely tied with other relational analysts such as Stephen Mitchell (1988) and Lewis Aron (1996). Within the rubric of relational psychoanalysis, Benjamin's work is particularly important because she has shown the ways in which feminism is integral to psychoanalytic discussions of intersubjectivity.

Benjamin's approach to intersubjectivity has its roots in infancy research, feminist thought, and continental philosophy. Her book, *The Bonds of Love* (1988), represents the first attempt to integrate these themes in a theory of intersubjectivity. Benjamin is critical of classical psychoanalytic theory, which frequently depicts human development in terms of a trajectory from undifferentiated (symbiotic) oneness to separateness. She also criticizes previous analytic theory for its treatment of the mother solely as an object, and not as an individual in her own right, and elaborates an intersubjective scheme that stresses the importance of the infant's recognition of the unique and separate qualities of the mother.

In terms of infancy research, Benjamin credits Margaret Mahler with bringing about a gradual shift to an object relations approach in psychoanalysis. Yet she is critical of her notion that the infant begins life in a state of undifferentiated oneness with mother. Instead, Benjamin cites Daniel Stern (1985), who argues that the infant is never totally undifferentiated, and has the innate capacity to engage the other. Stern demonstrates how crucial is the relationship of mutual influence between the infant and mother and designates the phase from eight to nine months, when the infant becomes affectively attuned to the other, as "intersubjectivity." Benjamin accepts this basic precept, but sees intersubjectivity as an ongoing process that begins even earlier in the infant's life. According to Benjamin, the notions of separation and connection should not simply be seen as opposite endpoints of a longitudinal trajectory. Rather, they form a tension that continues beyond the phase of affective attunement. And it is precisely this tension that constitutes the basis for her elaboration of intersubjective relatedness.

For Benjamin, the struggle for recognition characterizes how we relate to the other person as an independent consciousness, someone who is like us, yet different. Implicit in this approach is her concern to show that the mother is a subject, and not merely an object, even from the infant's point of view. The mother is not simply an extension of the infant's developmental needs, but an agent with her own emotions and desires. In other words, from the very outset, self and other are each subjects who seek to assert themselves. The recognition of another person as separate from one's self occurs through a paradoxical process of finding real people (as opposed to mental objects) and realizing that one's own subjectivity is dependent on recognition from them. Thus, for Benjamin, a generative tension is sustained through an individual's self-assertion of her own will and the mutual recognition of the other's will "that allows self and other to meet as sovereign equals" (Benjamin 1988, 12).

In analyzing the power relations between men and women, Benjamin focuses on the desexualization of women and their lack of agency within a wider sociopolitical context. Like Nancy Chodorow (1978, 1989), Benjamin sees the contemporary gender system as reducing the mother to a submissive, desexualized position, while it exalts the dominance, autonomy, and agency of the father. However, Benjamin moves beyond Chodorow, for whom the psychic life of the child mirrors this gender asymmetry, and argues for the need to understand and change the patterns of "identificatory love" between child and parent by which gender patterns in our society are established. The problem is that children of both sexes cannot maintain their identificatory love for mothers whom society devalues. As a result, boys identify with their dominant fathers and learn to diminish women, while women are deprived of the opportunity to fully embrace their own desire. The subsequent idealization of male power is matched by the denigration of women who seek to be autonomous, sexual beings.

For Benjamin, the cultural devaluation of women means that any attempt to transform existing gender structures through a change in parenting will be insufficient. Extending a line of argument developed by Frankfurt school theorists, Benjamin argues that the instrumental orientation and the impersonality that govern modern social organization should be understood as masculine. This means that male domination, like class domination, is no longer a function of personal power relationships (though these do exist), but something inherent in the social and cultural structures independent of what individual men and women want (Benjamin 1988, 186–87).

In order to achieve nonrepressive gender relations, change needs to take place at both the personal and societal levels. Above all, the cultural split of a dominant, autonomous father against a submissive, dependent mother must be replaced with new sexual roles that allow for more fluid sexual identifications. In the process of socialization children would learn to express their identities in relation to a socially autonomous and sexual mother, and an empathic, caring father. By moving beyond determinative gender identities, it thus becomes possible to recognize that in the sexual domains of contemporary culture, the constitution of gender is a fluid rather than fixed process. This pluralistic perspective eschews generalized gender roles and has become dominant in much current psychoanalytic discourse on gender (see, for example, Flax 1991).

Benjamin's contributions on intersubjectivity rely more on theoretical argument and exegesis than on clinical case examples. Her emphasis on mutual recognition demonstrates her philosophical debt to the Hegelian dialectic. Hegel described the battle that engages two subjects in order that each may dominate the other. Benjamin's discussion of the dialectic, like that of Sartre, Lacan, and many others, is indebted to Kojève's (1934–1935) influential interpretation of *Phenomenology of Spirit,* which had a major impact on contemporary continental understandings of Hegel. Kojève emphasized the role of conflict and tension in the early stage of the dialectic, in which the self-conscious emerges out of a cycle of desire and of the satisfaction of desire.

As described by Kojève, the Hegelian dialectic is a "life and death struggle" taken up by two subjects who would prefer the condition of solipsism to awareness that otherness exists in the world. The first experiential moment of intersubjectivity, thus, is one of rupture and disunity. According to this view, physical need leads human subjects into a fundamental dependence upon external objects. This outward search for satisfaction results in a power play of dominance and submission as each seeks to ward off the awareness of the other's subjectivity. Recognition of the other occurs begrudgingly.

Despite her indebtedness to Kojève, Benjamin does not depict the first phases of intersubjectivity in such starkly adversarial terms. Indeed, her emphasis on the pleasure and reciprocity in the early mother-child relationship recalls the philosophy of dialogue. Yet Buber's theory of I and Thou, with its concept of reciprocal interaction and togetherness, stands in stark contrast to the emphasis on the primacy of conflict in Hegel's dialectic, and references to the philosophy of dialogue are curiously absent here. Binswanger's (1993a) reflections on Hegel, Buber, and intersubjectivity predate Benjamin's efforts by many years and parallel them in striking ways (Frie 1997). Benjamin actually presents a view akin to Buber and Binswanger when she stresses the role of agency within the dialectic of recognition. For Benjamin (1988), mutual recognition "allows that self to realize its agency and authorship in a tangible way" (12). Not surprisingly, perhaps, Benjamin's view of agency has led her to express reservations about the essential exclusion and denial of psychic agency in postmodernism because it overlooks the motivations, needs, and desires of the subject. In contrast to postmodern constructionist perspectives on gender, Benjamin retains a conception of the agency as central to women's gender identity and sexual expression.

In addition to Hegel and Buber, various implicit and explicit philosophical influences can be traced in Benjamin's work. Benjamin, for example, cites Habermas and acknowledges a debt to his social theory. Indeed, the concept of intersubjectivity entered the discourse of the social sciences circa 1930 with George Herbert Mead, who inspired many of Habermas's ideas. Similarly, the dialectics of recognition started to surface in the discourse of the mental health professions at around the same time, with Buber and Binswanger. Benjamin's turn to these continental philosophical sources thus provides a means to navigate beyond the strict psychical focus of early psychoanalysis into the realm of sociopolitical experience and symbolic forms of gender constitution. As Benjamin states, "What psychoanalysis considers the problems of overcoming omnipotence is thus always linked to the ethical problem of respect and the political problem of nonviolence" (Benjamin 1999a, 94).

Benjamin continues to insist that subjectivity is a developmental achievement of social interaction in infancy. But if she adheres strictly to this position and does not allow for subjective experiences that predate the dialectic of recognition, problems arise. After all, how does the infant know that it was *he or she* who was being recognized? As Fichte demonstrates in his critique of the reflection model of self-consciousness, without a prereflective self-awareness, there would be no way of knowing that my reflection is in fact *my own* consciousness (Frie 1997). And as Stern's (1985) research has shown, months before the infant is aware of other minds, he or she can differentiate his or her own body from those of others. This bodily based grasp of difference occurs before what Benjamin considers to be intersubjectivity proper. Indeed, it seems that the latter is contingent on the former, and that the very notion of recognition should be reconceptualized along the lines of what Merleau-Ponty (1968) describes as bodily based interaction between "incarnated minds."

Robert Stolorow, George Atwood, Donna Orange, and Benjamin Branschaft

While Benjamin's ideas have had considerable influence, the work of Robert Stolorow, George Atwood, Donna Orange, and Benjamin Branschaft is most often identified with intersubjectivity in psychoanalysis. Although Binswanger, Lacan, and others developed clinical perspectives on intersubjectivity as early as the 1930s, it is largely through the efforts of Stolorow and his colleagues that the concept of intersubjectivity has become popularized in the North American psychoanalytic field. Unfortunately, the tendency of most psychoanalysts to distance themselves from the findings of philosophy is a major reason inter-subjectivity did not receive the attention it deserved until the 1970s. Since that time, Stolorow and his colleagues have developed what they call "intersubjectivity theory" in various stages (Stolorow and Atwood 1979; Atwood and Stolorow 1984; Stolorow, Brandchaft, and Atwood 1987; Stolorow and Atwood 1992; Orange, Atwood, and Stolorow 1997; Stolorow, Atwood, and Orange 2002). As their ideas have become more nuanced and defined, these authors have sought to distinguish their theory from the work of others.

Intersubjectivity theory developed out of research undertaken by Stolorow and Atwood into the subjective origins of personality theories. Intersubjectivity theory seeks to comprehend psychological phenomena as forming at the interface of reciprocally interacting subjectivities, not as products of isolated intrapsychic mechanisms. Its implications are both theoretical and clinical. Intersubjectivity theory is closely akin to Heinz Kohut's self psychology because it accepts that the sources of psychoanalytic inquiry and understanding, as well as self-experience, are all radically context-dependent. But in contrast to Kohut, Stolorow is critical of the notion of a preexisting nuclear self. And by emphasizing the development and maintenance of the orga-nization of experience, intersubjectivity theory asserts that all self-hood develops and is maintained within the interplay between subjectivities, a view that is similar to Sullivan's interpersonal approach.

For Stolorow and his colleagues, clinical work takes place in the field formed by the interplay of two subjective worlds. Thus, intersubjec-tivity theory, like the interpersonal approaches of Sullivan and Fromm, denies the validity of analytic neutrality. The myth of neutrality is described as an expression of an objectivist epistemology that envisions the mind in isolation, separated from the external reality that it per-ceives, which the authors refer to as the "myth of the isolated mind" (Stolorow and Atwood 1992, 7). In its place, they suggest an "empathic-introspective inquiry" that seeks to account for the analyst's impact on the patient's experience within the intersubjective field of analysis.

The rejection of the objectivist epistemology of classical psychoanalysis renders "one person psychology" obsolete. But Stolorow and his col-leagues go further, rejecting so-called "two person psychology," which they say perpetuates the notion of isolated and separate minds. Instead, they suggest the term "contextual psychology," which accounts for the constitutive role of relatedness in the making of all experience (Orange, Atwood, and Stolorow 1997). According to this viewpoint, the individual and his or her intrapsychic world are included as a subsystem within a more encompassing relational or intersubjective suprasystem. As Stolorow and Atwood state in *Contexts of Being:*

> The concept of an intersubjective system brings to focus both the individual's world of inner experience and its embeddedness with other such worlds in a continual flow of reciprocal mutual influence. In this vision, the gap between the intrapsychic and interpersonal realms is closed, and, indeed, the old dichotomy between them is rendered obsolete. (1992, 18)

This bold attempt to undercut traditional distinctions accounts for the radical nature of intersubjectivity theory. But it also raises important questions about its theoretical premises.

For Stolorow and others intersubjectivity can exist between any two subjects, and at any time. It does not refer primarily to a developmental achievement. Thus, they distinguish their conception from the work of Stern and Benjamin, for whom intersubjectivity is, at least in part, a developmental achievement or process. Similarly, Benjamin seeks to distance herself from Stolorow and his colleagues, "whose definition of intersubjectivity refers to all interplay between different subjective worlds. That definition," says Benjamin, "does not tell us how the intersubjective differs from the interpersonal . . . nor does it sufficiently distinguish subjects from objects" (Benjamin 1999b, 201). Although the work of Stolorow and others has numerous similarities with relational and interpersonal theory, it is probably their thoroughgoing emphasis upon contextualism that sets them most apart from these perspectives.

Not surprisingly, perhaps, Hegel's impact on Stolorow's intersubjectivity theory cannot be overstated. The Hegelian notion that self and other are reciprocally constituted is taken up and expanded upon by Stolorow and colleagues, even if the elements of conflict, tension, and dialectic within it are deliberately downplayed. But in contrast to Stern and Benjamin, Stolorow and his co-authors move beyond the conception of mutual recognition. In its place, they propose a contextualist epistemology in which the subject (or self) is always already inherent in an intersubjective field. In order to achieve their radical contextualism, Stolorow and others rely on a phenomenological account of the self and its organizing principles. In contrast to Husserl, however, their aim is to elucidate the way in which perception and self-experience is invariably embedded. Thus, Husserl's transcendent ego is rejected and replaced with a new, thoroughly contextualized subjectivity. Whether such a concept of subjectivity really remains within the purview of phenomenology is open to debate.

In arguing that nothing can be known or experienced apart from the context in which it appears, Stolorow and colleagues credit both Heidegger (Stolorow, Atwood, and Orange 2002) and his student, Hans-Georg Gadamer (Orange, Atwood, and Stolorow 1997). Drawing on Gadamer, they suggest that the historical matrix in which we are embedded provides the ground for all interpretation and understanding. Gadamer's hermeneutics owe much to Heidegger. Indeed, the connections between Heidegger's concept of being-in-the-world and the contextualist perspective are perhaps most clearly evident in the title of their recent work, *Worlds of Experience* (2002), a direct reference to the notion of world as used in the existential-phenomenological tradition. Following Heidegger, we exist in a *world* of historical and ontological contexts that forms the ground of our understanding of ourselves and others. In like fashion, Stolorow and his colleagues argue that the intersubjectively oriented psychoanalyst is always embedded in a "constitutive process" that links temporality and ontology: "We regard the past and the future as inevitably implicated in all present moments" (Orange, Atwood, and Stolorow 1997, 97).

On this basis, then, understanding becomes thoroughly contextualized. A subject that exists within this contextualized, intersubjective field could hardly be more different than the discrete and disembodied Cartesian mind that forms the basis of objectivist epistemologies. In place of the Descartes's autonomous, unified subject, Stolorow and his colleagues present the notion of the subject as a set of "organizing principles." Nevertheless, when all is said and done, they still maintain a conception of personal subjectivity, however minimal. This streak of humanism stands in marked contrast with much postmodern philosophy, which rejects *any* notion of subjectivity as a Cartesian artifact. Indeed, for many postmodernists, the very term "intersubjectivity" retains its Cartesian origins since it implies a plurality of discrete, individual subjects who are related in a particular way. Nor do Stolorow and colleagues embrace the linguistic turn of much recent intersubjective philosophy. In contrast to Habermas, for instance, they emphasize the presymbolic nature of intersubjective experience. Seen from this perspective, Stolorow and his colleagues seek to decenter and "rewrite" the subject, rather than reject it altogether. However, the way in which they carry this out is somewhat problematic.

Throughout their work, Stolorow and colleagues acknowledge the role played by phenomenology in the development of intersubjectivity theory. Phenomenology is concerned with the nature of experience. In essence, it asks, what does it mean to experience something? If experience is intentional, as Husserl maintained, we must presuppose a subject for whom "experiencing" takes place. At times, they seem to realize this, as for example, when they say that "The organizing activities of both participants in any psychoanalytic process are crucial." At other times, the authors merely refer to a vague "set of organizing principles." Clearly, experience is only possible if there is a self *for whom* the experience exists.

In the final analysis, it appears that Stolorow and his colleagues want to have it both ways: to overcome an objectivist epistemology through their embrace of contextualism, yet to retain a vestigial concept of subjectivity that their own approach criticizes as implicitly Cartesian. Their stated objective is to create a metatheory — an intersubjective suprasystem — that overcomes traditional differences between one and two person psychologies and renders the distinction between intrapsychic and interpersonal experience obsolete. This is an ambitious goal that sets their work apart from other intersubjective perspectives. Whether they can succeed in this task or have simply reintegrated these philosophical conundrums into their version of intersubjective theory remains to be seen.

The concept of intersubjectivity thus provides a new and exciting way of understanding interaction in the clinical situation. For the interpersonal, relational, and intersubjective analyst or therapist, the subjectivity of the therapist is not just "in the room" with the patient's, it is in the world with the patient. This is a radical departure from classical Freudian psychoanalysis. For revisionist analysts and therapists who identify with the discussion of intersubjectivity, clinical phenomena can only be understood in the contexts in which they take form. The patient and therapist together form an indissoluble dyad, and it is this relationship that becomes a domain of therapeutic inquiry. Phenomena that have been the traditional focus of analytic and therapeutic investigation are not understood as products of isolated intrapsychic processes but as having been formed in an intersubjective or interpersonal field of existence. A primary role of therapy is to reach an understanding of such phenomena as they emerge in the interaction between therapist and patient.

With the rejection of Freud's deterministic model of the mind, new understandings of the self and interaction emerge where instinctual determinism once held sway. But in their embrace of intersubjectivity, some theorists and clinicians may overlook the need to retain a theory of the subject, however minimal. Without some conception of a continuous subject, it becomes difficult to account for agency and choice, or to understand their role in therapy, a topic we shall address in the next and final chapter.

Psychotherapy and Postmodernism

Current debates in the mental health professions — including, but not limited to the psychotherapy field — are often couched in terms of the tensions between modernism and postmodernism. This polarization takes many forms, affecting how researchers and clinicians practice their crafts. In place of foundational concepts such as objectivity and truth, which are the hallmarks of the natural science approach to psychology, postmodernists emphasize constructivism or perspectivism. In place of sweeping generalizations about "laws of behavior" or of human nature, they stress the primacy of difference and cultural embeddedness. While we applaud many of the ideas that emanate from the postmodern camp, some are also problematic. Based on our review of the literature so far, we wonder whether all modernists actually adhere to the notion of an immutable core self. And do postmodernists all see the self as illusory? Is there a place for modernist concepts such as agency and individuality in postmodernism? And if so, are modernist and postmodern approaches completely antithetical, as some people maintain?

More often than not, things are not so simple, and there is a frequent blurring of boundaries, an unconscious tacking to and fro, between modernism and postmodernism on these (and other) issues. This chapter addresses the divide between modernism and postmodernism, focusing on agency, individuality, embodiment, and authenticity, and explores the wider social, political, and ethical implications of the debate.

As we have demonstrated in some detail now, many ideas that are central to postmodernist versions of psychotherapy were anticipated by European psychoanalysts and psychiatrists who were broadly identified with existential phenomenology, including Karl Jaspers, Ludwig Binswanger, Medard Boss, Erich Fromm, the early Jacques Lacan and R. D. Laing, among others. These clinicians introduced the concept of a socially and historically constituted person, emphasized the interpersonal and embodied basis of human experience, and questioned the myth of therapeutic or analytic neutrality.

At the same time, however, these clinicians sought to elaborate a concept of the individual self within a relational context and thus underline the importance of the patient's agency in therapeutic change. By retaining a conception of the person as the locus of experience, the existential-phenomenological tradition navigates carefully between modernist essentialism and postmodern reductionism. Thus, Heidegger's philosophy introduced the decentering of the self and laid the foundation for much postmodern thinking. His emphasis on language and being strongly influenced Jacques Derrida's deconstructionism and French post-structuralism. Yet unlike many of Heidegger's postmodern followers, the early Heidegger never does away with the person entirely, coining the terms *Dasein* and "being-in-the-world" to refer to the instrument and process by which our conscious experience comes into being. Similarly, Sartre formulated a conception of the person that anticipates Lacan's "split subject" along with the postmodern attack on the unity of the mind. Yet Sartre's idea of "prereflective" or implicit consciousness keeps the experiencing person intact, and Sartre holds us ultimately responsible for our choices, regardless of how often or ingeniously we avoid confronting them in bad faith. As we have seen, Buber and Binswanger both emphasize the reality of the concrete other, thus making clear that the self can never be understood in isolation. When the other, or Thou, is recognized as the fundamental precondition of my own being, understanding is never entirely one-sided and takes place in a process of mutuality. At the same time, for Buber and Binswanger alike, the self discovers and realizes its uniqueness in dialogue with the other. Finally, Merleau-Ponty challenges the traditional psychological division between mind and body, or intellect and soma, by elaborating the notion of bodily experience. His formulation of the body-subject takes as its focus the lived experience of the patient and provides the basis for an embodied psychotherapy.

In general, then, the existential-phenomenological tradition suggests that although we are fundamentally relational beings, we are never wholly determined by the contexts in which we exist. What is important is not only the way in which persons are determined by their contexts, but also the extent to which they can influence them. Agency remains a vital part of this dialectical process of becoming that defines us as human beings. We are always more than our contexts. There is inevitably a surfeit of meaning that cannot be reduced to the contexts or constructs we use to explain experience.

The same is true of embodiment. Psychotherapy and psychoanalysis have traditionally relied on language: the articulation of thought, affect, fantasy, and dreams in words. As a result, the embodiment of understanding and cognition elaborated by Merleau-Ponty and others long remained outside the purview of psychotherapeutic theory and practice. When applied to the therapeutic setting, our foundations for self-reflexivity, understanding, and knowledge lie in our bodily sensations and rest in the "reversible properties of flesh." The roots of a dialectic of reciprocal recognition, the dance of I and Thou in infancy, precedes language acquisition (Burston 1996b). As a result, language is a necessary but not a sufficient condition of adult self-awareness (Frie 1997, 1999c) and, therefore, the lived experience of adults needs to be "fleshed out" in terms of a continual interaction between language and the body (Gendlin 2003).

Agency and Persons: Beyond Ideology

Some readers will balk at our repeated emphasis on agency. After all, in the postmodern imagination, earnest talk of agency is often linked with "hard" conceptions of individuality and autonomy, the myth of the so-called Marlboro man. Talk of agency is depicted as ignoring or understating the impact of our personal histories, unconscious motivations, and most importantly, of our embeddedness in social, political, and linguistic contexts beyond our control or outside of our awareness. According to this stereotype, the very notion of agency or individuality implies an ideology — *individualism* — that states that we are always the ultimate agents of our own experience. Therefore, concepts like agency or individuality are summarily dismissed as instances of Cartesian "isolated mind" thinking, or of epistemological rigidity and shallowness. Though they enjoy a great deal of currency and credibility at present, such criticisms are simply false. Talk of agency becomes hubris only if our sense of ourselves as independent subjects leads us to feel that we are powerful autonomous agents and the sole authors of our lives. The concept of agency we are endorsing is vividly anticipated in the work of Buber, Binswanger, Fromm, Sartre, Laing, and others, and is not a reification of the omnipotent Cartesian subject that single-handedly creates its own experience.

Probably the strongest argument against the role of agency within the clinical situation concerns those patients who are lacking a sense of themselves as agents. More disturbed patients will often experience feelings and thoughts as happening to them, rather than as generated by them. Among the few "postmodern" psychoanalysts who have written convincingly about agency and will, Stephen Mitchell cautions that the concept of agency is often connected with the notion of an integral and continuous self. Mitchell concedes the importance of continuity in self-experience, yet embraces a constructivist view of the self and is therefore skeptical about the role of agency in bringing about change. According to Mitchell, patients may learn to recognize the role of agency in events that were previously experienced more passively. Yet he goes on to suggest that "it seems strained to assume that the self (agent) that is experienced after analysis has facilitated the integration of experiences was there, although disclaimed, all along" (Mitchell 1993, 110). The problem as outlined by Mitchell and others is based on the riddle of whether agency actually facilitates change in the therapeutic setting, or whether agency is itself the consequence of that change. Unfortunately, the formulation of agency in the clinical setting often leads to a version of the chicken versus the egg dilemma: it is impossible to tell which came first. If we assume that agency is a fluid rather than static concept, then we can avoid this dilemma.

In the clinical situation, agency is rarely a matter of simple choice, just as therapeutic action is never a linear process. Patients desire change, but they are unable to bring it about on their own. From a therapeutic perspective, we can observe the way in which patients are often mired in familiar patterns of relating to the world that they feel helpless to alter. In order for change to occur, patients must become aware that they are relying on a view of the world that is a reflection or compilation of past and present experience. By recognizing that their patterns of relating are simply maintaining the status quo, patients can begin to understand their need for choice and self-determination.

The underlying difficulty is how to change patterns of relating. These patterns are familiar and although they may be a cause of fundamental discomfort and unhappiness, they can also appear safe because they enable us to avoid anxiety. Change requires both a desire and a will to open up new possibilities of being. When we come to understand ourselves as agents in our world, it becomes possible for us to imagine making different choices and begin relating to others and acting in our worlds in new and different ways. The assumption of agency is an important part of this transformation.

We see human experience as the product of an ongoing dialectic according to which we are both "constructed" and the "agents of construction." Or to put it a different way, we are both determined by, and exercise our agency in determining, the communicative contexts in which we exist. The primary issue is to acknowledge the inevitability and relevance of agency in the process of therapeutic change without reverting to a false conception of the omnipotent Cartesian self.

The self necessarily plays a role in the construction of experience, yet does not, and never can, wholly determine its contexts. Rather, "agency" refers to the limited but important capacity of humans to "self-determine" their actions and decisions in ways that are not entirely dictated by, and cannot be reduced to, the biophysical and sociocultural contexts in which they exist (Martin, Sugarman, and Thompson 2003). Among representatives of the postmodern approach in psychoanalysis, Irwin Hoffman has recently (1998) responded to the problematic status of individual subjectivity and personal agency in the social-constructivist paradigm. Whereas Hoffman's earlier work stresses the ambiguity of experience, he now portrays the world as offering both certainty and uncertainty in a single dialectical framework that he refers to as "dialectical constructivism." To this end, Hoffman (2000) espouses a notion of free will that suggests a major role for conscious choice in construction and demarcates it as "a space between the source of influence and its impact, a gap in which I am present as an agent, as a choosing subject" (vii).

In our view, this is a significant addition to the constructivist paradigm because it emphasizes the role of the individual agent in the construction of his or her reality and also includes an ethical dimension. As Hoffman (2000) puts it, "Only some aspects of reality are socially constructed, in the sense they are manufactured by human beings. Among those that are excluded is the fact that humans, by their nature, are active agents in the social construction of their worlds" (77). This statement allows for recognition of a subjective aspect of experience that cannot be reduced to the sociocultural or relational spheres in which we exist. Following Hoffman, even if we grant that the self is constructed and multiple, psychoanalysis still needs to be able to conceive of the person's singularity and continuity over time (see Holland et al. 1998). The position we are delineating is along the lines of this latter view: a more cohesive, though not unified, concept of selfhood, one that is both constructed and self-generated in communicative contexts.

Though couched in terms of postmodernism, Hoffman's dialectical constructivism is thoroughly compatible with an existential-phenomenological perspective. Indeed, we think that this perspective could best be defined as a rigorous exploration of our ways of making meaning — both consciously and unconsciously. One aim of therapy is to become aware of this shifting horizon of understanding so that different ways of feeling, thinking, and being become possible and meanings that were previously "prereflective" or unformulated become discursively elaborated. Exploring clients' difficulties in terms of their personal meanings and sociocultural roots and ramifications is quite different from symptom remediation, or an attempt to eliminate their suffering by the most efficient means possible. Instead, it provides the opportunity to elucidate the meaning of distress and suffering by means of insight, and to strengthen the powers of choice and limited self-determination within the constraints posed by everyday life. A candid assessment of the ways in which patients' agency is situated and constrained by their reality can also assist psychotherapists in identifying problems that are best addressed through intervention, advocacy, or activism at the community, cultural, economic, or political level, rather than in private consultations with a mental health professional (Martin and Sugarman 1999).

Moreover, Hoffman's approach avoids the conundrums that confront the postmodern philosophical attack on the subject. The dilemma facing "postmodern" psychotherapy is the intrinsic incompatibility between the epistemological attack on the subject, which forms the groundwork of postmodernist and poststructuralist philosophy and literary theory (Derrida 1978; Foucault 1977b), and the actual practice of psychotherapy, which relies on an experiential subject. Poststructuralist theory assumes the subordination of the subject to language, as famously expressed by Roland Barthes (1984): "Linguistically, the author is never more than the instance of writing, just as I is nothing other than the instance of saying I: language knows 'subject,' not a 'person,' and this subject, empty outside of the very enunciation which defines it, suffices to make language 'hold together,' suffices, that is to say, to exhaust it" (145). A related argument was developed in the early work of Michel Foucault, whose declaration of a new era beyond subjectivity gave impetus to the postmodern movement. According to Foucault (1977b), the subject is fragmented by language, concepts, and history, a view that led many of his poststructuralist followers to herald the so-called death of the subject.

In fairness to Foucault and Derrida, they both back-pedaled on this issue toward the end of their lives, reinstating the "subject" in their work in a manner as emphatic as it was ambiguous. But leaving the perplexing reversals of philosophical fashion aside, there are other, more compelling reasons why the postmodern attack on the subject is of peripheral relevance to psychotherapeutic discourse. The ability to organize experience and pursue a course of action is dependent on the existence of a person for whom that experience takes place, and for whom his or her choice has (actual and potential) consequences. Without a psychological subject who develops, changes, learns, and decides, the therapeutic process loses its intelligibility and fundamental raison d'être and threatens to degenerate into talk about ideology and impersonal social forces that function as automatisms outside the person's awareness or control. Admittedly, the risk we run in ignoring such factors — as many schools of therapy still do routinely — is that if the experiencing individual is interpreted solely as a self-determining system, personal agency gives way to omnipotent control or psychological compulsion. Conversely, however, if we ignore personal agency, the person becomes the heteronomous plaything of impersonal social forces like language, ideology, power, and so on.

In the postmodernist view, theories of self derive from the social and cultural practices specific to a historic epoch and currents of power whose interest it is to define the self in ideological terms. This Foucaultian perspective is invaluable for demonstrating the issues of power, politics, and patriarchy involved in all human experience. A difficulty with the postmodern approach to the self is that its central proposition, namely the discontinuity and multiplicity of the self, can work against its actual political objectives. Fragmented, dissociated selves have limited political meaning or value; what meaning they have lies in the language and metaphors of tragedy (Glass 1993). According to the theory of multiplicity, there is no cohesive self per se, but rather a series of multiple, contiguous self-states. The problem is that multiplicity, which entered into the vocabulary of postmodernism as an innovative theory of dissociative psychopathology, has the potential to render the subject helpless.

By denying the possibility of a cohesive, continuous self, our ability to confront real political challenges is actually undermined. Theory and practice are in conflict here. Without a coherent notion of agency, which points to our fundamental ability to make choices and see things in ways that are different, new, or fresh, it is as though we are adrift, succumbing to the currents of the political status quo. According to Marxist literary critic Terry Eagleton, "The Left, now more than ever, has need of strong ethical and even anthropological foundations." Without "any adequate theory of political agency . . . postmodernism is in the end part of the problem rather than the solution" (Eagleton 1996, 135). The problem is that although it is thoroughly intriguing from a purely theoretical standpoint, postmodernism actually undermines its own political relevance by skirting relativism at the same time that it dismantles any notion of agency. And without a substantive conception of political agency, it is hard to see how progressive forces can realistically make a difference.

The challenge for postmodern influence in psychotherapy and psychoanalysis is to demonstrate that it can transform as well as subvert. In our view, the uncovering of difference and multiplicity, while important, does not go far enough. Therapists and analysts must guard against stopping at the point where the self has been shown to be infused with otherness. Such concepts as difference, contingency, and multiplicity are only truly meaningful if linked with an understanding and appreciation of the importance of cohesion, continuity, responsibility, and agency. The current fascination with postmodernism has the potential to obviate this distinction.

Rather than seeking to establish psychotherapy and psychoanalysis as postmodern doctrine or as natural science, we should heed Paul Ricoeur's (1970) trenchant observations of Freud. Ricoeur argues that psychoanalysis is a form of hermeneutics, a systematic effort to disentangle the logic of double or ambiguous meaning. Ricoeur's arguments, first published in the late 1960s, were considered radical and did not gain many admirers among North American psychoanalysts, who mostly sought to adhere to the principles of the medical sciences. But in Europe, Ricoeur's writings found an appreciative audience among clinicians and theorists alike.

Clearly, from today's perspective, to assert that Freud was a philosopher, or that psychotherapy and psychoanalysis are forms of hermeneutics, does not in any way diminish the importance of what therapists do or imply that therapy falls "short of the mark" from a natural scientific standpoint. This approach stands in stark contrast to the current emphasis on manualized and empirically validated forms of treatment.

But it also demonstrates that the work of a therapist or analyst is never easy to quantify, and that the tools of therapy, particularly hermeneutics, can be used to make trenchant observations of contemporary society (compare Cushman 1996) in much the same way that existential-phenomenological clinicians and thinkers once did.

Embodiment, Gender, and Race

Another important issue from the perspective of psychotherapy as a human science is the theme of embodiment. According to Merleau-Ponty, as we saw in the previous chapter, our perception and understanding of the world is always grounded in bodily experience. When applied to the therapeutic setting, we see that the foundations of self-reflexivity, the basis for human understanding, empathy, and knowledge lie in our bodily sensations and rest in the reversible properties of flesh. This insight into the body's centrality to human cognition is hardly the select purview of phenomenology, however. Increasingly, it is shared by analytical philosophers, attachment studies, and neuroscientific research.

For example, in a manner akin to Merleau-Ponty, Lakoff and Johnson (1999) insist that the body's preconceptual meaning structure provides the possibility of human thinking. They show that our conceptualization of the world and ourselves is intrinsically linked to our sensorimotor make-up. The body's preconceptual meaning structure also provides the basis for primary metaphors of space and time with which we construct our subjective lives. And from the perspective of attachment studies Peter Fonagy and colleagues (2002) demonstrate the ways in which mentalization (reflective functioning) and affect regulation are fundamentally connected to the developmental dyads through which our embodied consciousness emerges.

The neuroscientist Antonio Damasio provides us with a very similar perspective. Damasio (1994) argues that the body is a "ground reference" for understanding the world around us:

> The body, as represented in the brain, may constitute the indispensable frame of reference for the neural processes that we experience as the mind;

that our very organism rather than some absolute external reality is used as the ground reference for the constructions we make of the world around us and for the construction of the ever-present sense of subjectivity that is part and parcel of our experiences; that our most refined thoughts and best actions, our greatest joys and deepest sorrows, use the body as a yardstick. (xvi)

Damasio is describing the fundamental involvement of the body in all human experience. His insights are particularly germane since the body, as we know, plays a crucial role in the psychoanalytic dyad. The patient's and the therapist's bodily existence are always implicit in the discourse of therapeutic practice and, as such, are integral to the problem of intersubjectivity. Reflecting on Damasio's view of the body, Edgar Levenson (1998) proposes that "it may well be that the mind is not master, but is formed and molded by the body . . . [and] that our psychoanalytic desideratum, understanding, is neither entirely verbal nor intellectual, but more a limited reflection on an ineffable felt experience" (240). The notion of felt experience points to the role of affects, which are themselves bodily sensations. And, as the therapeutic process suggests, affective experience only gradually reaches the point at which it can be articulated or named in language.

On this view, language elaborates our bodily sensations, but does not create them (Frie 1999c). A process of sensing one's environment through the body always exists prior to and alongside the use of language. Our bodies can be said to "sense" their environments prior to language. Eugene Gendlin (1992) suggests that it is important to understand bodily sensing not as external observation or as subjective and internal, but as a form of interaction. Our bodies continually interact with the space around us and with the situations we find ourselves in.

The theme of embodiment has also had a significant impact on the development of postmodern thinking in psychotherapy and psychoanalysis. Where once there was a focus only on internalized objects and object choices, psychotherapists and psychoanalysts now conceptualize human development in terms of interactions between embodied subjects, not objects. The role of bodily or somatic experience has become central to the study of dyadic interaction and has been spurred on by the postmodern investigations of sexuality, gender, and race. Though a detailed examination of these categories is beyond the confines of our discussion, we will provide a brief overview of the main developments.

Postmodern critics rightly emphasize that Western culture has been characterized by Enlightenment forms of rationality that assume superiority and are unconscious of their one-sided, repressive and repressed assumptions. These forms of rationality reflect the hierarchical nature of power in Western society and have traditionally represented male, heterosexual, and Caucasian or "white" racial values. The embodied subject exists within this hierarchy that privileges one perspective and represses the other. Not only sexual difference, but also racial difference is conceived in terms of this power structure in which the other is repressed, both consciously and unconsciously. From a postmodern perspective, then, notions of sexuality, gender, and race are essentially social and linguistic constructions that rest on hidden (and not so hidden) assumptions about power and authority.

Many of the thinkers considered here have contributed much to the current focus on the marginalized other. Beginning with the work of Simon de Beauvoir (1953), whose work both informed and inspired Sartrean existentialism, feminist theorists have sought recognition of the other, not as a female object, but as an equal and embodied subject. Dialogical philosophers such as Buber and Binswanger sought to do justice to the other, not as an object, but as a Thou, while Marxist-inspired theorists like Fromm and Marcuse sought to account for the role of economic exploitation in determining experience. And like earlier existential-phenomenological critics of Freud, contemporary postmodern critics take issue with classical psychoanalysis, particularly its deterministic account of childhood development, misogynistic theories of female sexuality, and universal assumptions about race.

Within psychoanalysis, feminists have developed a series of approaches that seek to account for and redress the traditional inequalities between genders. From a broadly object relations perspective, the work of Chodorow (1989) and Gilligan (1993) focuses on the emergence of gender asymmetries in childhood development. From an intersubjective and relational perspective, the work of Benjamin (1997), Dimen (2003), and Harris (2005) explores and elaborates the marginalization of women within wider social contexts. This theme also forms the basis for the work of French postmodern feminists such as Kristeva (1987), Irigaray (1985), and Cixous and Clement (1986), who specifically address the cultural, political, and linguistic forces at work in the creation of gender inequalities.

As a result of feminist psychoanalysis, we are now much more mindful of the ways in which gender and authority shape what transpires in the clinical setting, and the fact that our bodies and their representations are politically, socially, and culturally determined. This is particularly important for understanding and appreciating the experiences of traditionally marginalized populations such as gay, lesbian, bisexual, and transgendered clients. Indeed, the introduction of queer theory has sought to reverse the longstanding marginalization of homosexuals within psychotherapy and psychoanalysis. For many gay and lesbian clinicians, it is precisely the feeling of being on the margins that has led them to address the normative categorizing of identity, thus offering a unique perspective that can help to deconstruct these categories (see Rottnek 1999; Corbett 2001; Drescher et al. 2003).

The notion of the marginalized other is also relevant to the discussion of race within the therapeutic setting. The relationship of race to the structures of power in our society continually informs our cultural and personal understandings of racial similarities and differences. Contemporary critics (for example, Jenkins 1995) seek to overcome Enlightenment beliefs that structured classical psychoanalytic approaches to practice and affected perceptions of minority patients, particularly African Americans. Others (for example, Leary 1997; Suchet 2004) emphasize the need to explore and acknowledge race between the patient and therapist as it manifests itself within the treatment relationship.

Within the contemporary, postmodern influenced discussion of sexuality, gender, and race, there are also important distinctions to be made. This is particularly the case between writers who embrace a constructivist approach to experience (Butler 1999) and those who seek to retain a concept of the self as agent (Benjamin 1988; Chodorow 1999;

Jenkins 2001). From a human science perspective, as we have seen, the embodied self can never be fully reduced to its contexts. And it is precisely the tension that emerges between an awareness of our contextual embeddedness and our quest for an individual identity that breaks free of reductionistic categories that defines our agentic potential. The embodied self as agent remains a potent and valuable concept for theory and practice alike.

INSIGHT AND EXPERIENCE

Merleau-Ponty's attempt to articulate a philosophy that transcends the traditional dualisms of mind and body, subject and object, calls to mind another binary opposition that structures our everyday language and acts as a social filter on our fleshly experience. To the vast majority of people in the Anglo-American world, the words "objectivity" and "subjectivity" denote mutually exclusive or antagonistic states of mind, or ways of experiencing and interpreting the world. The more "subjective" one's attitude, presumably, the more it is colored by emotion, bias, projection, and so on. And correlatively, the more "objective" one's attitude, the more impersonal and less distorted by feelings it is presumed to be. In short, prevailing linguistic usage is riddled with rationalist assumptions that construe feelings as inherently irrational and preclude thinking in terms of rational emotions or a *grounded* ("fleshly") subjectivity. More importantly, many psychotherapists (who should know better) still resort to this way of thinking, both in formulating clinical issues or dynamics and in conversation with their patients.

Cognitivism, behaviorism, and the medical model shoulder much of the blame for this state of affairs, of course. With rare exceptions, these approaches to the study of mental disorder all align themselves with an objectivist epistemology in which the therapist is idealized or imagined as being "objective" by virtue of their training and detachment, while the patient's subjectivity is deemed inherently suspect or virtually irrelevant. But if we examine the historical record, it turns out that psychoanalysis also contributed to this state of affairs. For despite insightful challenges from Jaspers, Binswanger, and others, the theoretical underpinnings of analytic discourse were overwhelmingly positivistic for the first sixty-odd years of its existence. As a result, the protean properties of desire, the manifold qualities and intensities of rage, regret, guilt, anxiety, and despair were all construed as the overt expression of specific quanta of sexual or aggressive energy circulating in a "mental apparatus" or cathected to external "objects" whose interactions with kindred systems were regulated by motives and mechanisms that remained largely outside of domain the of consciousness. The aim of analytic technique was to disclose the patient to himself or herself by "making the unconscious conscious" and strengthening the reality-testing ego.

But the term "objectivity" had a peculiar meaning in this context, since the ultimate in "insight" was presumed to be the ability to interpret twisted passions glimpsed or released in clinical work in light of this utterly impersonal, mechanistic frame of reference with the aid of a detached expert. This was especially true for psychoanalysts in training, who were often treated to a lengthy course of indoctrination while trying to make sense of complex and disconcerting emotional experiences (Kirsner 2000). While often explained in terms of "mastery" or "working through," there was something extremely odd and self-defeating about this whole procedure. Erich Fromm objected to this kind of intellectualistic exercise and made ample room for the raw immediacy of passions experienced in the analytic setting *prior to* any interpretive interventions that might be called for later. Indeed, Fromm maintained that unless insight is preceded or accompanied by a visceral, bodily kind of understanding, it is not compelling, nor will it lead to any significant change in the way the patient organizes experience or relates to others. In the terminology favored by existential-phenomenological tradition, insight that engages the intellect alone and fails to engage the whole person lacks depth and authenticity. Insight, when it is genuine, is mental, emotional, and physical — all at once.

AUTHENTICITY

Insight and experience in psychotherapy and psychoanalysis is directly linked to the contested issue of authenticity. Within the postmodern debate, the notion of authenticity is often framed as being synonymous with self-contained individuality and is consequently dismissed. The problem, from the perspective of postmodern critics, is that authenticity is a variant of the modernist idea that we are coherent and continuous selves rather than the postmodernist notion that we are a series of discontinuous "self-states" that are exquisitely context dependent (compare Fairfield et al. 2002). We believe that both authenticity and the self are relevant to clinical endeavors. Yet, as a result of Sullivan's famous dismissal of the notion of a core self, authenticity has long been viewed as a tenuous concept in psychoanalysis. As Sullivan puts it, "the overweening conviction of authentic individual selfhood . . . amounts to a delusion of unique individuality" (Sullivan 1950b, 16). In one sense Sullivan makes an important point because to speak of "authentic existence" can suggest that there is a single way of doing or being that defines us. However, there is also another tradition that sees authenticity in terms of a continually changing and evolving self-understanding.

For Binswanger, as for Buber, acknowledgment of the other person, not as a means to an end, but in his or her totality, as a Thou, is the condition of possibility for an authentic, loving relationship. The duality of this interaction constitutes a relationship of mutuality. In their view, authenticity is achieved not in isolation or through the analysis of intrapsychic structures, but in mutual dialogue with another human being. Binswanger and Buber use the term "authenticity" to refer to a deeper level of self-understanding that is achieved *in the presence of another person*. As such, it has direct bearing for psychotherapy because patients do not only seek symptom reduction, but a greater sense of meaning and self-understanding in their lives.

In the present climate of discussion, the issue of authenticity is perhaps most often associated with the so-called middle group of British psychoanalysis: D. W. Winnicott, Harry Guntrip, and R. D. Laing, who, like Sullivan, developed clinical vocabularies in which patients were alleged to have more than one "self." However, their distinctions between a patient's "true" and "false" selves are often glibly equated with authentic and inauthentic existence, respectively. Oddly enough, though extremely prevalent, this is a serious misreading. In fact, for Winnicott (1960), the distinction between the "true" and "false" self was less about establishing authenticity per se than about elaborating the notion of falsehood. He suggested, "there is little point in formulating a True Self idea except for the purpose of trying to understand the False Self, because it [the True Self] does no more than collect together the details of the experience of aliveness" (1960, 148). According to Winnicott, a false self is the result of developmental conflict encountered in the child-mother relationship. As a result, a false self is constructed as a defensive system that remains unconsciously maintained. Conversely, the true self originates in the capacity of the infant to recognize and enact spontaneous needs for self-expression: "Only the True Self can be creative and only the True Self can feel real" (1960, 148).

For R. D. Laing, by contrast, the "True Self" is even more ephemeral. Like Winnicott and Guntrip, Laing said that the False Self develops because of a pervasive lack of acceptance, attunement, and reciprocity in the mother-infant dyad, where the mother expects dutiful compliance with her prescriptions and ideas, and rewards calculated insincerity on the child's part. But in the wake of this sweeping (if subtle) invalidation of the child's experience, and the insistent feelings of invisibility and self-betrayal that haunt such patients, the "true self" that the schizoid patient defends or idealizes is *not* the patient's authentic self. On the contrary, as Laing describes it, the "true self" of the schizoid (or ontologically insecure) person is ultimately uncommitted, emotionally disengaged, and profoundly disembodied. It is a reified abstraction, a figment of the patient's desperate desire to shed the communal and corporeal dimensions of human existence (Burston 1996b). In short, it is inherently inauthentic and a poor substitute for a fully human existence.

By contrast with the "true self," in Laingian terminology, the term "authenticity" refers to any experience, expression, or action that *enlivens* the patient and brings their potential for honest self-expression and empathy with others into play. Conversely, attitudes, actions, or utterances that deaden or diminish the vitality and integrity of the person, deepening their sense of self-estrangement or self-betrayal, are deemed inauthentic, even if these actions, attitudes, and so on are highly "adaptive," or likely to yield intense short-term gratification (Laing 1961, chap. 9). Finally, though it is not stated in quite so many words, it is apparent from the context that Laing, like Sartre, conceived of "authenticity" as a state that fosters candid self-disclosure and self-expression, and diminishes the person's need for deception and self-deception.

In some senses, Laing's terminology is the complete opposite of Winnicott's, despite the fact that they are addressing the same phenomena. Still, there is a deeper consensus at work here. Both Winnicott and Laing based their work with deeply disturbed patients on the therapist's ability help patients' shed their deadened and defensive "False Self." But for Laing, who drew deeply on existential phenomenology, authenticity is a quality of experience or self-expression that is only possible in the context of embodied subjectivity, in the context of the I-Thou relationship. It is therefore incompatible with the dedicated pursuit of a "true self" that is fundamentally divorced from the body and from others. Contrast Laing's notion of authenticity with the postmodern critique of authenticity.

Postmodernists often relativize the notion of authenticity through constructivism. Taking the constructivist view of the self as his cue, for example, Stephen Mitchell writes, "the sense of authenticity is always a construction, and as a construction, is always relative to other possible self-constructions at any particular time" (131). Mitchell's aim is to demonstrate the inherently ambiguous nature of authenticity by linking it to the theory of multiple selves, thus freeing authenticity from any explicit connection with a single core of true self. He suggests that speaking in terms of authentic experience versus inauthentic experiences frees us from the problem of locating a core or true self because such experience is always and inevitably a construction and, as such, is always open to change.

The postmodern elaboration of the problem of authenticity in psychoanalysis allows for consideration of different types of self-experience. Because of its inherent ambiguity, however, this constructivist version of authenticity bears little resemblance with earlier philosophical and sociopolitical versions that emphasized norms and values like honesty and self-knowledge in human behavior. For many in the existential-phenomenological tradition, the notion of authenticity still implies a deeper understanding of ourselves in light of the world around us. Self-understanding does not occur in isolation, but through interaction with others and the world in which we live. As such, authenticity permits us to achieve a greater connection to others and the world. This self-understanding is not only very personal, it is also the source from which we make choices and undertake actions that affect our world.

Postmodernism, in turn, has shown us that knowledge is always embedded in specific contexts and that understanding can be characterized by difference and uncertainty. Even if we accept that self-understanding is central to the therapeutic process, such an understanding is often based on recognition of uncertainty in life and is always open to change. From a postmodern perspective, the notion of authenticity can seem inherently ambivalent or fleeting because it is always and inevitably a construction. The postmodern perspective on authenticity is summarized by Susan Fairfield, who seeks to deconstruct authenticity as a "modern" concept:

> A postmodernist would ask, how in the world could you possibly know which of the patient's subjective components are "authentic" ones — know this, that is, despite your own overdetermined subjective biases, the patient's conscious and unconscious strategies of concealment, and the shaping of the patient's material by the analytic situation itself? With which of *your* subjective components do you discern "authenticity," and on what basis do you grant this component the privileged status of objective judge? (Fairfield et al. 2002, 84–85)

Fairfield, moving beyond Mitchell, views authenticity as a construction relative to other possible self-constructions. For her, self-constructions are akin to self-states (or what used to be referred to as states of mind), leading to a situation in which authenticity can never be fully discerned.

In contemporary psychotherapy and psychoanalysis, there is often much talk of self-states (Bromberg 1998), but limited discussion of the self per se. The problem with accounting for human experience in this way is that individual self-states are representations of the person, but no combination of these self-states can actually yield an image of the person (Frederickson 2000). A self-state in isolation has nothing in common with the whole embodied in it. Self-states point *toward* a person, but are nevertheless *not* a person. The self is not materialistic, but an active, constantly unfolding process. Postmodernists struggle with the issue of authenticity when they relate it to a fixed core self. But the concept of authenticity does not require us to think of the self as static; rather, we can think of the self as emergent and dynamic. By conceptualizing authenticity and the self in this way, there is no need to embrace the problematic notion of multiple self-states.

Obviously, such terms as "authenticity" and "the self" are used in so many vague and over-encompassing ways that they have justifiably become a focus for skepticism. In a reply to Fairfield, Mitchell actually defends authenticity: "Aren't I being more authentic when I am telling what I believe is the truth then when I am deliberately lying? And am I not being more authentic when I am presenting what I think . . . rather than mimicking what I believe someone else thinks?" (Mitchell 2002, 107–8). Mitchell prefaced his response by cautioning that we must presume complex and ambiguous notions of who "I" am and what "truth" actually means. In his last years, Mitchell, like a number of postmodernist theorists, qualified his earlier support of postmodernism by moving from an outright embrace of constructivism (Mitchell 1993) to an acknowledgment of its limitations (Mitchell 2002).

Now, at the turn of the twenty-first century, the status and meaning of terms like "truth" and "illusion" have become moot in some philosophic circles, to the point where people who claim that we can, and indeed, *must* make such judgments in our clinical work are sometimes accused of being "positivistic." Edmund Husserl furnishes a splendid example of a human science theorist who commends natural scientists for their search for truth, but declines to endorse or adapt their methods to the study of the mind. In a related manner, Fromm commends Freud for his love of truth, but rejects his positivist metapsychology.

We similarly commend postmodernism for its trenchant analysis of the ways in which power and desire shape and inform our individual and collective mentalities, but the suggestion that selfhood is an illusion and that truth and authenticity are mere fictions is problematic at best. In spite of the societies in which we live, we all assume and, indeed, depend upon a system of beliefs and values that guide our behaviors and actions. Our ability to act on these beliefs may very well be constructed. But this ability also relies on an underlying continuity of action that is taken for granted in ourselves and others, and only explicitly acknowledged when challenged or placed in serious doubt. Similarly, even if we accept the notion of multiple constructed self-states, this self-system relies on an underlying continuity of selfhood that stands in the way of psychic disintegration and allows for self-perception and understanding over time. Otherwise, how is change possible? Thus, we maintain, there is a clear need to temper the constructivist impulse in postmodern theory to leave a space for individual will and agency, which is related to authenticity and self-understanding.

A potential difficulty for integrating postmodern philosophy into psychotherapy is that by reducing the subject and subjectivity to the by-products of relationships or contexts, the separateness of the other — that which is fundamentally irreducible — is lost or denied. Following the French phenomenologist Emmanuel Levinas (1974), we believe that therapists have an ethical obligation to recognize the singularity and the *separateness* of the other. Levinas emphasizes the "absolute otherness of the Other"; an otherness that cannot be explained in terms of relationships or contexts. He argues that if the other is reduced to a schema of who that person is — whether for us, or for others — then that person's irreducibility would be lost. In such cases, a "totalization" of the other takes place and an act of violence is committed.

With its singular focus on contexts and constructs, postmodernism has the potential to neglect the relevance of the individual sphere of human experience. By contrast, we believe that the lucid appreciation and enhancement of human singularity should be a matter of ultimate concern for all therapists. Moreover, a deepened or renewed awareness of our separateness and singularity can be a potent agent of transformation, especially in those for whom it was absent or relatively weak. Realizing that no one experiences or acts in the world in precisely the same way as I do, that no one else is responsible for the choices I make, and that I have but one life in which to experience and express the full range of my embodied subjectivity imparts a deep sense of urgency, clarity, and resolve. This awareness of separateness and singularity is fostered through the sense of togetherness in dialogue with the therapist and does not imply that the self can find itself phenomenologically in its lone state. On the contrary, psychotherapy and self-understanding exist within a thoroughly relational context. To paraphrase Hegel, although therapy may begin with an "I," it must always end in a "we." Separateness and togetherness, like singularity and duality, always exist in dialectical relationship to one another.

ALIENATION AND ENGAGEMENT

Thus far we have argued that postmodern thinking about the self and society emphasizes the dislocation and fragmentation of contemporary human experience. In the postmodern world there is a pervasive suspicion of grand narratives and absolutes, a deconstruction of identity and heralding of the death of the subject, and a celebration of multiplicity and the indeterminate. Postmodernism is in many ways a reflection of postindustrial Western society, which has become more problematical, heterogeneous, and fractious. In the midst of these changes, postmodern theory has developed probing and sophisticated discourses on gender, desire, power, and illusion.

Since the advent of postmodernism, however, such themes as agency, embodiment, insight, and authenticity, which were once commonplace in many therapists' working vocabulary, have often become moot. We have challenged the postmodern belief that these concepts are outdated fictions and have argued that our therapeutic imagination is needlessly impoverished if we reject them altogether. At the same time, we emphasize that, practiced in the proper spirit, psychotherapy and psychoanalysis are inherently critical, political discourses. To the extent that psychoanalysis is, of necessity, also a "socioanalysis," as Sartre, Laing, and Fromm insist, it is incumbent upon therapists to think about their patients' personal histories and everyday lives in terms of the social, political, and economic forces that impact their existence.

This raises the crucial question of human needs. For Freud, as for Marx, how our needs are met or frustrated by prevailing cultural norms and practices is always a key concern. Indeed, it was precisely the gaping disparity between the nature and urgency of human needs and the frustrating or disfiguring effects of the prevailing social structure that drove their social criticism. During the cold war era, the question of human needs was closely linked to the theme of alienation. At that time, discussion of alienation was ubiquitous in the social sciences but was subject to rigorous philosophical analysis by Hegelian-Marxists like Jean Hyppolite and Herbert Marcuse, who sought to affect a kind of Freud-Marx synthesis as a basis for critical social theory. In a similar spirit, the concept of alienation was introduced to psychotherapists by Erich Fromm (1961) and R. D. Laing (1967).

Given how central alienation was to therapeutic discourse a half century ago, its absence in the literature today is striking. One reason is that the many of the most profound and prolific writers in this genre were associated with a movement known as "Marxist humanism," which emerged as an alternative to the now defunct ideology of Soviet Marxism. Another reason is that talk of alienation has become anathema to the postmodern sensibility. Like the word "authenticity," "alienation" is often said to imply the existence of an essential human nature or a singular core of immutable selfhood from which one becomes estranged, perhaps as a prelude to a return or recovery of one's original ground. It is also associated with the idea of "humanism" which, in the wake of Heidegger, many theorists deem antiquated and parochial. While these critiques have merit, we are once again in danger of throwing out the baby with the bathwater. As with agency and authenticity, contemporary polemics often blind us to notions that are of enduring importance for psychotherapy. For all its openness to otherness and difference, postmodernism can be as rigid as the orthodoxies it criticizes.

Marx's concept of alienation was based on insights into the role of labor in human ontology as gleaned from Hegel's master-slave dialectic.

On this view, workers become estranged from work, from others, from their own bodies, and from nature when work ceases to engage the whole person and is reduced to a mere commodity. Though the burden of class divisions falls far more heavily on the poor, capitalism constrains rich and poor alike to address their material needs in ways that violate or run contrary to their basic human needs. The main difference between the rich and the poor, apart from the unjust allocation of resources, is that the wealthy often place their own class interests ahead of their human interests, while the poor, having nothing to lose, are more conscious of their alienation and therefore more capable of advancing the cause of general human emancipation.

In retrospect, of course, Marx thoroughly misjudged the proletariat, and wrote while capitalism was still in its infancy. Psychotherapy was not yet invented, and even when it was, proletarians never sought psychotherapy in large numbers. But does that render his ideas irrelevant to therapists today? One of the tasks for the future, says Marx, is to abolish the division between mental and physical labor that has reinforced class divisions since ancient times. If endowed with dignity and respect, he says, physical labor need not be slavish, and mental labor need not be the province of the educated, the rich, and the powerful alone. Admittedly, today's dwindling, embattled middle class usually pursues some form of "mental labor" for a living, so it is frequently forgotten that Marx was implicitly attacking the social practices that inscribe and perpetuate the Cartesian mind-body split, both in theory and in practice. In this, he anticipated many existential, phenomenological, and postmodern theorists. And though working professionals tend to avoid back-breaking labor, they can be just as profoundly alienated from nature and their own bodies. They may find that their work lacks meaning, or violates their conscience, or requires so much time that their families and communities are short-changed by their absence.

Today's workers are just as likely to be alienated as their proletarian predecessors. As a result, basic human needs — such as intimacy, community involvement, honest self-expression — are often frustrated in order to fulfill material needs. Alternatively, if the patient's material needs are already well provided for, but they continue to work incessantly, their work becomes a symptom, rather than a cause, of their self-estrangement.

Postmodernism often questions the notion of generic human needs, arguing that this way of framing needs is essentialistic — that is, it posits the existence of an immutable "human nature" that is the same in everyone and thus denies difference and multiplicity. But absent some fundamental bedrock of common needs and interests, it is difficult to imagine how humans could experience or cultivate empathy, solidarity, or even simple communication with one another. These needs are always historically and socially mediated, yet provide a ground from which to understand, criticize, and change the contexts in which we find ourselves. And without them, where would that leave psychotherapy?

Psychotherapy is both possible and necessary because we are profoundly alike in some ways, and yet profoundly different in others. There is no paradox, nor any hint of contradiction in this statement. Indeed, nothing in the attempt to elucidate the impact of generic or fundamental needs on human behavior negates our singularity or compels us to conclude that we are somehow more alike than different. A *socio-analysis* of the sort we are suggesting is rooted in an appraisal of the tensions and disparities between human rights and needs and the prevailing cultural and economic constraints that obstruct or preclude their fulfillment. In social change, as in therapeutic action, theory is intended to shape and inform praxis, to transform and humanize the social order.

How did we arrive at this curious state of affairs? Theorists like Freud and Marx thought that the task of reason was to illumine the ways in which society frustrates human needs and deforms human subjectivity. Postmodernism drew on the irrationalist impulse in existential phenomenology, above all in Nietzsche, and demonstrated ways in which the use of reason often masks an underlying ideology of power. Reason can become an instrument of power, an extension of arbitrary authority. Reason that is bereft of imagination and compassion, a sense of justice and of common decency, is indeed destructive. But reason that is not divorced from the body and emotions, that is informed and infused with a lucid appreciation of human needs and interests, has the principles of personal autonomy, uncoerced consensus, and reciprocal understanding as its normative basis.

For the German social theorist, Jürgen Habermas (1994, 1987), this vision of emancipation is implicit in language itself and provides a means by which social life might be transformed. In a similar vein, from the perspective of psychotherapy, the articulation of affect, need, and desire in language allows for the formulation of conscious and unconscious processes in the clinical encounter. In the face of postmodernity's celebration of fragmentation and dispersion, Habermas holds fast to the Enlightenment goals of autonomy and personal identity, which, he says, can only be realized through the dialectics of intersubjectivity. Yet, as the practice of psychotherapy demonstrates, the language we use is suffused with unconscious affects and desires, human needs, and personal pathologies. They are as much a productive part of the dialogic process of emancipation as they are a potential barrier to its realization. Therapy is made possible by attending to and recognizing the continual interweaving of the rational and irrational; each is a fundamental part of a process that is at once intellectual, emotional, embodied, conscious and unconscious, private and public.

Clinical Postscript

Contemporary psychotherapy is often portrayed as an empirically based treatment technique practiced by professionals in a medical setting. According to this account, the patient has a discrete form of psychopathology, while the therapist is an expert with the requisite knowledge and skills to remove the patient's symptoms as quickly and painlessly as possible. Yet the push toward "evidence-based" and standardized, highly scripted treatment protocols often obscures the fact that psychotherapy is not principally a matter of technique, but a special relationship between two unique human beings — one whose outcome is inherently unpredictable. Unfortunately, the medical model of psychotherapy overlooks human science therapies such as existential analysis, revisionist forms of psychoanalysis, and depth psychology, which are not easily quantified. The human science perspective rests on a philosophical foundation that enables practitioners to grasp, or at any rate to glimpse, what it means to be fully human, and to relate the concrete specificity of the patient's complaints to a more comprehensive and encompassing view of human existence.

Our reflections on psychotherapy as a human science have sought to provide the experienced practitioner, trainee, and interested reader with a theoretical foundation that is too often absent in today's clinical milieu. We are not interested in displacing empirical forms of psychotherapy or psychopharmacology, both of which have made significant advances in the treatment of specific symptoms. Rather, we wish to demonstrate that the mastery of a particular technique or treatment approach is only half the story, and that a balanced approach to therapy needs theory as much as technique. Many clinicians practice today without fully understanding the theoretical underpinnings of clinical practice, or the important theoretical controversies that affect their everyday work. Our aim has been to provide a history of the ideas that make up the human science perspective and to explain current controversies about clinical practice that are grounded in these complex and compelling theoretical differences.

PART I: THE HUMAN SCIENCE PERSPECTIVE IN CLINICAL PRACTICE

In this section, we will review some of the clinical implications raised by our exploration of philosophy and psychoanalysis. This overview will describe the main themes and controversies that encompass the field, but without providing detailed technical guidance.[1] In our experience, having taught a wide spectrum of trainees and experienced therapists — from undergraduates and doctoral candidates in psychology to psychiatric residents and candidates in psychoanalysis — we have found that students actively seek knowledge beyond the boundaries of natural science. Although many of our students were trained within a medical model, and some have little or no prior exposure to the humanities in general or to philosophy in particular, there is often a desire to learn more about fields outside of medicine and empirical psychology. This intellectual curiosity has much to do with

---

1. There are a number of useful texts, only some of which we can describe here, that elaborate the dynamics at work in psychotherapy from a human science perspective. See, for example, Yalom 2002; Curtis and Hirsch 2003, 69–106 (this book contains a number of other useful chapters as well), Schneider 2003; and Ehrenberg 1992. Each of these sources provides clinical examples along with theoretical discussion. While there are many texts that explain specific therapeutic techniques, none can take the place of expert supervision. In our view, the practice of psychotherapy is best learned through intensive supervision and is aided by a personal "training" therapy so that therapists can understand the role of their individual psychology and the way it impacts their work. A personal therapy can also enable therapists to empathize with their patients about what it is like to experience therapy. In addition, useful theoretical guides to clinical practice from a human science perspective include Fiscalini (2005), Benjamin (1988), and Chodorow (1999).

how the practice of psychotherapy is experienced by the clinician. Even if we view therapy in terms of manualized practice regimes, in which the various stages of the therapy are laid out with step-by-step instructions, nothing prepares the trainee or the experienced therapist for the vagaries of human interaction or their own reactions to the therapeutic experience.

Therapists want to make sense of what they do, to find out what works, what does not, and, above all, why. They want to understand their patients' experiences and to find out how to relate to them in ways that can make a difference in their patients' lives. This requires not only the ability to empathize, but to develop a thorough appreciation for human experience — both their own and that of their patients, which is not an easy thing to learn when training focuses on quantitative issues and approaches. Indeed, we have found that our students are not overly concerned with the latest result of studies on empirically based treatments. They do not ask what scientific evidence can tell them about psychotherapy outcomes. Rather, our students primarily tend to be interested in understanding what it is like to be sitting in a room with an anxious, depressed, or even psychotic person who repeats the same patterns of behavior or enters the same type of relationship over and over again. They want to know what motivates people. They want to understand the ways in which the patient's subjective experience is a result of psychological development as well as socioeconomic and political factors. Above all, therapists seek to understand their own myriad reactions to their patients — commonly known as countertransference — and the ways in which they can use their subjective experiences in the therapeutic setting.

In dealing with such issues, the philosophical foundations of psychotherapy are helpful. The nature of human relatedness has been a dominant theme of continental philosophy since Descartes, and is commonly referred to as "intersubjectivity" (the interaction of two or more individual subjectivities). Theories of intersubjectivity were developed in direct response to the Cartesian focus on the isolated individual mind (or subjectivity). Interest in intersubjective experience flowed from the realization that solipsism is an untenable position, a reflection of schizoid detachment or delusional existence and that, in the end, a monadological or self-enclosed existence is never actually possible. There are many approaches to the problem of intersubjectivity, ranging from emotive and linguistic to embodied and political. Ultimately, these different approaches cannot be completely disentangled since each plays a role in our experience and understanding of other people — be it our emotional reactions to one another, our use of language, our experience of our own bodies or the bodies of others and what they represent to us, or the role of culture and politics in shaping our understandings of one another.

Alongside the issue of intersubjectivity, the question of individual subjectivity continues to remain pertinent to clinical practice. The reactions that the patient and the therapist have to one another, referred to as "transference" and "countertransference," respectively, are inherently linked to one's subjective experience of the setting we find ourselves in. From a human science perspective, elucidating the transference and countertransference (or patient's and therapist's subjectivity) is a crucial part of the therapeutic process. While the patient's reaction to the therapist and the therapeutic setting (transference) and the therapist's reaction to the patient and the therapeutic interaction (countertransference) are both indelibly contextualized, that is, constructed by what goes on in the therapy and beyond, they are also a result of the each person's unique individuality, developmental history, and perspective — hence one's direct "subjective" experience. As our philosophical investigations of subjectivity have shown, however, even direct subjective experience occurs through a set of uniquely personal and ideological filters that are both culturally and politically constructed. As a result, countertransference reactions can never be understood solely as a consequence of the therapist's own unique character or difficulties, because they are always a reaction to the intersubjective interactions between therapist and patient and are affected by broader contextual factors. What a therapist does with his or her countertransference is something we will examine below in more detail.

The concepts of subjectivity and intersubjectivity are also implicit in the fourfold schematic we used to explain the relevance of the history of continental philosophy to psychotherapy. Beginning with our contrast between religious and irreligious thinkers, we have sought to show the ways in which religious beliefs are relevant to human experience, be they entirely private and subjective or more obviously intersubjective, cultural, or even political in nature. Psychoanalysts used to tell a joke that illustrated the division between analysis and religion. It went something like this: "If you like sex, you become a Freudian, but if you like religion, you become a Jungian." Although this was an unfair simplification, the early division between Freud and Jung on the meaning of religion and religious symbolism has had a lasting effect. To this day, Jungian and post-Jungian therapists are sought for their openness to issues concerning spirituality and religious belief, whereas patients who work with Freudian psychoanalysts often broach spiritual questions with some trepidation. Existential analysts and revisionist psychoanalysts, by contrast, are much more open to religion than their Freudian colleagues have traditionally been. Regardless of a therapist's brand of religiosity, or lack of it, we have found that an openness toward the nature and meaning of religious belief is vital to the process of allowing a therapy to unfold and develop.

The second of our conceptual schematics was the distinction between rationalism and irrationalism. This division is implicit throughout the history of philosophy, and is fundamental to the contemporary practice and understanding of psychotherapy. While we drew careful distinctions between thinkers who emphasized the primacy of reason, and those who acknowledged the existence of less discursive or intellectual ways of knowing and apprehending the world, we also sought to show that this distinction is somewhat malleable and a reflection of the specific time, place, and context in which it is made.

What often happens in contemporary clinical settings is that human behavior is observed with the purpose of judging the extent to which it is rational, and hence healthy, or irrational, and hence disordered. While such judgments are relevant in clinical settings that deal with acute and chronic disturbances such as delusional and psychotic behaviors, there are dangers in applying such invidious distinctions to less vivid or disturbed behavior. Indeed, as the history of radical and reactionary political movements in the modern era has shown, labeling behavior "insane" (and hence unsafe) was often politically motivated and used to stifle dissent.

The current diagnostic categories developed and used in the Diagnostic and Statistical Manual of the American Psychiatric Association (DSM), while useful in facilitating communication between professional mental health workers, are often overly reductive because they fail to capture the lived experience of the person being diagnosed. The problem is that human experience often defies our attempts at categorization. Moreover, the DSM's categories are themselves reflections of the social mores and norms of the time and place in which they were devised, as exemplified by the astounding fact that until 1974, the DSM labeled homosexuality a mental disorder.

As most of the thinkers and therapists we examined have pointed out, humans always have the capacity to demonstrate both rational and irrational behavior. Indeed, both are integral to human experience. The popular conception of falling in love is but one example of the way in which society seeks to explain the potentially irrational behavior of those who are smitten by another. Conversely, the need to maintain a rational perspective on the way one works in a postmodern, capitalistic society is often held up as a prerequisite of good citizenship or a hallmark of mental health, even though adherence to these norms can be profoundly alienating and anything but salutary for individual happiness or well-being. Clearly, how "rational" and "irrational" are defined, and by whom, entails issues of control, power, ideology, and authority, all of which are implicit in the therapeutic relationship.

The third of our classifications, the distinction between utopian and anti-utopian thinkers is remarkably relevant to the question of social interaction, whether within or outside the therapeutic setting. Whereas one group of thinkers and therapists we examined views human beings as essentially at variance with one another, and therefore destined to suffer from the effects of interpersonal conflict and unfulfilled desire, another group stresses the human ability to socialize and to maintain relationships with others based not on selfish desire, but on the ability to transcend inner and interpersonal conflict. This distinction is apparent in much therapeutic work, yet it often remains unformulated because it is not openly addressed.

When we teach trainees or therapists, we often ask whether they believe that humans are essentially selfish, or whether they can live together in ways that are harmonious enough to overcome our basic desires to have our personal needs fulfilled at the expense of other's needs and freedoms. The question initially strikes most students as odd, not so much because of its simplicity, but because the answer is almost always deemed to be self-evident. Further discussion of this issue invariably discloses that even experienced therapists entertain *very different points of view* on these fundamental questions, and yet do not realize the extent to which these viewpoints bear substantially on how they practice. We believe that these disparate perspectives affect the way in which a therapy is carried out. They influence the type of questions therapists ask as well as what therapists choose to focus on and the objectives they see in their work.

Freud's pessimism about human nature, which was shared by Lacan, was based on the belief that the desire for gratification can never be fulfilled, with the result that human experience is characterized by frustration or by a perpetual lack — which may or may not register in consciousness, of course. Yet for other theorists and therapists, the ability to bestow love on another human being, without continually needing to be loved in return, suggests the possibility of a very different view of human experience. These therapists tend to focus on the nature of a patient's relationships and seek to understand human behavior in terms of the ability or inability to maintain positive, loving relations with others. They view love as a mode of relatedness rooted in a vivid appreciation of the presence and immediacy of another person. And it is the ability to achieve this level of mutuality within the therapeutic setting that is seen as crucial to the efficacy of therapy.

The last of our four schematics is the distinction between modernism and postmodernism. We have demonstrated that although the label "postmodernism" is a recent occurrence in psychotherapy, the onset of postmodernism in philosophy was anticipated by earlier thinkers, above all by Nietzsche. Postmodernism is deeply suspicious of such notions as objectivity, truth, and reason, emphasizing constructivism and perspectivism. In contrast to the isolated and supposedly sovereign rational entity that characterizes the modernist self, the postmodern therapist sees the self as generated and maintained by the relational, linguistic, and cultural contexts in which it is embedded. As a result, the reliance on the analytic neutrality and objectivity that defined traditional Freudian psychoanalysis has given way to a therapeutic relationship based on greater mutuality in which traditional assumptions about authority and reason are infused or simply replaced with an emphasis on ambiguity and uncertainty.

A human science perspective in psychotherapy embraces aspects of modernism and postmodernism alike, and can be described as a form of "critical modernism." Indeed, on close inspection, a strict bifurcation between the two is difficult to formulate or maintain with any exactitude. For example, a therapist who uses a human science approach will view human interaction and individual experience as constructed and context bound, but may simultaneously acknowledge the role of personal agency or choice in the way the patient co-constructs his or her reality with others. In other words, although the self is seen as inherently relational, a limited degree of agency, autonomy, and individuality remain an important part of the human science lexicon. Similarly, the human science therapist will focus not only on how gender, race, sexual, and social class identities play out in treatment, but also on the ways in which they are representations of the society in which both the patient and therapist live. Such notions as identity and autonomy are also retained, lest human experience and relationships are reduced to epiphenomena of their cultural or relational contexts.

PART II: CLINICAL THEMES AND THEIR APPLICATIONS

In this final section, we will seek to understand what makes the actual practice of therapy from a human science perspective distinctive. We will examine a number of key clinical themes, including diagnostic assessment, two-person versus one-person psychology, authority and mutuality, the questioning of sociopolitical realities, and the role of transference-countertransference dynamics and dreams.

From a human science perspective, symptoms are recognized first as forms of communication. Properly understood within a supportive, therapeutic setting, symptoms present the opportunity for reflection and redirection — in essence, for changes in the problems of living. The process of diagnosis involves an assessment of the way in which patients relate to the world and other people around them, based on a detailed inquiry into past and present experience. From a human science perspective, personality is a function of experiential learning. As such, the aim of therapy is to help patients learn new ways of being and becoming by emphasizing strengths and fostering an awareness of difficulties. Problems in relating to others are a core focus, and therapy seeks to expand the possibilities of being with oneself and others.

Because therapists within a human science perspective eschew conformist norms of behavior, they prefer to understand symptoms in terms of problems in living, rather than the formal diagnostic approach of the American Psychiatric Association (DSM). Many symptoms that are defined under the traditional rubric of psychopathology, be they anxiety, distress, depression, and so on are seen as permanent possibilities of human functioning *in extremis,* rather than simply symptoms of "mental illness" per se. By contrast, the DSM's utility is more evident in the assessment of severe disturbances such as psychotic or delusional behavior. Human science therapists are versed in standard diagnostic categories, make assessments of the level of functioning, and are judicious in their recommendation or prescription of medication. In this context, it is important to note that a human science perspective can be practiced by any number of different clinicians in diverse settings, be they psychiatrists or psychiatric nurses in a hospital, social workers in a clinic, clinical psychologists in private practice, or counselors in an academic environment. The difference, though, is that many traditional medical settings increasingly limit the possibilities for flexibility and openness in the understanding and treatment of patients.

From a human science perspective, medication should be recommended when therapy is no longer a sufficient or satisfactory option. As much as possible, medication is used in conjunction with therapy, so that patients may achieve not only symptom reduction, but gain a deeper understanding of why they are suffering from specific symptoms to begin with. In order to reach decisions about the need for medication, it is vital that therapists rely on sound judgment derived from adequate training and experience, and also avail themselves of advice from psychiatrists if they themselves are unable to prescribe. Human science therapists see personality as shaped by social factors, not just by biological factors or learned behavioral patterns, and thus they tend to be critical of a traditional, one-sided disease model.

For many therapies within the medical model, the efficacy of treatment depends chiefly on the knowledge and expertise of the practitioner. Within this paradigm, the therapist's role tends to be analogous to the scientist who is capable of viewing the patient's mind and behavior with objective detachment. Analogous with the medical model is traditional psychoanalytic therapy, in which the analyst seeks to control and distance his or her own feelings to make possible a clinical environment free of the influence of the other person in the dyad. This approach is often referred to as a one-person psychology because it discounts the role of the therapist's subjectivity in the therapeutic focus.

In contrast, human science therapists view the ostensible benefits, or even the very possibility of achieving therapeutic neutrality, with considerable skepticism. Instead, they see therapy as a *collaborative process* in which the therapist works *with* the patient, rather than simply offering objective advice or insight to the patient. From the very beginning of a treatment, the human science therapist works with the patient to set goals for the therapy and actively fosters the patient's own goal setting. A one-person psychology is thus rejected in place of a collaborative, relational approach that undoes the strictures of both the medical model and the traditional psychoanalytic relationship. In the process a host of clinical possibilities are opened up.

Once therapist and patient form a dyad, the relationship also becomes the context for therapeutic inquiry. Clinical observations are made and understood within the interpersonal contexts in which they occur. The patient's experiences are not viewed as isolated processes that are only biologically derivative or behaviorally determined. Rather, they have been formed within an interpersonal context. Every therapy, properly carried out, is also a "socioanalysis" that elucidates the patient's enveloping social and political context, the sources of their distress, and their role in the experience of that distress. The aim of therapy is to understand the patient's often unformulated experience as it emerges within therapeutic interaction, thus evoking and potentially transforming the patient's experiences outside of the therapeutic setting.

A crucial part of the human science perspective is the inclusion of the social and political world in which both the patient and therapist live. Therapy cannot be divided from the wider context in which it takes place. This presents an important contrast to the traditional model, in which there tends to be a singular focus on the patient's biologically or behaviorally determined symptoms. Similarly, the classical psychoanalytic approach focuses on the patient's intrapsychic experiences, neglecting the patient's so-called "external" reality. In contrast, the human science perspective eschews talk of internal and external because it sees the human being fundamentally as a "being-in-the-world." And as beings-in-the-world, the patient and therapist can never be separated from the social and political contexts in which they exist.

For classical Freudians, in particular, the possibility of taking a patient's sociopolitical experiences at face value is excluded because the focus is on the patient's transference relationship to the analyst. In the process, the patient's political viewpoints tend to be interpreted as projections of or as resistance to the actual work of analysis. In contrast, a more realistic approach to the patient's political reality would be to acknowledge the patient's sociopolitical experience. But rather than get caught up in a singular discussion about political issues or differences, the therapist would attempt to see the patient's point of view as a representation or metaphor for her lived experience. This approach would seek to validate objective political concerns and then help to understand their significance in terms of the patient's own individual psychology. In the process, the therapist's sociopolitical contexts and their effect on the therapy would also need to be accounted for.

The human science perspective is premised on a steadfast acknowledgment of the sociopolitical reality as it emerges in the process of therapy. This reality may take many forms, such as gender discrimination, racial prejudice, the politics of sexual identity, or socioeconomic inequality and political injustice. In our contemporary society there is no shortage of these experiences. In each case, the first step would be to recognize the pervasive reality of the issue and then examine its possible meanings within the therapeutic dyad and beyond. Exploration of our immediate sociopolitical reality might begin with the patient's experience of the therapist's gender, race, or sexual orientation and what it means for them. This would be coupled with an acknowledgment of the inequalities and injustices that exist in the society we live.

The therapist may also help the patient take active steps to address his or her reality, either through the achievement of shifts in identity and ideology or through direct political involvement. A central part of this process is the recognition that the therapist and patient are agents who can facilitate change, yet are always limited, and to some extent defined by the constraints of the relational, social, and political contexts in which they find themselves. If issues like these do not arise spontaneously, a therapist may ask a patient about their sociopolitical perspective in the belief that human experience is always a fundamentally social enterprise. This approach seeks to help patients foster an awareness of the sociopolitical nature of all experience, and to understand the connections between the shape of a patient's sociopolitical world and the potential suffering it causes.

In sum, the human science therapist does not see or depict himself or herself chiefly as the expert or authority, nor claim that the progress of therapy is determined primarily by the decisions he or she makes. Indeed, human science therapists are sensitive to the role of power relations within the therapy, while nonetheless recognizing the obvious and irreducible differences between therapist and patient. Being concerned and empathic with patients does not preclude a certain degree of professional distance, which is not to be confused with traditional psychoanalytic notions of a blank screen and neutrality.

Leaving disparities in power aside, transference also plays an important role in the progress of the therapy. The patient brings to the therapeutic relationship attitudes and expectations born of previous relationships. The aim of exploring transference is to illuminate his or her subjective reality. But it is not assumed that the therapist is the sole arbiter of what constitutes "reality" in the clinical setting. Thus, the patient's transferences are analyzed both in terms of their real meanings *and* possible distortions. As therapy progresses, the patient learns to recognize interactions with the therapist as not only a repetition of old patterns of interaction, but as something potentially new. This makes possible the learning and acceptance of new and different ways of being and relating to others.

Analysis of transference is only half the equation, however. The other half concerns the therapist's own countertransference. Once, the therapist is no longer seen as either a blank screen or entirely objective, it becomes possible to acknowledge and investigate the inevitable interaction (intersubjectivity) of two subjectivities in the therapeutic dyad. For therapists from a human science perspective, countertransference is an important therapeutic tool because it provides a means to deepen and enhance our understanding of the patient, ourselves, and the therapeutic process.

Countertransference reactions to the patient and the therapeutic situation may include a range of responses from specific feelings and fantasies to embodied and behavioral responses. These are individual and often seemingly irrational responses to direct subjective experiences within the therapeutic setting that have to be unraveled and made sense of. The question of how to use these responses and whether or not to share them with the patient is currently a matter of debate among therapists. Some recommend the judicious and affective disclosure of countertransference feelings, while others believe that countertransferential data are a source of valuable information that should be kept private. It may be futile to seek a one-size-fits-all solution to this issue and may ultimately depend upon the needs of the individual patient.

While mutuality within the therapeutic relationship opens up a host of possibilities, it also highlights the issue of effective therapeutic boundaries between the patient and therapist. For human science therapists, mutuality allows for new dimensions of affective complexity and exploration. The aim of mutuality is not to dissolve the individual sense of its participants, however. Nor does an emphasis on mutuality imply that "anything goes." Distinctions between the therapist and patient in terms of their roles, functions, and power differentials must be openly acknowledged and valued. Two-person interaction is only possible if personal boundaries are respected and individual difference is recognized. Mutuality is, in fact, facilitated by acknowledging the limits of what is possible at any given moment in the dyad. Conversely, ignoring these limits precludes genuine interaction between therapist and patient.

Many human science therapists also rely on the clinical use of dreams. Their approach to dream interpretation varies greatly, depending on whether the therapist's orientation is predominantly psychoanalytic, Jungian, or existential-phenomenological. Freud interpreted dreams as a reflection of repressed childhood wishes and desires that were subject to heavy censorship and distortion, in the interest of enabling the dreamer to minimize internal conflict and maintain a neurotic equilibrium. By contrast, Jung argued that Freud's approach privileged the dreamer's past over their present. He emphasized the compensatory function of dreams, suggesting that their real function is to call attention to blind spots or distortions in the conscious ego's attitude to reality. In the process, Jung also sought to show ways in which dreams can link the dreamer's personal unconscious with the collective unconscious. From an existential-phenomenological and revisionist psychoanalytic perspective, dreams actually provide illuminating glimpses into the patient's personal past and its lingering impact on their behavior, and furnish a lucid commentary on the dreamer's current situation and relationships, including features that they are unable or unwilling to experience or express in their normal waking state. For human science practitioners, dreams ultimately are best understood within an interpersonal and social context, and furnish access to the patient's unformulated experience of his or her world. Regardless of the therapist's interpretive emphasis, dreams can provide important insights into the experiences of the patient and the interactions of therapy.

On this basis, then, the human science therapist demonstrates that relatedness is central to self-understanding and a sense of well-being. The therapeutic relationship is seen as crucial to this process because it is the vehicle through which change takes place and thus becomes a curative factor. Throughout the process of therapy, the therapist is not simply treating the patient, but also sharing in the existence of the patient.

Thus, to facilitate the therapeutic process, the human science therapist relies on a number of tools or techniques, including but not limited to the process of mutual goal setting, the development of a detailed personal history and analysis of the patient's contemporaneous social relationships, the exploration of sociopolitical realities and the ways these affect or impair the patient's prospects for well-being, the understanding of transference and countertransference interactions, and the exploration of dreams. The overall objective of a human science approach is to create the expansion of self-awareness in the patient and thereby to foster openness to new experiences and new ways of being and relating with others in the world.

Our aim in arguing for the broader acceptance of a human science perspective is to move beyond the narrow technical concerns of professionalized psychotherapy. As a result of a number of powerful forces — pressures from insurance companies, the growing influence of academic psychology, and pervasive descriptive psychiatric diagnoses — psychotherapy has become more concerned with curbing symptoms than with offering a healing relationship that treats the person as a whole. We have sought to show that many of the basic themes and perspectives that inspire or preoccupy contemporary therapists are vividly foreshadowed in the history of continental philosophy. In our view, psychotherapy is not only a learned technique, but also rests on a set of ideas, concepts, and theories that provide the foundation for understanding and experiencing the vagaries of human existence. A deeper appreciation of human experience is also necessary if therapists are to maintain their role as observers and critics of contemporary culture and society, and not become subsumed into the very set of values and beliefs they have traditionally questioned. Therapists have the ability to not only engage their patients in a truly personal and meaningful way, but also to question and transform the increasingly bureaucratic mental health systems in which they practice and the sociopolitical contexts in they live.

REFERENCES

Arendt, H. 1978. *The Life of the Mind*. New York: Harcourt Brace Jovanovich.

Aron, L. 1996. *A Meeting of Minds*. Hillsdale, N.J.: The Analytic Press.

Atwood, G., and R. Stolorow. 1984. *Structures of Subjectivity: Explorations in Psychoanalytic Phenomenology*. Hillsdale, N.J.: The Analytic Press.

Avineri, S. 1974. *Hegel's Theory of the Modern State*. London: Cambridge University Press.

———. 1976. *The Social and Political Thought of Karl Marx*. London: Cambridge University Press.

Avnon, D. 1998. *Martin Buber: The Hidden Dialogue*. London: Rowman and Littlefield.

Barthes, R. 1984. "The Death of the Author." In *Image, Music, Text*. New York: Hill and Wang.

Benjamin, J. 1988. *Bonds of Love: Psychoanalysis, Feminism, and the Problem of Domination*. London: Virago.

———. 1995. *Like Subjects, Love Objects: Essays on Recognition and Sexual Difference*. New Haven, Conn.: Yale University Press.

———. 1999a. *The Shadow of the Other*. New York: Routledge.

———. 1999b. "Afterword to Recognition and Destruction: An Outline of Intersubjectivity." In *Relational Psychoanalysis: The Emergence of a Tradition,* edited by S. A. Mitchell and L. Aron, 201–10. Hillsdale, N.J.: Analytic Press.

Binswanger, L. 1922. *Einführung in die Probleme der allgemeinen Psychologie*. Berlin: Julius Springer.

————. 1947. *Ausgwählte Vorträge und Aufsätze, bd. I: Zur phänomeno-logischen Anthropologie.* Bern: Francke.

————. 1949. *Henrich Ibsen und das Problem der Selbstrealisation in der Kunst.* Heidelberg: Schneider.

————. 1955. *Ausgewählte Vorträge und Aufsätze.* Vol. 2, *Zur Problematik der psychiatrischen Forschung und zum Problem der Psychiatrie.* Bern: Francke.

————. 1956. *Erinnerungen an Sigmund Freud.* Bern: Franke.

————. 1957. *Schizophrenie.* Pfullingen: Günter Neske.

————. 1992. *Ausgewählte Werke Band 1: Formen mißglückten Daseins.* Edited by Max Herzog. Heidelberg: Asanger.

————. 1993a. *Ausgewählte Werke Band 2: Grundformen und Erkenntnis menschlichen Daseins.* Edited by M. Herzog and Hans-Jürgen Braun. Heidelberg: Asanger.

————. 1993b. *Dream and Existence: Michel Foucault and Ludwig Binswanger.* Edited by Keith Hoeller. Atlantic Highlands, N.J.: Humanities Press International.

————. 1993c. *Ausgewählte Werke Band 3: Vorträge und Aufsätze.* Edited by M. Herzog. Heidelberg: Asanger.

————. 1994. *Ausgewählte Werke Band 4: Der Mensch in der Psychiatrie.* Edited by Alice Holzhey. Heidelberg: Asanger.

Borch-Jacobsen, M. 1991. *Lacan: The Absolute Master.* Translated by D. Brick. Stanford, Calif.: Stanford University Press.

Boss, M. 1957. *Psychoanalyse und Daseinsanalytik.* Bern: Kindler, 1957.

————. 1963. *Daseinanalysis and Psychoanalysis.* New York: Basic Books.

————. 1979. *Existential Foundations of Medicine and Psychology.* Translated by S. Conway and A. Cleaves. New York: Aronson.

Bowie, A. 1990. *Aesthetics and Subjectivity: From Kant to Nietzsche.* Manchester: Manchester University Press.

Brett, G. 1965. *Brett's History of Psychology.* Abridged version. Cambridge, Mass.: MIT Press.

Bromberg, P. 1998. *Standing in the Spaces.* Hillsdale, N.J.: The Analytic Press.

Bronner, S. 1994. *Of Critical Theory and Its Theorists.* London: Blackwell.

Brown, J. A. C. 1964. *Freud and the Post-Freudians.* London: Penguin.

Brunner, J. 2001. *Freud and the Politics of Psychoanalysis.* New Brunswick, N.J.: Transaction Publishers.

Buber, M. 1965a. *Between Man and Man.* Translated by R. G. Smith. New York: Macmillan.

———. 1965b. *The Knowledge of Man.* New York: Harper & Row.

———. 1970. *I and Thou.* Translated by W. Kaufmann. New York: Charles Scribners & Sons.

———. 1973. *Martin Buber Briefwechsel aus sieben Jahrzehnten, bd I I: 1918–1938.* Edited by Grete Schaeder. Heidelberg: Lambert Schneider.

———. 1983. *Ich und Du.* Heidelberg: Lambert Schneider.

———. 1992. *Das Dialogische Prinzip.* Gerlingen: Lambert Schneider.

Burston, D. 1986. "The Cognitive and Dynamic Unconscious: A Critical and Historical Perspective." *Contemporary Psychoanalysis* 22, no. 3: 133–57.

———. 1991. *The Legacy of Erich Fromm.* Cambridge, Mass.: Harvard University Press.

———. 1996a. "Conflict and Sociability in Hegel, Freud and Their Followers: Tzvetan Todorov's 'Living Alone Together.'" *New Literary History* 27, no. 1: 73–82.

———. 1996b. *The Wing of Madness: The Life and Work of R. D. Laing.* Cambridge, Mass.: Harvard University Press.

———. 1997. "Divided Loyalties: Cultural Weltanschauungen and the Psychology of the Unconscious." *Harvest: Journal of Jungian Studies* 43, no. 2: 123–37.

———. 1999. "Archetype and Interpretation." *The Psychoanalytic Review* 86, no. 1: 35–62.

———. 2000. *The Crucible of Experience: R. D. Laing and the Crisis of Psychotherapy.* Cambridge, Mass.: Harvard University Press.

———. 2003a. "Existentialism, Humanism and Psychotherapy." *Journal of the Society for Existential Analysis* 14, no. 2.

———. 2003b. "Nietzsche, Scheler and Social Psychology." *Journal of the Society for Existential Analysis* 14, no. 1: 2–13.

Butler, J. 1999. *Gender Trouble.* New York: Routledge.

Cannon, B. 1991. *Sartre and Psychoanalysis: An Existentialist Challenge to Clinical Metatheory.* Lawrence: University Press of Kansas.

———. 2003. "Sartre and Psychoanalysis." In *Understanding Experience: Psychotherapy and Postmodernism.* Edited by R. Frie. London: Routledge.

Casement, A. 2003. *C. G. Jung.* London: Sage.

Chodorow, N. 1978. *The Reproduction of Mothering: Psychoanalysis and the Sociology of Gender.* Berkeley and Los Angeles: University of California Press.

———. 1989. *Feminism and Psychoanalytic Theory.* New Haven, Conn.: Yale University Press.

———. 1999. *The Power of Feelings: Personal Meaning in Psychoanalysis, Gender, and Culture.* New Haven, Conn.: Yale University Press.

Cixous, H., and C. Clement. 1986. *The Newly Born Woman.* Minneapolis: University of Minnesota Press.

Clagget, M. 1963. *Greek Science in Antiquity.* New York: Collier Macmillan.

Cocks, C. 1991. "The Nazis and C. G. Jung." In *Lingering Shadows: Freudians, Jungians and Anti-Semitism,* edited by A. M. Maidenbaum. Boston: Shambala.

Connerton, P., ed. 1978. *Critical Sociology.* Harmondsworth: Penguin.

Cooper, D. 1967. *Psychiatry and Anti-Psychiatry.* Harmondsworth: Penguin.

Corbett, K. 2001. "Faggot = Loser." *Studies Gender & Sexual* 2: 3–28.

Craig, E. 1988. "An Encounter with Medard Boss." In *The Humanistic*

Psychologist, Especial Issues, edited by Erik Craig, Psychotherapy for Freedom, The Daseinsanalytic Way in Psychology and Psychoanalysis.

Critchley, S., and P. Dews. 1996. *Deconstructive Subjectivities.* Albany, N.Y.: State University of New York Press.

Curtis, Rebecca, and Irwin Hirsch. 2003. "Relational Approaches to Psychoanalytic Psychotherapy." In *Essential Psychotherapies: Theory and Practice,* edited by Alan S. Gurman and Stanley B. Messer. New York: Guilford Press.

Cushman, P. 1996. *Constructing the Self, Constructing America: A Cultural History of Psychotherapy.* New York: Addison Wesley.

Damasio, A. 1994. *Descartes' Error: Emotion, Reason, and the Human Brain.* New York: Avon Books.

———. 1999. *The Feeling of What Happens: Body and Emotion in the Making of Consciousness.* New York: Harcourt Brace.

de Beauvoir, S. 1953. *The Second Sex.* New York: Vintage, 1989.

Derrida, J. 1978. *Writing and Difference.* Chicago: University of Chicago Press.

Descartes, R. 1949. *A Discourse on Method.* New York: Dutton.

Dews, P. 1987. *Logics of Disintegration.* London: Verso.

Dilthey, W. 1989. *Selected Works.* Vol. 1. Princeton: Princeton University Press.

Dimen, M. 2003. *Sexuality, Intimacy, Power.* Hillsdale, N.J.: The Analytic Press.

Drescher, J., A. D'Ercole, and E. Schoenberg, eds. 2003. *Psychotherapy with Gay Men and Lesbians: Contemporary Dynamic Approaches.* New York: Harrington Press.

Dupont, J. 1988. *The Clinical Diaries of Sandor Ferenczi.* Cambridge, Mass.: Harvard University Press.

Eagleton, T. 1996. *The Illusions of Postmodernism.* Oxford: Blackwell.

Ehrenberg, D. 1992. *The Intimate Edge: Extending the Reach of Psychoanalytic Interaction.* New York: Norton.

Ellenberger, H. 1970. *The Discovery of the Unconscious*. New York: Basic Books.

Erikson, E. 1958. *Young Man Luther*. New York: W. W. Norton.

Fackenheim, E. 1970. *The Religious Dimension of Hegel's Thought*. London: Faber.

Fairfield, S., L. Layton, and C. Stack, eds. 2002. *Bring the Plague: Towards a Postmodern Psychoanalysis*. New York: Other Press.

Fancher, R. E. 1996. *Pioneers of Psychology*. New York: W. W. Norton.

Farber, L. 1966. *The Ways of the Will*. New York: Basic Books.

Farias, V. 1989. *Heidegger and Nazism*. Philadelphia: Temple University Press.

Feuerbach, L. 1957. *The Essence of Christianity*. Translated by G. Eliot. New York: Harper & Row.

———. 1972. "Principles of the Philosophy of the Future." In *The Fiery Brook: Selected Writings of Ludwig Feuerbach,* edited by Z. Hanfi. Garden City, N.J.: Doubleday.

Fichte, J. G. 1975. *Versuch einer neuen Darstellung der Wissenschaftslehre*. Hamburg: Felix Meiner.

Fichtner, G., ed. 1992. *Sigmund Freud und Ludwig Binswanger Briefwechsel, 1908–1938*. Frankfurt: Fischer Verlag.

Fiscalini, J. 2004. *Coparticipant Psychoanalysis*. New York: Columbia University Press.

Flax, J. 1991. *Thinking Fragments: Psychoanalysis, Feminism, and Postmodernism in the Contemporary West*. Berkeley and Los Angeles: University of California Press.

Fonagy, P., G. Gergely, E. Jurist, and M. Target. 2002. *Affect Regulation, Mentalization and the Development of Self*. New York: Other Press.

Foucault, M. 1977a. *Discipline and Punish: The Birth of the Prison*. Translated by A. Sheridan. Harmondsworth: Penguin.

———. 1977b. "Nietzsche, Genealogy, History." In *Language, Counter-Memory, Practice: Selected Essays*. Ithaca, N.Y.: Cornell University Press.

————. 1980. *The History of Sexuality*. Vol. 1. New York: Vintage.

————. 1993. "Dream, Imagination and Existence: An Introduction to Ludwig Binswanger's 'Dream and Existence,'" trans. F. Williams. In *Dream and Existence: Michel Foucault and Ludwig Binswanger*, edited by Keith Hoeller. Atlantic Highlands, N.J.: Humanities Press International.

Frank, M. 1988. *What Is Neostructuralism?* Translated by S. Wilke and R. Gray. Minneapolis: University of Minnesota Press.

Frederickson, J. 2000. "There's Something Youey about You: The Polyphonic Unity of Personhood." *Contemporary Psychoanalysis* 36: 587–617.

Freud, S. 1900. *The Interpretation of Dreams*. Vols. 4–5. Translated by J. Strachey. London: Hogarth Press, 1974.

————. 1901. *On the Psychopathology of Everyday Life*. Vol. 6. Translated by J. Strachey. London: Hogarth Press.

————. 1905. *Three Essays on the Theory of Sexuality*. Vol. 7. Translated by J. Strachey. London: Hogarth Press, 1974.

————. 1911. "Formulations Regarding the Two Principles of Mental Functioning." Translated by J. Riviere. In *Sigmund Freud: Collected Papers*. Vol. 4. Edited by M. Khan. London: Hogarth Press, 1971.

————. 1912a. "The Dynamics of the Transference." Translated by J. Riviere. In *Sigmund Freud: Collected Papers*. Vol. 2. Edited by M. Khan. London: Hogarth Press, 1971.

————. 1912b. "Recommendations for Physicians on the Psycho-Analytic Method of Treatment." Translated by J. Riviere. In *Sigmund Freud: Collected Papers*. Vol. 2. Edited by M. Khan. London: Hogarth Press, 1971.

————. 1913. "Further Recommendations in the Technique of Psychoanalysis. On beginning treatment . . ." Translated by J. Riviere. In *Sigmund Freud: Collected Papers*. Vol. 2. Edited by M. Khan. London: Hogarth Publishers, 1971.

————. 1914. "Further Recommendations in the Technique of Psycho-Analysis. Recollection, Repetition and Working Through." Translated by J. Riviere. In *Sigmund Freud: Collected Papers*. Vol. 2. Edited by M. Khan. London: Hogarth Press, 1971.

————. 1915. "Further Recommendations in the Technique of Psycho-Analysis. Observations on Transference-Love." Translated by J. Riviere. In *Sigmund Freud: Collected Papers*. Vol. 2. Edited by M. Khan. London: Hogarth Press, 1971.

————. 1919. "Turning in the Ways of Psycho-Analytic Therapy." Translated by J. Riviere. In *Sigmund Freud: Collected Papers*. Vol. 2. Edited by M. Khan. London: Hogarth Press, 1971.

————. 1923. *The Ego and the Id*. Vol. 19. Translated by J. Strachey. London: Hogarth Press.

————. 1927. *The Future of an Illusion*. Vol. 21. Translated by J. Strachey. London: Hogarth Press, 1974.

————. 1930. *Civilization and Its Discontents*. Vol. 21. Translated by J. Strachey. London: Hogarth Press, 1974.

Frie, R. 1997. *Subjectivity and Intersubjectivity in Modern Philosophy and Psychoanalysis: A Study of Sartre, Binswanger, Lacan, and Habermas*. Lanham, Md.: Rowman and Littlefield.

Frie, R., ed. 1999a. "Existential Analysis." Special edition of *Humanistic Psychologist* 27.

————. 1999b. "Interpreting a Misinterpretation: Ludwig Binswanger and Martin Heidegger." *Journal of the British Society for Phenomenology* 29: 244–58.

————. 1999c. "Psychoanalysis and the Linguistic Turn." *Contemporary Psychoanalysis* 35: 673–97.

————. 1999d. "Subjectivity Revisited: Sartre, Lacan, and Early German Romanticism." *Journal of Phenomenological Psychology* 30: 1–13.

————. 2000. "The Existential and the Interpersonal: Ludwig Binswanger and Harry Stack Sullivan." *Journal of Humanistic Psychology* 40: 108–30.

————. 2002. "Modernism or Postmodernism? Binswanger, Sullivan and the Problem of Agency." *Contemporary Psychoanalysis* 38: 534–73.

Frie, R., ed. 2003. *Understanding Experience: Psychotherapy and Postmodernism*. London: Routledge.

Frie, R., and K. Hoffmann. 2002. "Binswanger, Heidegger, and Anti-semitism." *Journal of the British Society for Phenomenology* 30: 221–28.

Frie, R., and B. Reis. 2001. "Understanding Intersubjectivity: Psychoanalytic Formulations and Their Philosophical Underpinnings." *Contemporary Psychoanalysis* 37: 297–327.

Friedman, M., ed. 1994. *The Worlds of Existentialism: A Critical Reader.* Atlantic Highlands, N.J.: Humanities Press.

Fromm, E. 1941. *Escape from Freedom.* New York: Holt, Rinehart & Winston.

———. 1947. *Man for Himself: An Inquiry into Psychology and Ethics.* Greenwich, Conn.: Fawcett.

———. 1955. *The Sane Society.* New York: Holt, Rinehart & Winston.

———. 1956. *The Art of Loving.* New York: Harper & Row.

———. 1959. *Sigmund Freud's Mission: An Analysis of His Personality and Influence.* New York: Harper & Row.

———. 1961. *Marx's Concept of Man.* New York: Frederick Ungar.

———. 1962. *Beyond the Chains of Illusion.* New York: Simon & Schuster.

———. 1970. *The Crisis of Psychoanalysis: Essays on Marx, Freud and Social Psychology.* New York: Holt, Rinehart & Winston.

Fromm-Reichman, F. 1990. "Loneliness." *Contemporary Psychoanalysis* 26: 305–30.

Gendlin, E. 1988. "Befindlichkeit: Heidegger and the Philosophy of Psychology." *Journal of Existential Psychiatry and Psychology: Special Issue.*

———. 1992. "The Primacy of the Body, Not the Primacy of Perception." *Man and World* 25: 341–53.

———. 2003. "From Concepts through Experiencing." In *Understanding Experience: Psychotherapy and Postmodernism.* Edited by R. Frie, 100–115. London: Routledge.

Gergen, K. 2001. "Psychological Science in a Postmodern Context." *American Psychologist* 56: 803–13.

Gilligan, C. 1993. *In a Different Voice*. Cambridge: Harvard University Press.

Glass, J. M. 1993. *Shattered Selves: Multiple Personality in a Postmodern World*. Ithaca, N.Y.: Cornell University Press.

Greenberg, J., and S. A. Mitchell. 1983. *Object Relations in Psychoanalytic Theory*. Cambridge: Harvard University Press.

Guntrip, H. 1961. *Personality Structure and Human Interaction*. London: Hogarth Press.

———. 1968. *Schizoid Problems, Object-Relations and the Self*. London: Hogarth Press.

———. 1969. *Schizoid Phenomena, Object Relations and the Self*. New York: Basic Books.

Habermas, J. 1975. *Knowledge and Human Interests*. Translated by J. Shapiro. Cambridge: Polity Press.

———. 1984. *Theory of Communicative Action*. Vol. 1. *Reason and the Rationalization of Society*. Translated by T. McCarthy. Boston: Beacon Press.

———. 1987. *Theory of Communicative Action*. Vol. 2. Translated by T. McCarthy. Boston: Beacon Press.

———. 1993. "Martin Heidegger: On the Publication of the Lectures of 1935." In *The Heidegger Controversy*. Edited by R. Wolin. Cambridge, Mass.: MIT Press.

Harris, A. 2005. *Gender as a Soft Assembly*. Hillsdale, N.J.: The Analytic Press.

Hauke, C. 2000. *Jung and the Postmodern: The Interpretation of Realities*. London: Routledge.

Hegel, G. W. F. 1948. *Early Theological Writings*. Translated by T. M. Knox. Chicago: University of Chicago Press.

———. 1942. *The Philosophy of Right*. Translated by T. M. Knox. Encyclopedia Britannica. Oxford University Press.

———. 1967. *The Phenomenology of Mind*. Translated by J. B. Baillie. New York: Harper & Row.

———. 1979. *Early Theological Writings*. Translated by T. M. Knox. Philadelphia: University of Pennsylvania Press.

Heidegger, M. 1959. *An Introduction to Metaphysics*. Translated by Ralph Manheim. New Haven, Conn.: Yale University Press.

———. 1962. *Being and Time*. Translated by J. Macquarrie and E. Robinson. Oxford: Basil Blackwell.

———. 1971. *Poetry, Language, Thought*. Translated by A. Hofstadter. New York: Harper & Row.

———. 1977. *Basic Writings*. Edited and translated by David Farrell Krell. London: Routledge.

———. 1978. *Wegmarken*. Frankfurt am Main: Vittorio Klostermann.

———. 1980. *Holzwege*. Frankfurt am Main: Vittorio Klostermann.

———. 1982. *The Basic Problems of Phenomenology*. Translated by A. Hofstadter. Bloomington: Indiana University Press.

———. 1987. *Zollikoner Seminare*. Edited by M. Boss. Frankfurt am Main: Vittorio Klostermann.

———. 2001. *Zollikon Seminars: Protocols — Conversations — Letters*. Evanston, Ill.: Northwestern University Press.

Henrich, Dieter. 1982. *Selbstverhältnisse*. Stuttgart: Reclam.

Herzog, M. 1994. *Weltentwürfe: Ludwig Binswangers phänomenologische Psychologie*. Berlin: Walter de Gruyter.

Heuer, G. 2003. The Devil under the Couch: The Secret Story of Jung's Twin Brother. *Harvest: International Journal for Jungian Studies* 49, no. 2: 130–44.

Hoffman, I. 1998. *Ritual and Spontaneity in the Psychoanalytic Process: A Dialectical-Constructivist View*. Hillsdale, N.J.: The Analytic Press.

———. 2000. "At Death's Door: Therapists and Patients as Agents." *Psychoanalytic Dialogues* 10: 823–46.

Hogenson, G. 1983. *Jung's Struggle with Freud*. Notre Dame, Ind.: Notre Dame University Press.

Holland, D., W. Lachicotte, D. Skinner, and C. Cain. 1998. *Identity and Agency in Cultural Worlds.* Cambridge, Mass.: Harvard University Press.

Holzhey-Kunz, A. 1990. "Ludwig Binswanger: Daseinsanalyse als wissenschaftlich exakte Untersuchung von Weltentwürfen." *Daseinsanalyse* 7: 81–101.

Husserl, E. 1960. *Cartesian Meditations.* Translated by D. Cairns. The Hague: Martinus Nijhoff.

———. 1962. *Ideas: General Introduction to Pure Phenomenology.* Translated by W. R. B. Gibson. New York: Collier.

———. 1964. *The Idea of Phenomenology.* Translated by W. P. A. a. G. Nakhnikian. The Hague: Martinus Nijhoff.

———. 1970. *The Crisis of the European Sciences and Transcendental Phenomenology.* Translated by D. Carr. Evanston, Ill.: Northwestern University Press.

Irigaray, L. 1985. *The Sex Which Is Not One.* Ithaca, N.Y.: Cornell University Press.

Jaspers, K. 1913. *Allgemeine Psychopathologie.* Berlin: Springer Verlag.

———. 1952. *Reason and Anti-Reason in Our Time.* Translated by G. Stanley. New Haven, Conn.: Yale University Press.

———. 1962. *Kant.* New York: Harcourt Brace Jovanovich.

———. 1965. *General Psychopathology.* Translated by J. Hoenig and M. Hamilton. Chicago: University of Chicago Press.

Jenkins, A. H. 1995. *Psychology and African Americans: A Humanistic Approach.* 2nd ed. Needham Heights, Mass.: Allyn & Bacon.

———. 2001. "Individuality in Cultural Context: The Case for Psychological Agency." *Theory and Psychology* 11: 347–62.

Jonas, H. 1963. *The Gnostic Religion.* Boston: Beacon Press.

———. 1966. *The Phenomenon of Life: Toward a Philosophical Biology.* New York: Harper & Row.

Jones, E. 1967. *Sigmund Freud: Life and Work.* Vol. 2. London: Hogarth Press.

Jung, C. G. 1904. *Word Association Experiments.* Vol. 2. Translated by R. F. C. Hull. Princeton, N.J.: Princeton University Press.

———. 1910. *On the Nature of the Psyche.* Vol. 8. Princeton, N.J.: Princeton University Press.

———. 1916. *Psychology of the Unconscious.* Translated by B. Hinkle. New York: Moffatt.

———. 1956. *Symbols of Transformation.* Vol. 5. Translated by R. F. C. Hull. Princeton, N.J.: Princeton University Press.

———. 1961. *Memories, Dreams, Reflections.* Translated by R. and C. Winston. New York: Vintage.

Kellner, D. 1984. *Herbert Marcuse and the Crisis of Marxism.* Berkeley and Los Angeles: University of California Press.

Kierkegaard, S. 1968. *Attack upon "Christendom."* Translated by W. Lowrie. Princeton, N.J.: Princeton University Press.

Kirsch, T. 2000. *The Jungians: A Comparative and Historical Perspective.* London: Routledge.

Kirsner, D. 2000. *Unfree Associations: Inside Psychoanalytic Institutes.* London: Process Press.

Kohut, H. 1977. *The Restoration of the Self.* New York: International Universities Press.

Kojève, A. 1969. *An Introduction to the Reading of Hegel.* Edited by Allan Bloom. Translated by J. Nichols. Ithaca, N.Y.: Cornell University Press, 1980.

Kristeva, J. 1987. *Tales of Love.* New York: Columbia University Press.

Kunz, H. 1949. "Die Bedeutung der Daseinsanalytik Martin Heideggers für die Psychologie und die philosophische Anthropologie." In *Martin Heideggers Einfluss auf die Wissenschaften.* Edited by A. Carlos. Bern: Franke.

Lacan, J. 1977a. *Ecrits: A Selection.* Translated by A. Sheridan. New York: Norton.

———. 1977b. *The Four Fundamental Concepts of Psycho-analysis.* Translated by A. Sheridan. Harmondsworth: Penguin.

————. 1988a. *The Seminar of Jacques Lacan, Book I: Freud's Papers on Technique, 1953–54.* Edited by J.-A. Miller. Translated by J. Forrester. Cambridge: Cambridge University Press.

————. 1988b. *The Seminar of Jacques Lacan, Book II: The Ego in Freud's Theory and in the Technique of Psychoanalysis, 1954–55.* Edited by J.-A. Miller. Translated by S. Tomaselli. Cambridge: Cambridge University Press.

————. 1993. *The Seminar of Jacques Lacan, Book III: The Psychoses, 1955–56.* Edited by J.-A. Miller. Translated by R. Grigg. London: Routledge.

Laing, R. D. 1960. *The Divided Self.* London: Tavistock.

————. 1961. *Self and Others.* London: Tavistock.

————. 1967. *The Politics of Experience and the Bird of Paradise.* New York: Pantheon.

————. 1970. *Knots.* New York: Pantheon.

————. 1985. *Wisdom, Madness and Folly: The Making of a Psychiatrist.* New York: McGraw Hill.

Laing, R. D., and D. Cooper. 1964. *Reason and Violence: A Decade of Sartre's Philosophy.* New York: Pantheon.

Laing, R. D., and A. Esterson. 1964. *Sanity, Madness and the Family.* London: Tavistock.

Laing, R. D., H. Phillipson, and A. R. Lee. 1966. *Interpersonal Perception: A Theory and a Method of Research.* London: Tavistock.

Lakoff, G., and M. Johnson. 1999. *Philosophy in the Flesh: The Embodied Mind and Its Challenge to Western Thought.* New York: Perseus Press.

Layton, L. 1998. *Who's That Girl? Who's That Boy?* Hillsdale, N.J.: The Analytic Press.

Leary, K. 1997. Race, Self-Disclosure, and "Forbidden Talk": Race and Ethnicity in Contemporary Psychoanalytic Practice. *Psychoanalytic Quarterly.* 66, no. 2: 163–68.

Levenson, E. 1998. "Awareness, Insight, Learning." *Contemporary Psychoanalysis* 34: 239–49.

Levi, W. A. 1974. *Philosophy as Social Expression*. Chicago: University of Chicago Press.

Levinas, E. 1974. *Otherwise Than Being*. Pittsburgh: Duquesne University Press.

———. 1993. *Outside the Subject*. Translated by Michael B. Smith. Stanford: Stanford University Press.

Löwith, K. 1981. *Das Individuum in der Rolle des Mitmenschen*. In *Sämtliche Schriften*. Vol. 1. Edited by K. Stichweh. Stuttgart: J. B. Metzler.

Mahler, M. S., F. Pine, and A. Bergman. 1975. *The Psychological Birth of the Human Infant*. New York: Basic Books.

Maidenbaum, A. M. S., ed. 1991. *Lingering Shadows: Freudians, Jungians and Anti-Semitism*. Boston: Shambala.

———. 2002. *Jung and the Shadow of Anti-Semitism*. Berwick, Maine: Nicolas-Hays.

Makkreel, R. 1975. *Dilthey: Philosopher of the Human Sciences*. Princeton, N.J.: Princeton University Press.

Martin, J., and J. Sugarman. 1999. *The Psychology of Human Possibility and Constraint*. Albany, N.Y.: State University of New York Press.

———. 2000. "Between the Modern and the Postmodern: The Possibility of the Self and Progressive Understanding in Psychology." *American Psychologist* 55, no. 4: 397–406.

Martin, J., J. Sugarman, and J. Thompson. 2003. *Psychology and the Question of Agency*. Albany, N.Y.: State University of New York Press.

May, R., E. Angel, and H. F. Ellenberger, eds. 1958. *Existence: A New Dimension in Psychiatry and Psychology*. New York: Basic Books.

McGuire, W. 1982. *Bollingen: An Adventure in Collecting the Past*. Princeton, N.J.: Princeton University Press.

Mead, G. H. 1962. *Mind, Self and Society*. Edited by C. Morris. Chicago: University of Chicago Press.

Merleau-Ponty, M. 1964a. *The Primacy of Perception*. Translated by W. Cobb. Evanston, Ill.: Northwestern University Press.

———. 1964b. *Signs.* Translated by R. C. McCleary. Chicago: Northwestern University Press.

———. 1968. *The Visible and the Invisible.* Evanston, Ill.: Northwestern University Press.

———. 1989. *Phenomenology of Perception.* Translated by C. Smith. London: Routledge.

Mills, J. 2002. *The Unconscious Abyss: Hegel's Anticipation of Psychoanalysis.* Albany: State University of New York Press.

Milton, J. 2002. *The Road to Malpsychia: Humanistic Psychology and Our Discontents.* San Francisco: Encounter Books.

Mitchell, J., and J. Rose. 1982. *Feminine Sexuality: Jacques Lacan and the École Freudienne.* London: Macmillan.

Mitchell, S. A. 1988. *Relational Concepts in Psychoanalysis.* Cambridge, Mass.: Harvard University Press.

———. 1993. *Hope and Dread in Psychoanalysis.* New York: Basic Books.

———. 2002. "The Treatment of Choice: A Response to Susan Fairfield." In *Bringing the Plague: Toward a Postmodern Psychoanalysis.* Edited by Susan Fairfield, Lynne Layton, and Carolyn Stack. New York: Other Press.

Mitchell, S., and M. Black. 1996. *Freud and Beyond: A History of Modern Psychoanalytic Thought.* New York: Harper Collins.

Modell, A. 1993. *The Private Self.* Cambridge: Harvard University Press.

Moran, D. 2000. *Introduction to Phenomenology.* London: Routledge.

Moses, I. 1988. "The Misuse of Empathy in Psychoanalysis." *Contemporary Psychoanalysis* 24: 577–94.

Needleman, J., ed. 1963. *Being-in-the-World: The Selected Papers of Ludwig Binswanger.* New York: Basic Books.

Nietzsche, F. 1956. *The Birth of Tragedy and the Genealogy of Morals.* Translated by F. Golfing. New York: Doubleday.

———. 1983. *Untimely Meditations.* Translated by H. Reginald. New York: Cambridge University Press.

O'Neill, J., ed. 1996. *Hegel's Dialectic of Desire and Recognition: Texts and Commentary*. Albany: State University of New York Press.

Orange, D., G. Atwood, and R. Stolorow. 1997. *Working Intersubjectively: Contextualism in Psychoanalytic Practice*. Hillsdale, N.J.: The Analytic Press.

Ott, H. 1993. *Martin Heidegger: A Political Life*. New York: Basic Books.

Pascal, B. 1995. *Pensées*. Translated by A. J. Krailsheimer. Harmondsworth: Penguin.

Rank, O. 1941. *Beyond Psychology*. New York: Dover.

Richardson, W. J. 2003. "Truth and Freedom in Psychoanalysis." In *Understanding Experience: Psychotherapy and Postmodernism*. Edited by R. Frie. London: Routledge.

Ricoeur, P. 1980. *Essays on Biblical Interpretation*. Translated by L. S. Mudge. Philadelphia: Fortress Press.

Roazen, P. 1971. *Freud and His Followers*. New York: Alfred Knopf.

————. 2000a. *The Historiographies of Psychoanalysis*. New Brunswick, N.J.: Transaction Publishers.

————. 2000b. "What Is Wrong with French Psychoanalysis? Observations on Lacan's First Seminar." In *Lacan in America*. Edited by J. M. Rabate. New York: Other Press.

Rockmore, T. 1995. *Heidegger and French Philosophy*. London: Routledge.

Rottnek, M., ed. 1999. *Sissies and Tomboys*. New York: New York University Press.

Rudnytsky, P. 1987. *Freud and Oedipus*. New York: Columbia University Press.

Russell, B. 1946. *The History of Western Philosophy*. London: Allen and Unwin.

Safranski, R. 1998. *Martin Heidegger: Between Good and Evil*. Cambridge, Mass.: Harvard University Press.

Samuels, A. 1985. *Jung and the Post-Jungians*. London: Routledge & Kegan Paul.

————. 1993a. "New Material concerning Jung, Anti-Semitism and the Nazis." *Journal of Analytical Psychology* 38: 463–70.

————. 1993b. *The Political Psyche*. London: Routledge.

Santaniello, W. 1994. *Nietzsche, God and the Jews: His Critique of Judeo-Christianity in Relation to the Nazi Myth*. Albany: State University of New York Press.

Sartre, J. P. 1955. *No Exit and Three Other Plays*. New York: Random House.

————. 1956. *Being and Nothingness*. Translated by H. E. Barnes. New York: Philosophical Library.

————. 1957. *The Transcendence of the Ego: An Existentialist Theory of Consciousness*. Translated by F. Williams and R. Kirkpatrick. New York: The Noonday Press.

————. 1967. "Consciousness of Self and Knowledge of Self." Translated by N. Lawrence and L. Lawrence. In *Readings in Existential Phenomenology*. Edited by N. Lawrence and D. O'Conner. Englewood Cliffs, N.J.: Prentice-Hall.

————. 1975. *The Emotions: Outline of a Theory*. Translated by B. Frechtman. New York: Citadel.

————. 1991. *Critique of Dialectical Reason*. Vol. 1. Translated by A. Sheridan-Smith. London: Verso.

Scanlon, J. 1992. "Persons and Their Worlds: Limits of Understanding." Paper presented at The Husserlian Foundations of Phenomenological Psychology, Simon Silverman Conference, Duquesne University.

Schafer, R. 1976. *A New Language for Psychoanalysis*. New Haven, Conn.: Yale University Press.

Scheler, M. 1973. *Selected Philosophical Essays*. Translated by D. Lachterman. Evanston, Ill.: Northwestern University Press.

————. 2000. *Ressentiment*. Milwaukee: Marquette University Press.

Schneider, K. J. 2003. "Existential Humanistic Psychotherapies." In *Essential Psychotherapies: Theory and Practice*. New York: Guilford Press.

Stadlen, A. 1999. "Demythologizing Daseinsanalysis." Transcript to the Lecture of the Fourth International Forum of Daseinsanalysis, Zurich, May 7.

Stepansky, P. 2001. *Freud and the Surgeons*. Hillsdale, N.J.: Analytic Press.

Stern, D. 1985. *The Interpersonal World of the Infant: A View from Psychoanalysis and Developmental Psychology*. New York: Basic Books.

Stern, D. B. 1997. *Unformulated Experience: From Dissociation to Imagination in Psychoanalysis*. Hillsdale, N.J.: The Analytic Press.

Stewart, D., and A. Mikunas. 1990. *Exploring Phenomenology: A Guide to the Field and Its Literature*. 2nd ed. Athens: Ohio University Press.

Stolorow, R., and G. Atwood. 1979. *Faces in a Cloud: Subjectivity in Personality Theory*. New York: Aronson.

———. 1992. *Contexts of Being: The Intersubjective Foundations of Psychological Life*. Hillsdale, N.J.: The Analytic Press.

Stolorow, R., B. Brandchaft, and G. Atwood. 1987. *Psychoanalytic Treatment: An Intersubjective Approach*. Hillsdale, N.J.: The Analytic Press.

Stolorow, R., D. M. Orange, and G. E. Atwood. 2002. *Worlds of Experience: Interweaving Philosophical and Clinical Dimensions in Psychoanalysis*. New York: Basic Books.

Storr, A. 1973. *Jung*. New York: Viking Press.

Suchet, M. 2004. "A Relational Encounter with Race." *Psychoanalytic Dialogues* 14, no. 4: 423–38.

Sullivan, H. S. 1950a. "The Illusion of Personal Individuality." In *The Fusion of Psychiatry and Social Science*, 198–226. New York: Norton, 1964.

———. 1950b. "A Note on the Implications of Psychiatry, the Study of Interpersonal Relations, for Investigation in the Social Sciences." In *The Fusion of Psychiatry and Social Science*, 15–29. New York: Norton, 1964.

———. 1953a. *Conceptions of Modern Psychiatry*. New York: Norton.

————. 1953b. *The Interpersonal Theory of Psychiatry*. New York: Norton.

Tanner, T. 2003. "Sigmund Freud and the Zeitschrift fur Hypnotismus." *Arc de Cercle* 1, no. 1: 75–142.

Theunissen, M. 1977. *Der Andere*. Berlin: Walter de Gruyter.

————. 1984. *The Other*. Translated by C. Macann. Cambridge, Mass.: MIT Press.

Walker, C. 1995. "Karl Jaspers and Edmund Husserl-III: Jaspers as a Kantian Phenomenologist." *Philosophy, Psychiatry and Psychology* 2, no. 1: 65–82.

Warnock, M. 1970. *Existentialism*. London: Oxford University Press.

Whitebook, J. 1985. "Reason and Happiness." In *Habermas and Modernity*. Edited by R. Bernstein. Cambridge, Mass.: Polity Press.

Winnicott, D. W. 1960. "Ego Distortion in Terms of True and False Self." In *The Maturational Process and the Facilitating Environment*. New York: International Universities Press, 1965.

————. 1965. *The Maturational Process and the Facilitating Environment*. New York: International Universities Press.

————. 1980. *Playing and Reality*. Harmondworth: Penguin.

Withers, Robert, ed. 2003. *Controversies in Analytical Psychology*. London: Brunner-Routledge.

Wolin, R., ed. 1993. *The Heidegger Controversy*. Cambridge, Mass.: MIT Press.

————. 2001. *Heidegger's Children: Hannah Arendt, Karl Lowith, Hans Jonas, and Herbert Marcuse*. Princeton, N.J.: Princeton University Press.

Wolstein, B. 1971. "Interpersonal Relations without Individuality." *Contemporary Psychoanalysis* 7: 75–80.

Wortis, J. 1954. *Fragments of an Analysis with Freud*. New York: Simon & Schuster.

Yalom, I. 2002. *The Gift of Therapy*. New York: Perennial.